Business Anthropology: New Progress in China

Modern China Series

Business Anthropology: New Progress in China

Chen Gang
Tian Guang

North American Business Press

Business Anthropology: New Progress in China

ISBN: 978-1-948915-27-4

NORTH
AMERICAN BUSINESS
P R E S S

North American Business Press
Atlanta, Georgia
Miami, Florida
New York, New York,
Toronto, Canada

FIRST PRINTING, 2022

About Modern China Series

As one of the oldest civilized regions globally, China has emerged as a "new world" because it embraces its essence and heritage and links them to viable economic strategies. In the last 25 years, China has made tremendous strides. The country and its people have every right to take pride in these accomplishments. Many Chinese leaders and intellectuals anticipate continuing growth with these successes. Furthermore, China's plans and strategies are often based on this premise.

There is tremendous interest in the U.S. in the Chinese economy and business environment. China has emerged as a global superpower, and scholars and business people in the U.S. are keenly interested in learning how this will affect them and do business with China. In response to growing interest from international and Asian scholars, North American Business Press is pleased to announce our Modern China Series (MCS) books. It is the first book series about modern China in the U.S., garnering tremendous interest in the U.S. and worldwide. With our first book reaching stores in September 2011, this initiative developed relationships between NABP and Chinese scholars. They desire to promote their academic and applied business writings to the rest of the world.

We have had an overwhelming demand for the Modern China Series from both authors who would like to publish in the series and people who would like to read the books. There are currently ten books published in the series, and we have a couple of dozen books that we are considering for the series. The books have been viewed by thousands of people from the U.S. and the rest of the world.

We have published books on several areas revolving around the Chinese business environment. We have a few that focus on the best practices in marketing in China; some are compared to "best practices" in doing business in China, and a few on the outlook of the Chinese economy. The market for the Modern China Series is enormous. There are tens of thousands of scholars that are keenly interested in the continued growth of the Chinese economy and the implications that it will have on the business world. Even more significant are the millions of business people interested in the impact that China will continue to have on the global economy. It is difficult to pin down the exact demand for the series, but it Is enormous.

We have big plans for growing the Modern China Series. It can be one of the most significant economic/business series ever produced. We are very selective with the books we will add to the collection, but we encourage scholars who think they have unique and exciting perspectives on China to submit their book manuscripts. From the readers' perspective, we are committed to producing high-quality books regularly so that readers should expect a steady stream of insightful books to be coming out for many years to come.

This initiative is headed by Dr. Robert Tian, a renowned researcher and academic. He spearheads our efforts in partnering with foreign authors and administering the day-to-day operations of this series. Dr. Tian, a Vice-President with North American Business Press and Editor of this series, spends much of his time in Beijing, Shanghai, and other Chinese cities, focusing on developing and managing our interests with authors and universities. Below is the list of the books we have published:

Enterprise Strategy: New Horizon authored by Zhang Xiuyu
Governance of Private Enterprises in Modern China authored by Zhong Qin
The Art of War and Enterprise Strategy Management authored by Fu Shouzhi
Marketing Issues in Modern China edited by Robert Guang Tian et al.
The Footprints of the Academician authored by Fu Zhouzhi
Marketing and Economics in Modern China (I) edited by Xiaoguang Qi et al.

Marketing and Economics in Modern China (II) edited by Wang Tianjin et al.

An Islamic Heritage in China authored by Ma Zhanming

China Environmental Anthropology authored by Wang Tianjin, Tian Guang, and Ma Jianfu

Can China Rule the New World authored by Tian Guang and Chen Gang

Critiques on Pan-marketization authored by Li Cunlin, Liu Hongfei, and Tian Guang

Economic and Business Anthropology in China edited by Xiaoguang Qi and Tian Guang

SME Managers Turnover in Modern China authored by Ji Yun

Political Connection and Financial Fraud in China authored by Peng Jinqian

China-Mongolia Economic Corridor authored by Eerdun Taoketao, Zhang Zhe, Wang Gang, and Wei Lisi

Anthropology of Chinese Foodways authored by Tian Guang and Chen Gang

Urbanization of Rural China authored by Li Taohong

The Science of Success in China authored by authored Zhang Xiuyu

Child Rearing in Rural China authored by Jiang Youchun and Yang Yunyi

ABW Management Theory and Practice authored by Zhang Xiuyu

Belt and Road vs. China and World authored by Tian Guang and Chen Gang

Modernization of China by Tian Guang, Luo Kanglong and Chen Qian

China in Xi Jinping Era by Shu Xiaohui, Li Yangkuo and Tian Guang

Business Anthropology: Progress in China by Chen Gang and Tian Guang

Table of Contents

Preface **1**

Acknowledgment **15**

Foreword **17**

Foreword **23**

Chapter 1 Development of Business Anthropology in China **41**

Introduction 41

Prologues for Business Anthropology in China 43

The Growth of Business Anthropology in China 48

Academic Activities and Organizations in China 52

China Needs Business Anthropology 56

Summary and Conclusion 59

Chapter 2 Urban-Rural Relationships in China in the Context of COVID-19 .... **61**

Introduction 62

New Meaning of the Urban-Rural Relationship 63

Urban and Rural Areas Affected by the Covid-19 70

Rural Rebuilding in the Post-Epidemic Era 77

Conclusion 85

Chapter 3 Changes in Structures and Functions of Border Markets **87**

Introduction 87

Traditional Structures and Functions of Markets in Yunnan 93

Transformation of Structures and Functions of Markets 102

Discussion and Conclusion 110

Chapter 4 Impacts of Roads on Dulong People and Their Coping Strategies **115**

Introduction 115

Research Site and Methods 117
The History of the Road Construction 118
Road and Social-Cultural Changes 120
Discussion and Conclusion 125

Chapter 5 The Role of Ethnic Enterprises and Entrepreneurs 127
Introduction 127
Literature Review 128
Theoretical Framework 131
The Analysis of the Data 132
Conclusion and Discussion 142

Chapter 6 Tobacco Growing and Cultural Impacts on Minority Female Smokers 147
Introduction 147
Methodology 149
Cultural Impacts 150
Environmental Analysis 152
Social and Culture Analysis 154
Social Systems and Education Factors 156
Discussion and Conclusion 158

Chapter 7 Foodservice Industry in Shantou 161
Introduction 161
Classic Brand Management 163
Research Site and Methods 166
Five Classic Brands in the Foodservice Industry 168
Issues of Brand Management in Classic-Brand Restaurants 173
Discussions and Suggestions 185
Conclusion 188

Chapter 8 NGOs in Southwest China 191
Introduction 191
Social Welfare and Civil Society in Post-Socialist China 192
The Development of NGOs in the West 195

NGOs in the Chinese Cultural Context 197
Practical and Conceptual Problems of NGOs in China 200
NGOs in Hong Kong and Taiwan 204
NGOs in Southwest China... 206
Conclusion 211

Chapter 9 Unsuccessful Factory Project by a Sino-Botswana Joint Venture... 215
Introduction 215
China and Botswana 218
Background of the Sino-Botswana Glass Factory Project................ 221
Cooperation and Difference during the Construction of the Glass Factory 224
Cultural Differences Between China and Botswana......................... 228
Chinese Socialism Meets with Botswana's Democracy.................. 229
When "Time is Money" Meets "There Is No Hurry in Botswana" .. 231
Conclusion 232

Chapter 10 Commercialization of Stone Pot Chicken in Klu-Nang of Tibet.. 235
Introduction 235
The Origin and Commercialization Stages...................................... 238
Characterization of Commercialization... 243
Inherent Adaptability of Commercialization 251
Conclusion 259

Epilogue... 261

References 265

Index 297

Afterword... 309

Preface

Anthropology was introduced to China at the beginning of the 20th century, along with other Western social sciences such as sociology and Western ideas such as Marxism. Western anthropology came to China through three channels: Chinese scholars who went to study anthropology in the west and returned to China to promote anthropology at universities or research institutes where they worked; anthropological works translated into Chinese that spread anthropological knowledge widely in China; and foreign anthropologists who came to teach and do fieldwork in China and increased impacts of anthropology as a discipline in Chinese society (Yang 2000:71).

Differing from Western anthropology, which began as a scientific discipline by studying tribal people, some Chinese anthropologists focused their research on Han Chinese society. In contrast, some other Chinese anthropologists studied Chinese ethnic minorities at the very beginning of the discipline in China. This outcome might result from the rural hardship in those years caused by endless civil wars and natural calamities and the Chinese intellectual tradition that every scholar has the responsibility to help the country when in danger. Chinese anthropologists were once deeply influenced by British functional theory. Thus, they were anxious to apply their learning from the west to identify Chinese social problems and find solutions to them. Fei Xiaotong's (1939) *Peasant Life in China* is an excellent example of this approach. It was regarded as a landmark in anthropological fieldwork and theory (Liang 2016:463). The Sino-Japanese War (1937-45) pushed many Chinese scholars to inland Yunnan Province, where many ethnic groups lived. Some scholars thus turned to study the ethnic people.

In 1949, the Chinese Communist Party (CCP) came to power in mainland China. Some Chinese anthropologists moved to Taiwan or overseas, but the majority stayed in mainland China, intending to contribute their part to building a new China (Wong 1979:37). In the early 1950s, the Chinese government restructured higher education by following the Soviet model. Anthropology was eliminated from universities with sociology, whereas ethnology was kept as a discipline of minority studies. For the following 20 years, anthropology disappeared from the Chinese academic world. China was then virtually closed to Western anthropologists. Anthropologists interested in Chinese study had to do fieldwork in Taiwan, Hong Kong, and the overseas Chinese communities. Freedman (1979:413) called this phenomenon the residue of "China," or sitting in an armchair reading archive and interviewing "the dead"; or interviewing refugees in Hong Kong or the United States, or working on their data collected before 1949. Very few lucky western anthropologists, such as William Geddes, were granted permission to visit some showcase communities in China.

In 1978, China opened up again to the Western world. The first anthropology department was reestablished at Sun Yat-sen University in Guangzhou in 1981(Zhou 2006:23). The First National Symposium on Anthropology was held at Xiamen University in 1981. The Chinese Anthropological Society was established at this conference, marking the revival of anthropology as an academic discipline in China (Ma 2012:27). The open-door policy allowed Western anthropologists to conduct fieldwork in China, who came in large numbers in the mid-1980s. The end of the 1980s and the early 1990s witnessed publications of their works, such as Huang Shu-min's *Spiral Road: Change in a Chinese Village through the Eyes of a Communist Party Leader* (1989); Helen F Siu's *Agents and Victims in South China: Accomplices in Rural Revolution* (1989); Sulamith Heins Potter and Jack M. Potter's *China's Peasants: The Anthropology of a Revolution* (1990); William R. Jankowiak's *Sex, Death, and Hierarchy in Chinese City: An Anthropological Account* (1993); Mayfair Yang's *Gifts, Favors, and Banquets* (1994); Andrew B. Kipnis' *Producing Guanxi* (1997); Ann Anagnost's *National Past-Times: Narrative, Representation, and Power in Modern China*(1997). These anthropologists and their works have tremendous impacts on Chinese anthropology.

Han Chinese society and rural China have gradually dominated Chinese anthropological research. After the 1980s, Chinese anthropologists continued their study of the traditional cultures of ethnic peoples. At the same time, they studied the new situation and new problems that resulted from China's reform and appeared in the minority areas in the course of "modernization." Examples of the research topics at this time included "the study of the movement of Chinese ethnic groups," "the study on the issue of modernization of Tibet," and "the study on the opening West and ethnic relations" (Liu 2003:221).

In the 1990s and 2000s, many Chinese students who had earned master's and doctoral degrees in anthropology outside China returned to academic careers in China, thus integrating Chinese anthropology into world anthropology (Pieke 2014: 124). The 16th Congress of the International Union of Anthropological and Ethnological Sciences (IUAES) held in July 2009 at Yunnan University of China demonstrates this integration. About 5,000 scholars and students from 116 countries and regions attended this Congress. Its programs included 239 academic sessions/panels with more than 5000 paper abstracts, six cultural exhibitions, five Study Tours and 23 films, exploring the theme of "Humanity, Development, Cultural diversity." (Zhang 2009) Some Chinese scholars predicted that this Congress would be a landmark in the development of Chinese anthropology (Xu 2007:1).

What has Chinese anthropology contributed to world anthropology in general? Chinese anthropology has made achievements in studying kinship systems, religion and ritual, comparative politics, and economic cultures worthy of pride (Wang 2005:9). Hundreds and thousands of ethnographies have been published covering all ethnic groups in China. Chinese anthropologists and ethnologists conducted large-scale research on economic and socio-cultural situations and the development of China's ethnic peoples, first in the 1950s and 1960s, and then in the 1980s and 1990s, producing a large number of academic monographs and investigation reports containing new information theories or theories methods. Heated discussions have been held in China on patterns of society, marriage and family, ethnicity and nationality, issues of modernization in ethnic areas, protection of cultural diversity, and preservation of the heritage of material cultures. These discussions have significant impacts on the discipline (He 2008:13-18).

Another vital contribution of Chinese anthropology is setting up an example in localizing (*bentuhua*) anthropology. When anthropology was first introduced to China, many Chinese scholars put forward ideas of establishing China's anthropology from different perspectives. Apart from translating canonical works, pre-1949 Chinese anthropologists argued that the social sciences needed modification and adaptation before being applied in China by collecting and organizing traditional Chinese societal and historical materials and combining them with selective Western theories (Liang 2016:463). After 1949, localizing anthropology and other social sciences continued de-westernization in conjunction with the Communist state's ideological and political agenda.

The Chinese government has been promoting to development of China's social sciences with Chinese attributes. Marxist-Leninist-Stalinist approaches were adopted to study minorities in the 1950s and 1960s. Since the revival of anthropology in China's universities, the localization of anthropology has moved to a stage of comprehensively analyzing western anthropological theories and combining them with Chinese realities. Localizing anthropology in China can be seen in Chinese anthropologists' study of Han Chinese society, which often combines historical research and anthropological fieldwork. China's rich historical documents have been used as local knowledge in anthropological studies and theorizing.

What can Chinese anthropology contribute to world anthropology? It can broaden the discipline's range of study. Apart from those traditional research topics on ethnic peoples mentioned above, more areas of interest have emerged in conjunction with the significant changes that Chinese society has undergone since the early 1980s. These can be found in the anthropological study of communities (rural, urban, and in between), of individuals' lives, including gender and sexuality, family and marriage, childhood and education, consumption and leisure, and the nation and its constituent ethnic and regional parts (Harrell 2001), of social transformation and cultural transformation (Zhao 2015), of new social order, of politics and government, of population, class, consumption and belonging, and modernization and globalization (Pieke 2014).

China's rise as a global power has provided a rare opportunity for Chinese anthropologists to make lasting contributions to world anthropology. Chinese anthropologists can contribute by thinking in new ways and writing about society, not just about another culture. In addition, they can provide ethnographic witness to the process of global domination, expansion and exploitation from the vantage point of emerging centers and make ethnographic comparisons with other civilizations beyond China's borders (Pieke 2014:132-133).

As a subfield of applied anthropology, business anthropology uses anthropological theories and methods in exploring and solving problems in the real business world. It studies how to improve business efficiency and work processes by observing how people perform in their workplace. It can help business people understand an organization's culture by studying group behavior. It allows managers to deal with organizational change issues due to the merger of companies (Tian, Van Marrewijk, and Lillis 2013). Business anthropologists can provide suggestions on marketing strategies by studying consumer behavior. They can help in product design by discovering what consumers want and assist multinational corporations in understanding the cultures of the many countries in which they operate in the trend of globalization and diversity that has involved the business world (Jordan 2010).

China has undergone tremendous economic and social change since its economic reform in the late 1970s. It gradually abandoned its closed, centralized economic planning system and brought China into a world market-oriented economy. After over forty years of development, China has become a locomotive in the world economy and a manufacturing base of consumer goods globally. Measured on a purchasing power parity (PPP) basis that adjusts for price differences, China in 2012 stood as the second-largest economy in the world after the U.S. (Central Intelligence Agency 2012). China's products can be seen in all corners of the world, and Chinese businesspersons are now going out of China to do business in all continents of the world.

However, China lacks in-depth research on the globalized market, business organization and cultural factors of other countries. Chinese businesspersons have faced many problems in foreign countries. Their products were even confiscated or burned down in some countries, bringing tremendous loss to Chinese companies. Inside China, the transition to the market economy has affected business strategies to meet international market needs across many industries. Chinese business leaders now realize that to better market their products and services internationally. They must better understand the global market environments from a cross-cultural perspective (Paliwoda and Ryans, 2008; Yu et al. 2006).

At this critical period in China's economic development, business anthropology was introduced and promoted in Chinese universities as a subfield of anthropology. Since 2005, Tian Guang, a business anthropologist trained in the USA, has run seminars on business anthropology at Peking University, Minzu University of China, and Fudan University, among many others. He visited the Business School of Shantou University in 2011. He was later appointed as a foreign expert professor to offer business anthropology courses to graduate and undergraduate students at the school. In May 2012, Tian Guang and Zhou Daming edited a textbook on Business Anthropology, which Ningxia Renmin Publishing House published. On May 17, 2012, Sun Yat-Sen University in Guangdong, one of the most prestigious universities in China, held the first international conference on business anthropology in China. At the same time, Minzu University and the Renmin University of China, another two most prestigious universities, jointly hosted a conference on business anthropology in Beijing.

At these two conferences, some Chinese scholars pointed out that many companies would have to set up a new senior management position with other senior executives, entitled Chief Anthropologist, to give advice and suggestions for the company's long-term development. The Chief Anthropologist could be the best candidate for promoting harmony among the company's internal staff to improve the working efficiency of employees (Wu 2012; Zhong and Liu 2012). The mainstream public media widely reported the two conferences in China. Their influence is far-reaching. Before the COVID-19 pandemic broke out, an international conference on business anthropology was held each year by different universities in China. Well-known European and American business anthropologists include Marietta Baba, Allen Batteau, Dominique Desjeux, Ann Jordan, Timothy Malefyt, Alfons van Marrewijk, Maryann McCabe, Brain Moeran, Patricia Sunderland, among many others, attended the conferences.

Since 2012, lectures on business anthropology have been given in universities across China. Undergraduate business anthropology courses and graduate programs in business anthropology have been offered at Sun Yat-Sen University, North Minzu University, South-Central Minzu University, Ningxia University, Jishou University, and Yunnan University. At the same time, more and more research projects, papers and books related to business anthropology have been coming out in China.

All these events stated above show that business anthropology has a bright future in China and will soon boom in China as an academic discipline as China's social and economic development continues fast. This book is about the progress of business anthropology in China. It provides concrete examples to show what Chinese business anthropologists work on and how they handle them. Chapter One discusses the development of business anthropology in China from a historical perspective. It is initially published in the Human Organization, and Dr. Tian Guang, a professor at Huaihua University, is the principal author of the chapter. This chapter highlights some significant accomplishments in business anthropology and summarizes a few critical scholars' contributions to the discipline in China.

Chapter 2 is authored by Jianhua Fan, a professor at the National Research Centre of Cultural Industries in Central China Normal University, and Ran Qi, a Ph.D. candidate at the School of Cultural Industrial Management in Communication University of China. It studies the urban-rural relationships in China. It points out that rural villages are the foundations of Chinese Society. City and the countryside have supported each other for thousands of years in China. But today, the city is advancing. The countryside is declining. A city is a consumption group, and it does not have a production function, and the raw materials needed for urban development are all obtained from the countryside. Unlike cities, rural areas have always been production bases. However, limited by the scarce economic structure of self-sufficiency, if a rural village wants to prosper, it must rely on the urban market. As a result, the dual nature of the interaction between urban and rural economic development has conditioned that the urban-rural relationship is an interdependent, mutually restrictive and inseparable balanced one. It also means that the fundamental essence of urban-rural integration is rebuilding the rural social pattern from a modern perspective. In the spring of 2020, COVID-19 disconnected China's rural and urban areas, which caused a significant blow to cities and rural areas. By examining the urban-rural relationship under the epidemic, the authors point out that the countryside has become a buffer for social distress and a refuge for urban crises. In the post-epidemic phase, rebuilding a more flexible and resilient organic cycle is the theme of urban-rural relations.

Dr. Yin Jiandong, a professor and Liu Weiwei, a lecturer at the School of Humanities of Yunnan Minzu University, authored Chapter 3. It points out that the border areas of Yunnan show complex and diverse ecological environments and unique geographical locations, which make their rural markets, bear typically ethnic, regional and open features of cross-border exchanges. The structures and functions of the border markets are undergoing a significant modern transformation with the development of the market economy, rapid urbanization and construction of towns in the border areas. This chapter explores how the space and time structures of the markets have been reshaped in modern changes. In contrast, the traditional economic function of the needs has been gradually weakened, and a trend of increasing social and cultural functions has emerged. This factor reflects that Yunnan's border markets, rural societies, and ethnic and cultural traditions undergo structural changes, bringing about diversity in the marketing system.

Chapter 4 is written by Dr. Gang Chen, a professor at the Center for Social and Economic Behavior Studies at Yunnan University of Finance and Economics and his student Jiyuan Zhao. It studies the socio-cultural changes that the Ethnic Dulong people have experienced since constructing a 96.2-kilometer long mud road in 1999. The Dulong ethnic group lives in the Dulong River Valley in Nujiang Prefecture, China's Yunnan Province. On April 10, 2014, a tunnel that closely connects the beautiful valley with the outside world was completed. The construction of this road has enormous impacts on the ethnic Dulong communities and the ecosystem in the valley. It has put the Dulong people into the turmoil of modernization and globalization. The authors claim that the Dulong people have been adjusting themselves and their cultures to the changing world with which the Dulong River Highway connects them.

Dr. Zhang Jijiao, a professor at the Institute of Ethnology and Anthropology of the Chinese Academy of Social Science, wrote chapter 5. He studies the urban migrants in China, focusing on ethnic enterprises and entrepreneurs. Based on first-hand information collected recently in some cities in China, the author uses the "ethnic enclave" and its economic circle theory to show that various factors affect the formation of the ethnic economic-cultural pattern in cities. The ethnic enterprises and the ethnic entrepreneurs play the most critical and substantial roles, which epitomize ethnic minorities' livelihood strategy and economic strength in the city. The author points out that an ethnic enterprise is a social organization and the foundation for changing or creating ethnic economic-cultural patterns. Depending on the situation, the ethnic entrepreneurs can utilize their own cultural identity, ethnic values, family and community social networks to venture capital, gain cheap labor and commercial credit, etc., creating a favorable environment for the development of the ethnic enterprises.

Chapter 6 is authored by Dr. Liu Ting, a Yunnan Academy of Social Sciences professor. Based on the anthropological fieldwork on women smokers, the author points out that smoking is prevalent among ethnic minority women in mountainous areas, especially older women. These women are mainly among Yi, Wa, Hani, Lahu, Miao, Zhuang, Dai, and Tibetan peoples living in the southeastern, northwestern and southern parts of Yunnan province. Factors affecting smoking include socio-cultural, environmental, religious, gender, educational, and health-care causes, which should be considered when smoking control policies are implemented.

Chapter 7 was written by Dr. Tian Guang, Ms. Liu Yala, a graduate of Shantou University, Dr. Zhao Jianhua, a professor at the University of Louisville in the U.S, and Dr. Liu Yu, a business professor at Shantou University. Based on an in-depth ethnographic study of five classic brands in the foodservice industry in Shantou City in Guangdong province, this chapter examines issues surrounding branding facing these classic brands. It suggests concrete measures for these restaurants to modernize their brand management from a business anthropological perspective. The authors argue that the traditional brand-named firms must keep their traditions to win in the current highly competitive business environment.

Chapter 8 is contributed by Dr. Shu-min Huang, a professor at the Institute of Anthropology at the National Tsing Hua University of Taiwan. It discusses the origin and operations of a dozen indigenous Chinese NGOs working to promote the social welfare of the marginalized ethnic groups in southwest China's hilly regions bordering Yunnan, Guizhou and Sichuan provinces. The author found that these NGOs exhibit several shared characteristics even though they have different specific goals, including poverty reduction, post-disaster reconstruction, community development, environmental conservation, cultural preservation, etc. They were all initiated by community elites with broad-based information networks and connections. Most of them also received initial inputs in funding, operation space, technical training, and advisory supervision from international NGOs.

Chapter 9 is authored by Dr. Xu Wei, an associate professor at the Institute of African Studies, Zhejiang Normal University. This chapter is based on a long-term and in-depth fieldwork on a glass factory project owned by a Sino-Botswana joint venture, which failed and was auctioned in 2016. It reveals the cooperative and conflictive aspects embedded in the construction of the factory from synchronic perspectives. These include operation mode, Chinese company's adaption to Botswana local laws and regulations, the gaming between the partners, industrial diversification of Botswana, impacts from the political struggle in Botswana to the project, etc. The author finds that cultural differences and conflicts between the two parties involved in the project and political influences led to the failure. The author concludes that the key to the success of such a cross-boundary, cross-cultural and cross-social economic cooperative project is to find the mutual rules and implement them firmly.

Dr. Yang Minghong, a professor at Yunnan University, Ms. Liu Jianxia, a Ph.D. candidate at Sichuan University, Dr. Tu Kaijun, an official of the Sichuan Province Government, and Dr. Xu Zhen, an associate professor at the School of Economics, Sichuan Normal University are the authors of Chapter 10. They study the commercialization process of Stone Pot Chicken in Tibet and found out that this process is the result of the integration of the local catering culture in Tibet and the inland catering cultures. They point out that the formation of the catering culture is related to the local ecology. Religion, economy and other factors are inseparable from each other. The commercialization of Stone Pot Chicken shows the process of Tibet's economic modernization from one aspect.

All these chapters have outlined how business anthropology has developed in China and what issues and topics Chinese business anthropologists have handled. Chinese business anthropologists have conducted fieldwork and ethnographic studies from cities to rural areas, from east coast provinces to remote west mountain provinces, and from

China to Africa. They have provided concrete examples to show that the sustainable development of the economy or business firms cannot succeed without taking local cultural factors into account. They have proved that anthropology can contribute to economic or business development for a better world in the future (Chen Gang and Tian Guang).

References

Fei, Xiaotong. (1939). Peasant Life in China: A Field Study of Country Life in the Yangtze Valley. G. Routledge and Sons, Limited.

Freedman, Maurice. (1979 [1969]). "Why China?" [Presidential Address, Royal Anthropological Institute]. In The Study of Chinese Society: Essays by Maurice Freedman. Selected and Introduced by G. William Skinner, 407-422. Stanford, CA: Stanford University Press.

Harrell S. (2001). "The Anthropology of Reform and the Reform of Anthropology: Anthropological Narratives of Recovery and Progress in China." Annual Review of Anthropology, 30:139–61

He, Xingliang. (2008). "30 Years of Chinese Ethnology and Anthropology: A Review and Prospect." Ethno-National Studies, 6: 11-21.

Jordan, A. (2010). "The Importance of Business Anthropology: Its Unique Contributions." International Journal of Business Anthropology, 1(1): 3-14.

Liang, Hongling. (2016). "Chinese Anthropology and Its Domestication Projects: Dewester-nization, Bentuhua and Overseas Ethnology." Social Anthropology, 24(4): 462-475.

Liu, Mingxin. (2003). "A Historical Overview on Anthropology in China." Anthropologist, 5（4）: 217-223.

Ma, Xue-fang. (2012). "The Division of Ethnology from Anthropology and the Multiple-path Anthropology Development: Anthropology Building in the mainland of China since the 1980s." Qinghai Journal of Ethnology, 23(1):26-33.

Paliwoda, Stanley J. and John K. Ryans, (2008). International Business vs. International Marketing. Cheltenharn, UK: Edward Elgar Publishing.

Pieke, Frank N. (2014). "Anthropology, China, and the Chinese Century." Annual Review of Anthropology, 43:123–38.

Tian, Robert G., Van Marrewijk, Alfons and Lillis, Michael (2013). General Business Anthropology (2nd Edition). Miami, FL: North America Business Press.

Wang, Ming-ming. (2005). "Chinese Anthropological Studies in the Past 25 Years: Achievements and Problems."Jiangxi Social Sciences, 12: 7-13.

Wong, Siu-lun. (1979). "Sociology and Socialism in Contemporary China." London, Boston and
Healey: Routledge & Kegan Paul.

Wu, Yan. (2012). "China Needs Business Anthropology." China Minzu Newspaper, June 28.

Xu, Jie-shun. (2007). "The Resumption and Development of Chinese Anthropology." Journal of Huaihua University, 26(10): 1-3.

Yang, Hui. (2000). "A Review of China's Anthropology Study in 50 years." The Ideological Front, 26(1): 71-76.

Yu, LiAnne, Cynthia Chan, and Christopher Ireland. (2006). China's New Culture of Cool: Understanding the World's Fastest-Growing Market. Berkeley, CA: New Riders Press.

Zhang, Xiaomin. (2009). "Report on the 16th Congress of the International Union of Anthropo-logical and Ethnological Sciences."http://www.iuaes.org/congresses/2009china.html.

Zhao, Xudong. (2015). "Toward a Chinese Phase of Anthropology." Journal of Social Sciences (Shanghai), 4: 74-85.

Zhong, Zhe and Liu Ning. (2012). "Business Anthropology Expending the Study Scope of Anthropology." China Newspaper of Social Science, July 20, 2012.

Zhou, Daming. (2006). "Chinese Anthropology Stepping into the 21st Century." Journal of Sun Yatsen University (Social Science Edition), 2: 23-27.

Acknowledgment

This work is deeply indebted to many Chinese scholars who did much to inspire it. In addition to the works by all the participants, we have referred to hundreds of articles and books published both in Chinese and in English. Thanks to Ms. Wang Jing and Dr. Russell Belk for their willingness to write the foreword for our book. Thanks to Dr. Jenny Banh for writing the epilogue for our book. We would like to thank the Academic and Scholastic Publishing Foundation of Huaihua University and the Center for Social and Economic Behavior Studies of Yunnan University of Finance and Economics for publishing this book. Thanks to Dr. Luo Kanglong and his team at the College of Culture and History Administration of Jishou University for financially supporting International Journal of Business Anthropology, which initially published most the articles used in this book. Finally, we would like to thank the editorial team of North American Business Press for their encouragement and dedicated work. Without it, this book may not be able to get published in time.

Foreword

Anthropology Facing the Humanity's Future

Wang Jing

CEO, Newland Technology Group

According to one point of view, the origin of anthropology is closely tied to the Renaissance following the Middle Ages. Western humanistic values regard human individuals as the ultimate essence of development and maximize individuals' value. On the other hand, Chinese anthropology upholds the principle of "serving the people." Its ultimate goal is to benefit the nation and the people. In 1980, Professor Fei Xiaotong proposed that anthropological studies should be people-centered.

Today, humanity has entered a new age of globalization and digitalization in our world. The value system of "the community with a shared future for mankind" proposed by Chinese President Xi Jinping can trace its root to the ideals of ancient Chinese intellectuals from over 2,000 years ago, who regarded "harmony" as the ultimate priority of the entire human development. For thousands of years, countless brilliant minds have been exploring the answer to that question - how do we maximize the value of humanity as a whole? In a recent video conference with US President Joe Biden, President Xi said, "our global village is faced with many challenges."

I began my exploration of anthropology when I started writing the book Human Destiny: A Brief History of Governance. I initially wanted to write a book about the "digital citizen." However, as I delved deeper into the writing, I realized that humanity had entered a brand new digital age. The study of human destiny is no longer restricted to the study of individuals. Instead, we should take a more systematic approach, thinking and exploring the destiny of individuals and communities and all humans as an entirety.

"The Science of Human Destiny" Facing the Future

Chinese President Xi emphasizes: "The world today is going through changes unseen in the past hundred years," and "it is a time that calls for theories and ideas and a time that must be capable of producing them. We must live up to its expectation." Therefore, it is significant to look into the future and take a critical approach to anthropology.

As in any transition of human social institution, humanity has always had to experience bloody revolutions in ideology, culture and governance at every crossroad. The Renaissance following the dark Middle Ages forced theology down from the pedestal and away from political power after its previous dominance in Europe for thousands of years. The Enlightenment ushered in the glory of capitalism and the industrial age that lasted multiple centuries. The New Culture Movement facilitated the spread of Marxism-Leninism in China, guiding the Chinese people to save the nation and themselves with socialism. Today, Xi Jinping Thought on Socialism with Chinese Characteristics for a New Era has made a new leap forward in adapting Marxism to Chinese conditions.

Throughout history, individuals have always been the most immediate victims of turmoils in the human world, nations and societies. Anthropology research in the new era should focus on human destiny and the core factors that impact it. It should help people understand the in-depth reasons behind the ups and downs of human history, the eternal laws of human society, and what essentially affects human destiny, guiding them to think systematically and explore a path out to future challenges.

Without changing the destiny of all humans, it is hard to change the destiny of nations and communities. Without changing the destiny of nations and communities, it is impossible to change the destiny of individuals. For that very reason, it is imperative to construct an academic system for anthropology that faces the future and systematically studies the destiny of individuals, communities and humanity as a whole.

In China, anthropology has historically been a discipline that "strengthens the nation, the campus and the people." Each theory has been developed under a specific condition of its time. Currently, much human thinking and behavioral patterns will inevitably be replaced and subverted by new ones of our time. Therefore, in the new era, I propose that we redefine anthropology as a discipline that "strengthens humans, nations and life," shifting the focus from "the study of people" to "the study of human destiny."

Understanding the Changes in Human Destiny

The development of human governance is a history of reform and innovation and the embodiment of human destiny. We can see how society evolved with the development of productive forces. When the productive forces developed to a certain degree, where the inherent relations of production were no longer compatible with them, new ideas and concepts would lead to a new governance model to replace or subversively transform the previous one. Governance runs through the whole process of the development of human society. Governance adapts the relations of production to the development of productive forces, resolves social conflicts and promotes social transformations.

In primitive times, the clans and tribes gave birth to the embryo of human governance-universal democracy, which was realized through open consultation, universal participation and collective decision-making. From the slave societies to the feudal societies, the emergence of the natural states gave birth to the oligarchy democracy model. Characterized by its pyramid structure to safeguard the ruling class's interests, it gradually developed into a governance system with contemporary significance. In capitalist societies, the proxy democracy model of sovereign states came into being and coordinated state relations by law instead of force, providing a peaceful and progressive option for humans to deal with international disputes.

Today, humanity has entered a pluralistic democratic society in the post-nationalist era. Social governance has developed from a single sovereign state to a multi-subject governance structure, such as the United Nations, the World Trade Organization, the International Monetary Fund, the International Olympic Committee, etc., resulting in various new authorities beyond state power. We can see that no governance model, from the universal democracy of primitive tribes tens of thousands of years ago to the pluralistic democracy of today, has eliminated the root causes of international conflicts. Therefore, it has not entirely overcome the primitive hostile complex, the restriction to human governance.

The world currently dominated by capitalism is more lost and helpless than ever before. Political, economic, technological, military, ideological, and other conflicts continue to rise yearly. Therefore, the destiny of humanity as a whole has been long stuck in a dark place. During an era of intensified changes, it has fallen into the "darkest moment" that humanity has ever seen. The governance of life impacts the destiny of individuals. The governance of a nation affects the destiny of communities. The governance of the globe impacts the destiny of all.

Socialism with Chinese Characteristics

In the new era, China is on the path of socialism with Chinese characteristics with President Xi at the helm. In addition to modernizing China's governance system and improving its governance capacity, China's insightful and forward-looking leaders have promptly seized the opportunities brought by the digital era and put forward the new concept of building a "digital China." It has undoubtedly provided a new engine and new lever for national governance.

"Digital China" aims to realize the concepts and top-level planning of modernized national governance through digital technological means and model building. It will help transform China's social governance from affair-centered to people-centered to give people a greater sense of "gain, security and happiness." China will gradually resolve the conflicts between unbalanced and inadequate development and people's ever-growing needs for a better life. China will also encourage enterprises to use technology for good causes, substantially reform the developmental pattern, and eventually achieve shared prosperity.

The COVID-19 pandemic has been a significant test of the global public crisis governance system and the governance capacity of all countries around the world. Thanks to its continuous improvement of digital infrastructure and governance capacity, China has implemented targeted prevention and control over the rampant virus. However, most countries have been unable to contain the pandemic, resulting in the loss of countless innocent lives. Even those who survive face an economic and social shutdown on top of the trauma of the virus.

China is a land with a significant cultural legacy and diverse social ecology. In the digital age, "Digital China" will become a testing field for national and global governance. The experiences China gains from its practices will also be replicable examples in human governance. Through the Belt and Road Initiative, China's wisdom and solutions in national and global governance will be shared with the entire world as examples to follow.

Global Governance is the Only Way to Change Human Destiny

Global governance will unquestionably be the most revolutionary progress in human history. If it can be truly realized, humans will completely transcend our primitive nature as animals and unfold a new page of human civilization.

The world we humans rely on for survival has now become one unity. We are all so intertwined that no country can stay inside its bubble. Humans today have to overcome the dual threats from the "state and society" and the "nature and earth." "Fragmented" governance models are due for a profound change. Humanity is expecting to shift from economic globalization to global economic integration and finally to a global governance model that integrates the entire world as one. This shift will take innovations in the system, culture, ideology, theories, and digital governance.

Humans today should be concerned with the governance of the physical world and the governance of the digital world in the future. We should not only focus on governing countries but also on governing the world as a whole. We should think about the past and present, and future. History has pushed us into a brand new era. No matter what happens in the world today, how many twists and turns there are ahead, or how bumpy the path will be, nothing can stop the wheel of human progress from moving forward.

"The community with a shared future for mankind" is a new concept, path and methodology of global governance put forward under the future-oriented framework of humanity. More importantly, it is the ultimate goal humans need to achieve to create a world of shared prosperity.

Caring about the destiny of humanity is not just the job of politicians and scholars but something all of us have to face together for generations to come. We are in an age of hopes and opportunities when revolutions will continuously break out in ideology, culture and governance. When people from a hundred or even a thousand years later look at what we do today, we could potentially become a new Renaissance, Enlightenment, and Awakening Age in history.

I believe that, either in academic research or participation in human governance, anthropology will be thriving and flourishing in the future, with active exchanges, heated debates and diverse ideas, and contributing to the realization of "the community with a shared future for mankind."

Foreword

The Fruits of Business Anthropology in China

Russell Belk

York University
Toronto

This book is an exciting compilation of ethnographies in Western China by Drs. Chen Gang and Tian Guang with their colleagues. But "exciting" is probably not the first reaction that surfaces in looking only at the chapter titles – roads, food service, NGOs, and entrepreneurs are topics that seem likely to arouse little interest except for those whose research lies in these areas. Likewise, female smokers, border markets, urban-rural relations, and stone pot chicken may be eccentric topics. But the talented ethnographers who conducted this research and wrote these chapters can develop their topics and make them come alive deftly. They then step back and allow us to contemplate the broader significance of the patterns of business and consumer behavior that they have discovered. They show how changes hailed as modernization affect several of China's 55 ethnic minorities and their engagement with Han Chinese and foreigners from Vietnam, Korea, Laos, and Myanmar. In one case, they can step even farther back and contrast Asian and African time styles and business styles and use the chapter to comment on China's soft power and its Belt and Road initiative in Africa.

This is not to say that any of these chapters are the final word on minorities, the Western provinces, or their engagement with economic development. This is part of an evolving story. Nor is it possible to foresee the future and imagine all the long-term consequences of the changes since the time of the ethnographies. Part of the beauty of these chapters is that they detail ordinary and everyday activities like eating, traveling, touring, and bargaining in places where Han Chinese and foreign visitors may find their Other. But this strength is also a weakness. By detailing certain practices, other practices are necessarily missed. For example, by focusing on Klu-Nang stone pot chicken from Tibet, the authors miss the more ubiquitous Tibetan momo, tsampa, and butter tea and the impact of Chinese foods on Tibetan cuisine (Wu and Chee-beng 2001; Wu and Cheung 2002). Similarly, the ethnographic chapters on ethnic minorities in the Western China province of Yunnan and the Tibetan Autonomous Region could have provided more background on the controversies regarding China and its ethnic minorities to put this material in a broader contemporary and historical context (e.g., Dillon 2018; Roberts 2020; Zang 2016). And in the welcome chapter on China's joint project to build a glass factory in Botswana, there might have been more critical attention brought to China's Belt and Road initiative and how it is changing business and consumer life in Africa (e.g., French 2015).

But ethnographies are not intended to be broad social commentaries. Furthermore, as Chinese citizens, the authors may be somewhat circumspect in what they say and how they say it. For example, in commenting on China's Cultural Revolution in Chapter 1, they note that it "...had many unfortunate consequences and today is regretted by most Chinese." After this momentous understatement, the remainder of the initial chapter is a very nice history of business anthropology in China. This is part of an effort in restoring anthropology in China after a long hiatus – an effort in which the authors have played a prominent part. They also credit a handful of other business anthropologists located in China and abroad who are doing research in China. They note, for example, the work of Yan (1996) on gift-giving in China, although they might have also noted the work of Yang (1994) and Joy (2001). At stake here are issues involving the continuum of guanxi reciprocal relations and when they are used for benign social purposes versus predatory coercive purposes. This is also an issue raised by Polanyi (1945) as the "fictitious commodities" of land, labor, and money became commodities for sale during the enclosure movement and the rise of proto capitalism in Europe. The issues are not quite the same in bringing marketization to the ethnic minorities of Western China (Fowler, Chu, and Fowler 2020), but there are some similarities. At issue is whether bringing large-scale commodification to the economies of China's ethnic minorities is necessarily a good thing, as Shi (1989) proposed. And is opposing such change merely a romanticism that tries to freeze minority lives in the past? The authors don't take a stand on this issue in their introductory chapter, which is better assessed in the specific ethnographies summarized in the book's remaining chapters.

Chapter 2 sets the tone for much of the remainder of the book by highlighting the relative absence of the COVID pandemic in the rural areas of Western China. It also sets the tone by romanticizing rural China as being pure and relatively free from the impurity of urban China. This is an old theme in Chinese history, literature, and film by the first half of the twentieth century (Lee 1999). The city was depicted as dank and evil, and the countryside was seen as free and good. In the treaty port foreign concessions of old Shanghai, the city was also an important site of Western consumer culture:

> The modern Chinese understanding of the "city," whether in terms of consumer culture, municipal administration, lifestyles, career opportunities, or political participation, was largely fashioned in Shanghai. Over the course of the twentieth century, the city has been alternately branded as China's pride and shame, a place of infinite glamour and unequaled squalor. These contrasting constructions said less about the conditions in the city than Shanghai's primary strategic significance in the never-ending contest between the countryside and the city (Yeh 2007: 5).

Yeh (2007) shows how the city organized spaces as urban multistoried buildings and rural parks and organized time as the world of urban corporate time clocks versus the timeless rural countryside. Of course, this imagery can be reversed, and the city can be seen as modern, sophisticated, safe, and "the country's best defense against the hopelessness of the countryside" (Yeh 2007: 119). Nor are these contrasting urban and rural life images unique to China (Seabrook 2007; Williams 1975). The two are also interdependent. The city depends on the resources of the countryside, including its human resources in the form of immigrants and migrant workers. And like the relationship between economically less and more developed countries, the countryside exports raw materials and imports developed goods from the city, perpetuating an exploitative imbalance.

Rural support was also essential to Mao's rise to power in revolutionary China (Averill 2002). This was symbolically important as well as strategic. During the Cultural Revolution, the countryside was not only a place of re-education but also of purification in the Down to the Countryside Movement (Brown 2012; Tsang 2021). Thus, China's move to modernize the Western provinces and bring the benefits of highways, trains, airports, tourism, and economic development to rural areas and the ethnic minorities who live there can also be seen as a loss of another way of life, including language, culture, self-sufficiency, and tradition. But it is more complicated than this, as the careful ethnographies of the present book reveal.

In Chapter 3, the authors draw on the work of Fei, Skinner, and even Braudel to describe how peasant markets work as a point of contact with cities and the Other. The Other, in this case in Yunnan's border areas, includes people from Vietnam, Laos, and Myanmar. Traders on both sides of the border often speak multiple languages because of their proximity and long contact history. In addition, socializing and drinking together are common after trading. That is, the exchanges are traditionally extra-economic and include socializing as well. The authors also note that relatives are often chosen as favored trade partners, and they may be given a good price or even be given goods for free. Thus, the boundary between market exchange and sharing may be fuzzy (Belk 2010). This can potentially become a problem if it threatens the viability of the business. European clerks are preferred in remote Australian Aboriginal community stores because they have no local relatives to whom they would be expected to show favoritism (Belk, Groves, and Askergaard 2000). A further change discussed more fully in the Chapter is that with the completion of the Dulongjiang Road, the region's isolation from November to May when snow blocks the mountain pass has been circumvented. The authors report in this chapter that while rapid development and urbanization have changed some of the traditional times and spaces of border markets in Yunnan, the markets continue to function as a point of contact between urban and rural China.

Besides increased year-round physical contact with city dwellers, most towns and villages in Yunnan now have access to electricity, television, cell phones, and the internet. Since these things quickly became the new normal, it is easy to underestimate their impact. In rural India, Tenhunen (2018) found that a similar simultaneous explosion of electricity and electronics led to better price information on agricultural produce, better access to medical care, empowerment of women, more love marriages versus arranged marriages, and greater empowerment of the young and educated. Similarly, in Eastern Europe after communism, although some of the nepotism and patronage favoritism needed to survive under communism continued (Ledeneva 2017), more subtle changes were emancipatory. They included the new availability of hair care, perfumes, deodorants, soap, toothpaste, underwear, pantyhose, lingerie, and sanitary napkins (Drakulić 1991). Although these seem like superfluous things (Clunas 2001/2004), it is precisely such superfluous things that can make a profound difference in how people feel about themselves.

Nevertheless, the Eastern European situation was one of pent-up demand for products that had been the desired forbidden fruit for many years. We long to know more in the case of rural Yunnan about what was desired and how elements of "foreign" cultures were received. Some of the fruits of development may be rotten or maybe desirable but poisonous.

The authors also observe that with the loss of rural population as more people move to the city for employment (legally or illegally), the social life of the plaza where people socialized, played, and were entertained on market days has largely disappeared except for a few older people who were left behind. I suspect this was also exacerbated as people cloistered themselves indoors to watch television or communicate with now distant loved ones via WeChat. The authors also lament the decline or disappearance of ethnic holidays and festivals, but in the same breath, they observe the growth of cultural tourism in Yunnan. Paradoxically such tourism has helped preserve some of these cultural celebrations, but at a cost. Likewise, the authors end the chapter by listing the accompanying costs of rationalizing and modernizing markets in rural Yunnan: counterfeits, smuggled cigarettes, drugs, pornography, gambling machines, and rampant AIDS. One thing that would be of help here is a timeline. These ethnographies were conducted over the years, and some are more recent than others. Since costs and benefits change over time, knowing the years covered by the different chapters would be good.

Chapter 4 is a general account of the tunnel created under the mountain that separated the Dulong minority from the rest of China. While the new highway shortens the distance by only 16 kilometers, it shortens the driving time from 9 hours to 3. Moreover, it lengthens the driving season from 6 months to 12. The tunnel and highway were completed in 2014 and 2015, respectively, and a team of Yunnan University faculty and graduate students began their ethnography in 2016. There were major landslides in 2017, and the highway, along with another highway in progress to Tibet, was closed until 2019, when Dulong valley was reopened to a limited number of tourists.

The research team also conducted a netnography, a study of social media posts (Kozinets 2019) on Baidu, CNKI, and other internet sources. Their report in this chapter is limited to descriptive statistics. Key among them is that the villages in the Dulong Valley and its 4300 residents now have highways, electricity, running water, telephone, internet, radio and television. The Dulong is also known as the tattoo face people, and the village studied, Longyuan, had 558 villagers living at 1800 meters above sea level. With the valley's opening, it became a hot spot for tourism and ethnographic research. The Shanghai government provided funds to construct brick houses to replace the wood and bamboo traditional houses that housed families on the second floor with livestock below. The new houses have five bedrooms and pigs in the back. Government efforts also helped shift local people away from agriculture and serve the tourist trade.

Among the other changes detected by the research team are that families no longer socialize outside; they are instead indoors, occupied with TV, phones, and the internet. With all of these changes happening in a short period, disruption of traditional ways of living is inevitable. The authors report that the low grain production in the high-altitude valley previously restricted alcohol production, but now cheap alcohol comes in by truckload. As a result, alcohol abuse has risen, and some villages are thinking of banning it (c.f., Groves and Belk 2001). Besides the decline in outdoor socializing, the dead are no longer buried near the family house. Even though, as Christians and animists, the Dulong believe that spirits are everywhere and affect the family's well-being.

There are no doubt other changes not reported in this brief chapter. One thing hinted at is the ironic duality of the Chinese government trying to modernize the Dulong by opening them up to the outside world and introducing a market-based economy on the one hand and trying to capitalize on the sensational "primitive" image that is such a tourist draw on the other hand. Llamas and Belk (2011) found something similar in ethnic minority villages of Yunnan, Old Towns like Shangri La (Dukezong) and Lijiang, and Chinese "folk culture villages" in Kunming, Shenzhen, and Hainan. These locales have all been reconfigured for tourism—primarily Chinese and global tourists. Museums have been built, local performances of ethnicity have been staged, hotels built, and tourist attractions like the world's largest prayer wheel have been built. Monasteries destroyed in the Cultural Revolution have also been rebuilt for touristic rather than religious purposes. Buddhist iconography like Dharma Wheels, Tibetan thangkas, and shortens have been appropriated and used as part of the décor of hotels, museums, and airport terminals. Souvenir stands and ethnic restaurants abound. Yet most of the revenues go to Han Chinese rather than local minority members. When much of the thousand-year-old Old Town of

Kukezong went up in flames in 2014, it was rebuilt to appear authentically old but modern fire-resistant materials. Like the tourist performances by actors in ethnic dress, the appearance is all-important, even at the price of authenticity.

Moreover, the expected disruptions of local life and authority to touristification, commoditization, and marketization emerged in these places as well (Belk and Costa 1995; Chaudhuri and Belk 2020). The authors of the present book detail some such changes and note, for instance, that Dulong residents of the newly constructed Longyuan find that it feels crowded and that the noise at night keeps them awake. Their former ability to commune with their ancestors has also been interrupted by the distance of the new village from their buried remains. But the authors conclude that the Dulong are doing their best to cope with the cultural changes imposed upon them, even at the cost of some suicides and conversions to Christianity.

In Chapter 5, the authors detail the role of ethnic entrepreneurs in four dispersed Chinese cities: Hohhot, Shenzhen, Kunming, and Qingdao. They also examine six ethnic groups: Dai, Hui, Yi, Bai, Mongolian, and Korean. The ethnic migrants to these cities comprise the "floating urban minorities." Hui migrants to Kunming have become dominant in cattle ranches, and beef and mutton are processed in their slaughter facility. Food, domestic service, healthcare, manufacturing, entertainment, cleaning services, and commercial trade are other dominant specialties with variations among the ethnicities and the cities studied. They also describe how the restaurant must add Han spices when Mongolian food is served to Han Chinese. This is similar to the adaptations of "Chinese" food in its diaspora to other cultures (Wu and Tan 2001; Wu and Cheung 2002).

These are the minority group members who have gone to the city to seek their fortunes. They concentrate on ethnic enclaves within the cities and rely on help, capital, and information networks. The authors characterize the more successful urban minority groups as enacting either a family "beehive" model, an ethnic "beehive," or a value-chain "beehive." In each case, they are led by a "queen bee" who is a "king without a crown." Similar patterns have been observed among international migrants, although Western treatments tend to emphasize issues of migrant identity (e.g., Halter 2000; Rapport and Dawson 1998; Tharp 2001).

Chapter 6 is an interesting chapter about cigarette smoking among females in some ethnic minorities in Yunnan province. There is an interesting backstory that could complement this chapter. It involves the anti-American and anti-Japanese boycotts of the first three decades of the twentieth century (Zhao and Belk 2008). BAT (British American Tobacco) was so successful in introducing its cigarette brands to China that tobacco was called "the opium of the twentieth century" (Wood, 1998: 197). It faced no serious local competition until the Nanyang brothers assembled a similar array of brands. Nanyang also played the nationalism card in promoting that BAT was American. This worked until BAT discovered that one of the Nanyang brothers had taken up Japanese citizenship to sell cigarettes there. Then, in an ironic advertising reversal, BAT announced that it should be the choice of good Chinese citizens because Nanyang was in league with the enemy.

The authors discovered that more ethnic minority women smoke than men is partly due to belonging to cultures (e.g., the Lahu people) with more equal gender rights. Han women, who are more influenced by patriarchal Confucian ideology, wouldn't dare to smoke. The same is true of Miao women who can't eat with their husbands' family members or go upstairs where these in-laws live. Secondly, there is a pragmatic reason the ethnography found that smoking helped prevent mosquito bites for women who work in the fields 12 hours a day. The authors found that smoking is "a way to release their sorrows apart from their addiction for those women who smoke." We are reminded of Richard Klein's (1993) witty tribute, *Cigarettes are Sublime.*

In Chapter 7, the authors examine surviving historical brands that have become classics. They focus on five classic foods in Shantou, some of which have won coveted state recognition. All are among the twenty-plus foodservice enterprises designated as classic brands by the local tourism bureau and the local social sciences association. Branded goods may have originated in prehistoric China, and some surviving brands of Chinese medicines, scissors, and other consumer goods have histories that go back hundreds of years (Eckhardt and Bengtsson 2010; Hamilton and Lai 1989; Pinheiro-Machado 2010; Wengrow 2008).

In the case of the classic brand foods and their restaurants in Shantou, their fame is sufficient to draw both locals and tourists. All current proprietors were previously "hated capitalist roaders" and were sent to the countryside for "re-education." They had learned hard work and discipline and put in long hours and a no-frills/no-waste approach that now serves them well in their restaurants. Buddhism is the dominant religion in Shantou and is based on Buddhist compassion. One owner gives food to beggars and others in need at 11:00 am each day. These and other practices like rejecting innovation fly in the face of brand management principles taught in marketing texts and classes. But these entrepreneurs' passion suggests that good food, sincerity, and authenticity may trump corporate marketing principles.

Chapter 8 asks, "Will the reduction of the Party-State control in China give rise to a genuine civil society?" Several factors are working on behalf of the growth of NGOs and civil society building in China. There are many holes in the Chinese social support system, and as one result, there are demands for workers' rights, consumers' rights, and environmental protections.

The chapter distinguishes Western and Chinese civil society organizations by noting, for example, that religious organizations founded many Western NGOs and that there was less need for Chinese NGOs under Mao's "iron rice bowl," in which state-owned enterprises and collectives offered complete care for those who worked for them. Different types of current Chinese NGOs are described, from those that serve common interests like qigong meditation to the many earthquake relief organizations that sprang up following the Wenchuan earthquake just before the 2008 Beijing summer Olympics.

In Chapter 9, the authors return to a full ethnography with a highly insightful study of a failed attempt to create a Sino-African glass factory in Botswana. They attribute the failure largely to the different temporal orientations of the two countries. Time is a precious commodity in East Asia and is not something to be wasted. People are early for appointments and are proud to meet deadlines and even finish ahead of time, not so in sub-Saharan Africa, where "African time" means a much more casual approach to life and a "better" work-life balance.

The ethnography is also a reality check on China's Belt and Road initiative in Africa, where China has made huge investments. Besides a clash of work cultures, there were other important differences between the Botswanan and Chinese business sides. They include different technological infrastructures, political models, levels of "corruption," and differences in state-ownership versus privately owned business ventures. Disruptions in funding and timing problems also led to a stop-and-go construction schedule. Ultimately the project was aborted, and the assets of the glass factory were auctioned off. This occurred amidst a swirl of rumors, as there was no media investigation in Botswana. The chapter provides an excellent cultural deconstruction of this failed bi-cultural construction project.

Chapter 10 finishes the book with an ethnographic account of the commercialization of Tibetan "Klu-Nang Stone Pot Chicken" in the city of Ninychi, Tibet. The resulting restaurants serve locals and an increasing number of tourists drawn by the fame of the city's stone pot chicken. This case is a microcosm of "Tibet's economic modernization in the authors' analysis." As such, it serves as a fitting conclusion for the book. It compares the costs and benefits of replacing indigenous culture with a commodified tourist culture and integrating Tibetan and Han cultures. Hopefully, the reader will ask what is gained and what is lost in such commercialization, cultural dilution, and touristification (e.g., see Bruner 2005; Chaudhuri and Belk 2020; Davis and Monk 2007; Desmond 1999; Llamas and Belk 2011; MacCannell 1976; Sheller and Urry 2004).

The stone pots for stone pot chicken were carved from relatively soft steatite found in area mountains. The pots allow cooking at altitude at high temperatures, which would otherwise require a pressure cooker. The Tibetan chickens are a special breed that can endure the altitude and winter cold. Tibetan herbs are also used to give a special flavor to stone pot chicken, and the rock transfers minerals that are good for health. The covered pot idea was borrowed from hot pot cooking in Chongqing. Machines now produce the once-handmade pots. Chicken farming has been corporatized. There is a chicken abattoir to supply chickens to the 30 restaurants and hundreds of hotels and inns in Ninychi that serve stone pot chicken. The success of these ventures has also spawned the breeding of Tibetan pigs, forest crops, and organic vegetables. Agricultural technology has also become more sophisticated, and acres of greenhouses extend the growing season. In July of 2019, when the ethnography was conducted, there were 124 stone pot chicken stores in the urban area of Ninychi. The tourist accommodations and attractions added jobs and injected money into the local economy. While all of this sounds good, the new jobs may be lower-level while Han Chinese, both local and distant, own the facilities and likely extract larger profits and enjoy more senior executive positions. However, ownership structure and revenue extraction were not examined in this ethnography, so this is a guess based on research elsewhere in Tibet and Yunnan (Llamas and Belk 2011).

The ethnography details that Yellow Sect Buddhists have had to make some concessions to allow the killing and eating of meat during the holy month of April (Tibetan calendar) since they previously were not allowed to kill or eat meat or sell stone pot chicken during this time. This is not the first time or place where religious practices have changed to accommodate commercial interests; consider European business openings on weekends.

The final chapter also touches on the experience of eating Klu-Nang stone pot chicken. It recognizes that memory is embodied and that food and fragrance memories are powerful in evoking broader experiences, as Proust (1996) found with petit Madeline's and lime blossom tea and as others have found more broadly (e.g., Banerji 2006; Falk 1994; Holtzman 2009; Howes 2005; Lupton 1996). The authors echo that "food [itself is] a kind of memory.

Conclusion

Suppose there was a need to demonstrate the fruits of business anthropology while also contributing to the small but growing literature of this small but growing discipline. In that case, this is the volume that will serve that need. The hope is that these fruits will now plant their seeds throughout the world, especially among those interested in Chinese consumer and producer interaction. I hope this book is translated into Chinese and can serve as a bridge between Chinese- and English-speaking researchers.

As a pan-cultural book focusing on Southwest China, this volume provides a tantalizing glimpse into the Chinese government's controversial economic development plan for minorities. The plan is demonstrably lifting people out of what appears to be poverty by some common metric. But this same development has provoked concerns, especially concerning once-isolated minorities and their strong religious practices and beliefs. This book goes some way in evaluating the results of this drive for harmony. Furthermore, it demonstrates the power of business anthropology to take on broader concerns regarding minority representation, harmonization processes, the Belt and Road initiative, touristification, and more. To me, and I hope it is an excellent provocation to you as well.

References

Averill, Stephen. (2002). “The Transition from Urban to Rural in the Chinese Revolution,” *The China Journal*, 48 (July), 87-121.

Banerji, Chitrita (2006), Feeding the Gods: Memories of Food and Culture in Bengal, Oxford: Seagull Books,

Belk, Russell (2010), “Sharing,” *Journal of Consumer Research*, 36 (5), 715-734.

Belk, Russell and Janeen Costa (1995), “International Tourism: An Assessment and Overview,” *Journal of Macromarketing*, 15 (2), 33-49.

Belk, Russell, Ronald Groves, and Per Østergaard (2000), “Aboriginal Consumer Culture,” *Research in Consumer Behavior*, 9, 1-45.

Brown, Jeremy (2012), *City versus Countryside in Mao's China: Negotiating the Divide*, Cambridge: Cambridge University Press.

Bruner, Edward (2005), *Culture on Tour: Ethnographies of Travel*, Chicago: University of Chicago Press.

Chaudhuri, Himadri and Russell Belk, eds., (2020). *Marketization: Theory and Evidence from Emerging Economies*, Singapore: Springer Nature.

Clunas, Craig (1991/2004), Superfluous Things: Material Culture and Social Status in Early Modern China, Honolulu, HI: University of Hawai'i Press.

Davis, Mike and Daniel Monk, eds. (2007), *Evil Paradises: Dreamworlds of Neoliberalism*, New York: The New Press.

Desmond, Jane (1999), *Staging Tourism: Bodies on Display from Waikiki to Sea World*, Chicago: University of Chicago Press,

Dillon, Michael (2018), *Lesser Dragons: Minority Peoples of China*, London: Reaktion Books.

Drakulić, Slavenka (1991), *How We Survived Communism and Even Laughed,* New York: W. W. Norton.

Eckhardt, Giana and Anders Bengtsson (2010), "A Brief History of Branding in China." *Journal of Macromarketing*, 30(3).

Falk, Pasi (1994), *The Consuming Body*, London: Sage,

Fowler, Jie, Rongwei Chu, and Aubrey Fowler (2020), "Within Country Migration, Marketization, and Liquid Identity," in Himadri Chaudhuri and Russell Belk, eds., *Marketizatuion: Theory and Evidence from Emerging Economies,* Singapore: Springer Nature, 221-234.

French, Howard (2015), China's Second Continent: How a Million Migrants are Building a New Empire in Africa, New York: Vintage.

Groves, Ronald and Russell Belk (2001), "Look at Them Blokes! Got No Bloody Control See': Alcohol Consumption and the Australian Aborigine," *Asia Pacific Advances in Consumer Research*, 4, 310-317.

Halter, Marilyn (2000), Shopping for Identity: The Marketing of Ethnicity, New York: Schocken.

Hamilton, Gary G., and Chi-kong Lai (1989), "Consumerism without Capitalism: Consumption and Brand Names in Late Imperial China," in Henry J. Rutz and Benjamin S. Orlove, eds, *The Social Economy of Consumption,* Lanham, MD: University Press, 253-279.

Holtzman, Jon (2009), Uncertain Tastes: Memory, Ambivalence, and the Politics of Eating in Samburu, Northern Kenya, Berkeley, CA: University of California Press.

Howes, David, ed. (2009). Empire of the Senses: The Sensual Culture Reader, Oxford: Berg.

Joy, Annamma (2001), "Gift Giving in China: A Continuum of Social Ties," *Journal of Consumer Research*, 28 (2), 239-256.

Klein, Richard (1993), *Cigarettes are Sublime*, Durham, NC: Duke University Press.

Kozinets, Robert (2019), Netnography: The Essential Guide to Qualitative Social Media Research, Los Angeles, CA: Sage.

Ledeneva, Alena (2017), "The Ambivalence of Favour: The Paradox of Russia's Economy of Favours," in David Henig and Nicolette Makovicky, eds., *Economies of Favour after Socialism*, Oxford: Oxford University Press,21-49

Lee, Leo Ou-Fan (1999), Shanghai Modern: The Flowering of a New Urban Culture in China, 1930-1945, Cambridge, MA: Harvard University Press.

Llamas, Rosa and Russell Belk (2011), "Shangri-La: Messing with a Myth," *Journal of Macromarketing*, 31 (September), 257-275.

Lupton, Deborah (1996), *Food, The Body and the Self*, London: Sage.

MacCannell, Dean (1976), *The Tourist: A New Theory of the Leisure Class*, New York: Schocken.

Pinheiro-Machado, Rosana (2010), "The Attribution of Authenticity to "Real" and "Fake" Branded Commodities in Brazil and China," in Andrew Bevan and David Wengrow, eds., *Cultures of Commodity Branding*, Walnut Creek, CA: Left Coast Press, 109-129.

Polanyi, Karl (1945), The Great Transformation: The Political and Economic Origins of Our Time, Boston, MA: Beacon Press.

Proust, Marcelle(1996), *In Search of Lost Time*, 6 volumes, London: Vintage.

Rapport, Nigel and Andrew Dawson, eds. (1998), Migrants of Identity: Perceptions of Home in a World of Movement, Oxford: Berg.

Roberts, Sean (2020). The War on the Uyghurs: China's Internal Campaign against a Muslim Minorities Internal Campaign against a Muslim Minority, Princeton, NJ: Princeton University Press.

Seabrook, Jeremy (2007), *Cities: Small Guides to Big Issues*, London: Pluto Press.

Sheller, Mimi and John Urry, eds. (2004), *Tourism Mobilities: Places to Play, Places in Play*, London: Routledge.

Shi, Zhengyi (1989), "Gap Acceleration and Equilibrium-An Exploration of the Economic Development Strategy in the Minority Areas," *Heilongjiang National Series*, 3, 29-45.

Tenhunen, Sirpa (2018), A Village Goes Mobile: Telephony, Mediation, and Social Change in Rural India, Oxford: Oxford University Press.

Tharp, Marye (2001), Marketing and Consumer Identity in Multicultural America, Thousand Oaks, CA: Sage.

Tsang, Gabriel (2021), "(Post-)traumatic Logic of Socialism, Hunger, and Masculinity in Shang Xianliang's*Mimosa* (1984), in Jooyeon Rhee, Chikako Nagayama, and Eric Ping Hung Li, eds, *Gender and Food in Transnational East Asia: Toward a Dialogue Across Boundaries*, Lanham, MD: Lexington Books, 203-220.

Wengrow, David (2008), "Prehistories of Commodity Branding," *Current Anthropology*, 49, 7-34.

Williams, Raymond (1975), *The Country and the City*, New York: Oxford University Press.

Wood, Frances (1998), No Dogs and Not Many Chinese: Treaty Port Cities in China 1843-1943, London: John Murray.

Wu, David and Tan Chee-beng, eds. (2001), *Changing Chinese Foodways in Asia*, Hong Kong: Chinese University Press.

Wu, David and Sidney Cheung, eds, (2002), *The Globalization of Chinese Food*, Honolulu: University of Hawai'i Press.

Yan, Yunxiang (1996), The Flow of Gifts: Reciprocity and Social Networks in a Chinese Village, Stanford, CA: Stanford University Press.

Yang, Mayfair Mei-hui (1994), *Gifts, Favors, and Banquets: The Art of Social Relations in China,* Ithaca, NY: Cornell University Press.

Yeh, Wen-Hsin (2007), Shanghai Splendor: Economic Sentiments and the Making of Modern China, 1843-1949, Berkeley, CA: University of California Press.

Zang, Xiaowei, ed. (2016), *Handbook on Ethnic Minorities in China*, Cheltenham, UK: Edward Elgar.

Zhao, Xin (2008), "Advertising Consumer Culture in 1930s' Shanghai: Globalization and Localization in Yue Fen Pai," *Journal of Advertising*, 37 (2), 45-56

Chapter 1
Development of Business Anthropology in China

Chinese scholars and practitioners embrace Business Anthropology (a branch of applied anthropology) that deals with distinctive ethnic groups and economic development impacts. Anthropologists worldwide can benefit from an analysis of these important and distinctive developments. That trend and its major contributors are discussed.

Introduction

Business anthropology (an interdisciplinary subfield integrating business disciplines with anthropology) has developed rapidly in the West and the United States. A significant part of applied anthropology attracts both scholars and practitioners (Caulkins and Jordan 2013; De Waal Malefyt and Morais 2017; Jordan 2017; Liu and Li 2009; Tian, Zhou, and Ma 2018). Nevertheless, although anthropologists contribute to the business world (Jordan, 2013), they have not been adequately phased into business research practices (Tian and Walle 2009). But progress is being made.

Although this chapter deals with business anthropology as it is practiced in China, the field is closely related to economic anthropology and ethno-economics. Due to these parallels, briefly distinguishing the three concerning each other is useful.

Economic anthropology is the theoretical and scholarly branch of anthropology that deals with economic relationships and the interconnections between these activities within culture and societies. It is distinct from neo-evolutionist theories such as Leslie White's (1959), although potentially friendly to them. Economic anthropology is, perhaps, best known for the debate between the formalists (who embrace a neoclassical paradigm, view economic behavior as rational and universal) vs. the substantives (who, being more culturally relativistic, believe that economic behavior is culturally specific and fueled by emotions and feelings, not merely rational calculation).

Ethno-economics deals with the same issues raised by economic anthropology, especially when dealing with economic development issues and the situations faced by ethnic minorities and rural communities. Although the subject matter of economic anthropology and ethno-economics is largely the same, ethno-economists tend to focus upon economic theories and methods and add anthropological perspectives as required.

Business anthropology adapts anthropological theories and methods to business and commerce. Seminal work has been provided by scholars and consultants, such as Edward T. Hall. More recent movements include the "Naturalistic Consumer Research" movement associated with business scholars Russell Belk and John Sherry. Providing an alternative to quantitative and "scientific" research, the Naturalists employ qualitative methods, such as participant observation and the ethnographic method, within business research. In the last 20 years, providing these qualitative research services has become an important part of business research in the West. Most of this work involves adapting anthropological techniques to serve mainstream companies. This is the theme, for example, in the groundbreaking edited volume Handbook of Anthropology in Business (Denny and Sunderland 2014) in addition to some pilot studies (Freeman 2000; Moeran 2005; Tett 2009; Zaloom 2006).

Adapting anthropological techniques of qualitative research to serve mainstream companies, for example, is the theme of Ann Jordan's Business Anthropology (2013). Although Jordan's work is largely practitioner-oriented, scholars such as John Sherry, John and Tonya Bradford (2015) provide scholarly examples of how techniques of cultural analysis used to study indigenous cultures can be applied to the modern world. This example reflects the observations of Marietta Baba (2014), who notes that anthropological techniques employed in exotic places can be put to effective use within mainstream locations.

While some Western business anthropologists offer a general view of business research and anthropology's role in it, others specialize in specific sub-disciplines of business, such as advertising (De Waal Malefyt and Morais 2012). Wide arrays of specialized uses of anthropology within the business are discussed in the groundbreaking volume Handbook of Anthropology in Business (Denny and Sunderland 2014). In a similar spirit of specialization, Alfons Van Marrewijk (2015) uses business anthropology to explore the principles and techniques of project management.

A minority of Western business anthropologists, such as Alf H. Walle (2013), apply business anthropology to questions regarding economic development involving ethnic minorities and rural regions. Walle observes (2013 xi): "The holistic orientation of business anthropology offers flexible alternatives that are useful and appropriate when dealing with indigenous cultures, rural communities, traditional peoples, and small ethnic enclaves." As will be demonstrated, this orientation is a significant aspect of Chinese business anthropology. As a result, the field is growing in prominence (Zhang 2014; Yang 1995). This chapter presents a summary of these achievements.

Prologues for Business Anthropology in China

According to Tang and Chen (2017), the first hints toward business anthropology in China can be traced back to 1925 when American anthropologist Daniel Harrison Kulp published *Country Life in South China, the Sociology of Familism*, an ethnographic study of a Han Village (the largest ethnic group in China). Kulp illustrated the core concept of "familism" to emphasize what he felt were distinctive Chinese social and economic characteristics. Many issues addressed by Kulp have re-emerged in contemporary business anthropology.

Although Kulp wrote a seminal monograph, few scholars followed his lead for decades. Instead, anthropologists (such as those in Hong Kong) focused on theoretical issues. An article published by Xu Zhengguang in 1974, entitled "On Economic Anthropology," focused on the relationship between economics and economic anthropology (Tian and Luo 2013; Shi 2002).

Except for these Taiwanese scholars, Chinese anthropology was evolving in relative isolation. During this era, Taiwan's economy soared, and its scholars benefited from frequent exchanges with Western scholars. Under these favorable conditions, Taiwanese anthropologists began examining industrial, commercial, social, and economic development issues (Zhu 2001).

In the early 1970s, Xu Zhengguang, a pioneering Chinese business and economic anthropologist, published "A Few Questions Concerning Economic Anthropology." This formative paper elaborates on the interconnections between economic anthropology and other issues, including the economic life of traditional peoples, the development of community economies, and the relationships (and differences) between economics and economic anthropology.

Addressing the well-known "formalist" and "substantive" debate in economic anthropology, Xu noted that some formalist scholars applied Western neoclassical economic theory to small communities in developing countries in a constructive manner. Coming to conclusions that reflected the spirit of these times, suggestions were made to replace "subsistence or "non-market economies" with wage labor and commodity production to embrace important aspects of Western economics and business (Xu and Huang 1999). In those years, however, the concept of business anthropology in China was still at an early stage of development and lacked independence.

During this period, few Westerners were conducting anthropological research in China. An exception in the mid-1960s is the work of American anthropologist William Skinner who published an ethnographic study in *Asian Studies Quarterly* that analyzed the function and status of traditional rural markets in China. In that work, he investigated the evolution of China's rural markets, describing and analyzing the reforms in the rural market system reform that had occurred since 1949. Skinner was the first foreign researcher to research economic anthropology after founding the People's Republic of China (Shi 2002; Tian and Luo 2013).

Although other precedents can be found, the theoretical foundation of modern business anthropology in China can be traced back to Fei Xiaotong's *Peasant Life in China,* which has been described as "a milestone in anthropological fieldwork and theory evolution" (Fei and Dai 2012).

Researching from the 1930s until the 1950s, Fei examined the life of Chinese peasants and suggested that subsidiary businesses could be established, which balanced with agriculture, animal husbandry, and forestry in systematic and sustainable ways. His work has been described as a pioneering anthropological study that dealt with rural life and its transformations (Shi 2013).

In 1949, Fei and his assistant published *Earthbound China: A Study of Rural Economic in Yunnan, significantly impacting* Western academics. Like many other Chinese during this era, Fei believed that industrialization was the only way to lift China's rural economy out of backwardness.

In 1981, Professor Fei noticed that the raising of sheep and rabbits that he first observed in the 1930s had become a subsidiary business for every household in the Jiangcun Village, accounting for half of the average income per capita. In some rural areas, the industrial labor force exceeded that of agriculture. Arguing that the new structure of the rural economy provided significant opportunities for industry, he believed the time had come to cease referring to such regions as "countryside" (Shi 2013).

Fei's viewpoint on rural industry triggered heated debate: the rural industry was accused of vying with large-scaled industries for raw materials, energy and markets. The Vice Prime Minister, then in charge of industry, ordered relevant governmental agencies to investigate the issue. It was even debated in the National People's Congress. Applied anthropologists strived to influence the decision-making process. Fei achieved that goal.

Fei made significant contributions to the anthropology of China. He is remembered for studying the distinctiveness of the ethnic minorities, their history, their economic and business behaviors, and their needs. In doing so, he used the theories of British structural/functional anthropologists that he acquired from his professor, the legendary Bronislav Malinowski. Although business anthropology was not yet well developed and influential within China, the foundation for future growth and influence emerged.

Applied anthropology exists to help leaders to make appropriate and informed decisions. As a result, the research conducted inevitably reflects the paradigms and models employed by those who will use the generated data. Even though this is true, anthropologists often suggest important perspectives that those lacking an understanding of local cultures might overlook.

Since the introduction of Chinese economic reforms in the 1980s, increased attention has been paid to disciplines such as sociology and anthropology. In addition, important works have been translated into Chinese, such as A. Allen's work on economic anthropology (1985 translated by Tian Guang). Professor Shi Zhengyi addressed the nature, features, and "laws" of ethno-economic development and change (Shi 2002; Tian and Luo 2013).

Analyzing the economic gaps of that era, from 1984 to 1986, Shi Zhengyi and others investigated and analyzed the differences between those living in rural ethnic regions and those in developed areas. This led to the advance of the theory of strategies for accelerating economic development in some areas and industries. Doing so dovetailed nicely with governmental policies abstracted by a model known as the Four Modernizations, first articulated in 1963 by Zhou Enlai (first Premier of the People's Republic of China) and established as public policy in 1977 after his death. During the Cultural Revolution (which had many unfortunate consequences and today is regretted by most Chinese), leaders often spoke of the "Four Olds" known as (1) Old ideas, (2) Old customs, (3) An old culture, and (4) Old habits of thinking). The Four Modernizations can be viewed as the mirror opposite the "Four Olds."

proponents of the cultural revolution believed that these characteristics were archaic and counterproductive and needed to be stamped out. Although policies related to the "Four Olds" vs. the Four Modernizations" might have led to excesses, the resulting policies allowed local decision-makers to gain more authority, such as paying workers based upon their actual contributions, not merely a uniform wage. This decentralization of power ultimately exerted a positive influence.

As time went on and economic growth increased, planners and decision-makers sought to take advantage of favorable opportunities and conditions. One intent was to allow the ethnic minorities to narrow the economic gap between the eastern and western regions and included plans to achieve advanced conditions among the ethnic minorities (Zhang 2015).

These actions need to be viewed within the context of the national policy of the era that emphasized "one center, two basic points." This slogan stems from a speech presented in 1987 by Zhao Ziyang, entitled "Advance Along the Road of Socialism with Chinese Characteristics." Zhao argued that at the center of Chinese strategic policies was economic development. However, accomplishing this goal required paying attention to specific social and cultural sensitivity issues and opening China to the outside world (Shi 1989). Although the Chinese leadership emphasized that promoting industry was the primary goal, it simultaneously began to focus on the distinctiveness of China and the Chinese people.

Today, the relative importance of industry and manufacturing in China has decreased, allowing economic development to be viewed more flexibly. As a result, attention is increasingly directed toward rural groups (such as the western ethnic minorities) and their specific needs (Zhang 2015). This trend makes culturally sensitive researchers and strategists increasingly important.

Shi believed that economic development initiatives must pay attention to ethnic and cultural considerations to nurture and protect the region's cultural and social resources (Fei 2001). He repeatedly stressed that developing a commodity economy was necessary for advancing economic development in China's western ethnic areas. He felt the government needed to transform subsistence peasant life into a commodity economy. Shi's research on the cultures within ethnic minority regions can even be viewed as the theoretical underpinning of early business anthropology in China (Qu 2014).

Several theories developed regarding ethnic minority areas. The "gradient theory" assigned a lower priority to western China and its ethnic minorities and concluded that their development could be delayed. As an alternative, the "surpass theory" or "counter-gradient theory" held that the West possessed an enormous potential and that the ethnic minorities should be treated accordingly. This paradigm argued that if the government provided sufficient support, these areas could catch up with and even surpass the developed regions (Li and Zhao 2008).

Thus, a wide variety of opinions existed. The "two-step theory" gave strategic priority to developing the eastern coastal areas before investing heavily in the western minority areas. The "collaborative theory" advocated the simultaneous development of all regions.

During this period, the decision-makers of China, including high-ranking governmental officials, increasingly relied upon social scientists when forging strategies and plans. In tandem, these social scientists adjusted their work in ways that these leaders could appreciate and employ.

The Growth of Business Anthropology in China

The Institute of Sociology and Anthropology of Peking University played a leading role in promoting localized views of economic anthropology. In 1995, it hosted a Social-Cultural Anthropology seminar and invited Taiwanese scholar Dr. Jiang Bin to deliver a keynote speech on "economic anthropology." Under these circumstances, Jiang introduced the anthropologists of Mainland China to the two rival viewpoints of economic anthropology, i.e., the formalist (that employs universal and rational theories of neoclassical economics) and substantivalism (that views economic behavior from within a specific cultural environment).

Wang Yanxiang (a scholar in ethnic economics who graduated from the Central University for Nationalities with a doctoral degree) emerged as another important contributor who published articles in the *National Economy* and *Journal of the Central University for Nationalities* that introduced Western economic anthropology concerning China's ethnic minorities (Luo and Tian 2014).

In 1997, Professor Wang Mingming from Peking University published *Social Anthropology and China Research* to introduce William G. Skinner's earlier work on economic anthropology in China's rural areas. In the same year, the book *Economic Anthropology,* written by the Japanese economic anthropologist Shinichiro Kurimoto, was translated into Chinese and published. It was the first comprehensive introduction to economic anthropology generally available to Chinese academics (Shi 2002:273-6).

In the 21st century, theoretical innovation and vision have led to breakthroughs in Chinese economic anthropology. Economic anthropologists are being trained and developing significant research streams (Tian and Luo 2013:332-5). Two books entitled Economic Anthropology was published in 2001 and 2002. Professor Chen Qingde from Yunnan University published one, and Shi Lin wrote the other.

In addition, ethnographies have been published that contribute to business anthropology. In his ethnographic study of a village in North China (Yan 2000), Yan Yunxiang built upon the work of Karl Polanyi's social integration model. Polanyi, of course, was the founder of the substantive school of economic anthropology that nests economic behavior within a cultural context.

Yan's research pointed out that the traditions of Chinese gift-giving resonated from and represented complex social relations that reflected the social hierarchy contrary to the substantive principle of reciprocity. Using the ethnographic method, he interpreted the "meaning" of wealth concerning cultural, economic, trade, and sacred aspects of the culture (Luo 2000). Luo Hongguang demonstrated that economic behavior is nested within a social context and associated with religion, consciousness, and cosmology. Thus, the culturally sensitive substantive model was making an impact.

Today, more universities and research institutions across China offer economical and business anthropology courses than before. Doing so coincides with a greater interest in Western China and its ethnic minorities. At the same time, discussions of economic anthropology are included in newly published anthropology textbooks (Fan 2009).

With the deepening of China's economic reforms and the gradual improvement of the market system, business anthropology has played an increased role in China. With the ongoing refinement of the discipline and the deepening of research, scholars in the discipline's relevance are growing and gaining the respect of decision-makers locally. Scholars with a background in business anthropology are urged to study specific problems in the industrial and commercial fields. Fully achieving this goal will take the further efforts of Chinese business anthropologists, but considerable progress is being made (Tian, Zhou and Ma 2018).

It is useful to speak of specific individuals and their contributions to portray this progress. By doing so, not only are notable people discussed, their examples point to the contributions of others because the development of any discipline cannot be separated from the scholars that give it life. In particular, Chen Gang, Guo Yi, Jiang Caifang, Luo Kanglong, Peng Zhengyin, Qi Xiaoguang, Sun Jianfu, Tian Guang, Yang Tingshuo, Zhang Jijiao and Zhou Daming have made vital contributions (Tang and Chen 2017).

As representative examples, the specific contributions of Zhou Daming, Zhang Jijiao, and Tian Guang are briefly discussed.

Zhou Daming

Zhou Daming's academic contributions mainly include his studies on immigration and urbanization, ethnic and regional culture, and anthropological research. His expertise has been utilized by the World Bank, the Asian Development Bank, related ministries and commissions of the State Council, the Guangdong provincial government, etc. He has recently directed a project that gathered and examined the social development indicators used to evaluate Guangdong Province: a project that has been highly praised (Zhang 2014).

He has studied migrant workers (Zhou 1992; Zhou and Zang 2006), peasant entrepreneurs (Zhou 2002), and family businesses (Zhou and Tian 2015). By doing so, he has laid a foundation for examining the field of business administration in China. His *Vicissitudes of Fenghuang Village* is an important monograph of business anthropology in Chinese.

Zhou has emphasized theories that reflect local conditions and traditions and argued for the development of business anthropology in China.

Zhang Jijiao

Zhang Jijiao calls his research "enterprise anthropology" (Zhang 2015). The term is, however, consistent with "business anthropology" because the field in China is sometimes referred to as "commercial anthropology," "industrial anthropology," and so forth (Liu and Zhang 2016). Zhang has studied private lending, private credit and institutional financial changes (an early focus of business anthropology in China (Zhang 1998). He has expanded business anthropology by studying different enterprises and entrepreneurs. The subjects he studied include ethnic enterprises and migrant entrepreneurial family businesses.

He coined the term "umbrella society" to describe the relationship between local governments and enterprises to understand local resource allocation and economic and social development. In addition, he put forward the concept of "cellular society" to depict folk people's economic and social landscape (Zhang and Liu 2015). With this pair of concepts, he has modeled China's economic and social transformations, which involves the innovative use of business anthropology in China.

Tian Guang

One of the principal promoters of the discipline's construction of business anthropology, Dr. Tian has a cross-disciplinary background in anthropology, economics, and business administration (Tian, Zhou, and Ma 2018; Tian, Feng, and Wang 2017; Tian and Tian 2014). Professor Tian's representative works in English, General Business Anthropology, was co-authored with Drs. Van Marrewijk and Lillis and published by an American publisher. Based on theories and methods of anthropology, the authors have studied cross-cultural management and marketing, food culture and consumer behavior, and anthropology and business administration education. Their research findings have become important literature in studying the anthropology of business. Over the years, Dr. Tian and his colleagues have practiced what they preach, offering business anthropology courses at Shantou University (Tian and Chi 2012) and giving lectures at various colleges and universities around China. In addition, Dr. Tian has taken the initiative to organize international conferences on business anthropology in China so that the Chinese scholars have greater exposure and a viable platform to communicate with business anthropologists from across the world.

These three scholars are representative of the breadth of business anthropology in China. Many others, of course, have made vital contributions, but limits of space prevent a more detailed analysis.

Academic Activities and Organizations in China

Journals have a vital role in the development of a discipline. With an international strategic vision, in 2009, Zhou Daming and other scholars launched the *International Journal of Business Anthropology*, which has emerged as one of the major international academic journals dealing with business anthropology. After Tian Guang served as the inaugural editor, he has turned editorial duties over to Dr. Chen Gang of Yunnan University of Finance and Economics. Other respected academic journals include the *Qinghai Journal of Ethnology,* the *Journal of Beifang Minzu University,* the *Journal of Guangxi Minzu University,* and the *Journal of Hubei Minzu University* published special issues on business anthropology in recent years.

In addition, textbooks and monographs related to the themes of business anthropology are emerging. *Business Anthropology* edited by

Tian and Zhou (2012), is the first book to introduce the main theories, methods and research works of Western business anthropology to Chinese scholars. It orients the readers toward organizational well-being as a set of processes that can be promoted and supported by business anthropology. The book contains several business ethnographic works by Chinese scholars on industrialization and modernization in China. To keep pace with international business anthropology, Tian and Zhou published their monograph *General Business Anthropology* by one of China's national leading publishers in the year 2013. In addition, discussing Western business anthropology focuses on China's evolution and development into a postindustrial and commercial society from an anthropological perspective, demonstrating the applications of anthropology in the business world. Tian and Zhou first propose that China needs business anthropology in the book. The Chinese anthropologists must take the responsibility to localize business anthropology in terms of the Chinese context and the Chinese business world (Tian and Zhou 2013).

Dr. Qi Xiaoguang's *Study of Organizational Culture from the Perspective of Business Anthropology* was published in 2016, based on his more than ten years of work experience and observation in a multinational company. From a business anthropological perspective, it analyzes the cultural characteristics of multinational organizations that have entered China. In the book, Qi studies two multinational organizations in Dalian engaging in the international shipping industry. It is with different "nationalities" in terms of their unique organizational culture development and construction in the daily business environment, thus demonstrating how the dynamics and nuances of culture can potentially influence business operations. Christopher Marquis, professor of management and organization studies from Cornell University, commented that although survey articles on this topic began to increase, the relatively basic organizational culture from the perspective of business anthropology has not been discussed.

Given that the research in this field is still in its infancy, Dr. Qi's work has an opportunity to be an important academic one that will influence basic research in this field in the future. Professor Christopher Marquis believed that the book provided a new perspective for understanding formal and informal organizations in the business context. Therefore, he posed that the book would bring new insights into the interdisciplinary study of anthropology and management. Dr. Qi's work is an exemplary demonstration of using the theories and methods of business anthropology to carry out research (Qi 2016).

With the development of business anthropology in China in recent years, many Chinese scholars have studied its localization. Li Wenrui and Chen Gang investigated and studied the taxi driver groups and the taxi industry in Kunming, the capital of Yunan Province, and illustrated how the informal social groups affect business competition (Li and Chen 2014). Chen Gang and Guo Rui studied the multinational enterprises represented by the Chinese operating in Southeast Asia. They concluded that cultural adaptation is the key factor for foreign business firms to succeed in China (Chen and Guo 2015). Wang Shaojie analyzed the construction of corporate culture and suggested that social responsibility is the key element for a company to create the core values for the corporate culture (Wang 2015). Scholars studied organizational culture by referring to product design (Tian and Zhu 2014) and developing a time-honored food branding in Shantou City (Tian, Liu and Liu 2015; Tian and Wang 2014). Xu Wei carried out long-term, in-depth field research on a Sino-Botswana joint project of building a glass plant and advised Chinese business firms to study the hosting country's culture first before developing any business relationship with the business firms in the targeted country (Xu 2016). In their study and research, these Chinese business anthropologists adopted the principles and methods of business anthropology. Their research thus gained unique charm, showing business anthropology's theoretical vigor and application value.

Studying the production and consumption of commodities from the perspective of anthropology, Liu Humeng and Zhang Yinfeng forecast the development prospects of business anthropology in China (Liu and Zhang 2016). In terms of business anthropology theory, research and discipline construction, the Chinese scholars teased out market and marketing from the perspective of anthropology (Tian 2016). Based on the principles of business anthropology, they explored the relationship between qualitative research and discipline construction of management science, clarifying the key role of business anthropology in the localization of management studies (Tian, Liu and Wang 2015).

In her study of ethnic relations in Ethiopia, Dr. Shi Lin, a professor from The Central University of Nationalities, pointed out that it would be more effective to study national governance by means stated below. First, through anthropological and ethnological work, we can understand the present situation of its ethnic groups and ethnic relations history. Then we can conduct "multi-dimensional" systematic research which combines "panoramic (overall) dimension" with "close shot (regional) dimension," longitudinal (diachronic) dimension and horizontal (synchronic) dimension, and ethnographic description with theoretical analysis (Shi 2016). In her book Economic Anthropology, she elaborated on the theoretical source for business anthropology -- the academic contributions of Malinowski, Michael Polanyi and others to economic anthropology (Shi 2002).

Since anthropology was introduced into China early in the 20th century, research-oriented universities like Peking University, Sun Yatsen University and the Chinese Academy of Social Sciences (among others) have established institutes of anthropology and offered anthropology courses (Zhou 2012). With the further development of anthropology, some universities and institutions have promoted the research and teaching of business anthropology. In the early 21st century, Shantou University was the first Chinese university to offer courses in business anthropology. Building upon this experience, Tian Guang, the course director, created courses that combine business anthropology with Chinese characteristics (Tian and Chi 2012). Currently, universities such as North Minzu University are following in Tian's footsteps.

Since 2013 Yunnan University has recruited graduate students specializing in business anthropology. In that program, students are introduced to anthropological theories and methods and principles of business and administration. Moreover, they learn to apply the theories and methods of anthropology within a practitioner context in ways that improve their managerial abilities (or those of the clients they serve). Currently, the Research Center for Social and Economic Behavior at Yunnan University of Finance and Economics is the editorial home of the *International Journal of Business Anthropology*, one of the field's premier journals. These institutions encourage business anthropology in China while honing the skills of scholars, researchers, and practitioners (Zhao 2016).

With the combined efforts of scholars like Zhou Damin, Tian Guang, and Chen Gang, among others, the first international conference on business anthropology was held at Sun Yat-sen University in May 2012 (Tian and Zhou 2013). The conference has emerged as a high-profile annual event for business anthropologists worldwide.

In short, in the last decade, business anthropology has grown significantly in China. Not only does it support and utilize domestic business anthropologists, but China has also reached out to the larger academic world to attract the participation of noted scholars and practitioners from the United States and the West. As a result, while the Chinese seek to develop a version of business anthropology suited to its unique needs, it simultaneously embraces the profession.

China Needs Business Anthropology

Although ethno-economics and economic anthropology differ in their history, similarities make them mutually reinforcing. Commonalities among the three are easy to find. Ethno-economics, for example, makes use of ethnographic fieldwork and comparative studies. Business anthropology is often indebted, in some way, to economics. Business anthropology is an interdisciplinary field involving anthropology, management science, economics, ethnology and psychology (Tian 2012).

Business anthropology is known for, among other things, the innovative development of business ethnography, bringing traditional fieldwork within the context of business, focusing upon the influence of cultural differences in business administration practice, and developing ways to deal with these influences. To some extent, China's early business anthropology theories originated from ethno-economics and economic anthropology. Professor Shi Zhengyi made huge contributions in this respect.

In the second place, all three disciplines study human behavior and lifestyles within a cultural context. Because China was historically predominantly rural, early ethno-economists and economic anthropologists focused primarily on this type of culture and economy. In the mid to late 20th century, China's economic policies emphasized industrial development. Today, the West of China and ethnic minorities are receiving more attention. Because of this increased diversity, business anthropologists have expanded their range of research and practitioner contributions (Tian, Liu, and Wang 2015).

Professor Shi Zhengyi began to study ethnic questions, cultural issues, and social problems from a wider perspective after becoming conscious of the limitations of traditional ethnology. His example provided insights to early ethno-economists and economic anthropologists and inspired them to extend their research scope to be more globally oriented. Thus, research agendas moved from a narrow horizon to deal with broader generalizations. With economic and cultural globalization accelerating, Chinese business anthropologists gradually expanded their research focus to include multinational issues, consistent with ethno-economics and economic anthropology developments. (Shi 2011).

In the context of the global economy, transnational business transactions in China have become common. As a result, many obstacles to trade are being viewed from a cultural perspective. China, a large and culturally diverse country, is significantly different from many trading partners. As a result, Chinese companies and individuals potentially face conflict or misunderstandings when working with Western companies.

It is well known that specific cultures are distinctive. For example, Geert Hofstede (1984) has developed a dimensions model of cultures that includes issues such as power distance and individualism to depict. Applying this model to the USA and China suggests, for example, that Americans tend to be highly individualistic while the Chinese people are more comfortable working collectively. If these differences are not recognized, they can lead to tensions. Business anthropologists can help mitigate these differences in ways that facilitate harmonious relationships.

In another well-known example, Edward T. Hall's The *Silent Language* (1959), different people relate to time in their ways. Americans tend to be more rigid and often insist on a strict schedule. The Chinese, in contrast, tend to be comfortable with greater flexibility. In China, for example, it is polite to arrive a few minutes earlier than the appointed time, but in English-speaking countries, doing so might be improper. As a result, cultural sensitivity is required (Tian 2011). Business anthropologists can serve as "coaches" who help their clients master the social conventions they encounter.

Multinational enterprises that operate in China can benefit from cross-cultural management. The opposite is increasingly true: many Chinese enterprises invest in factories abroad. Haier, for example, has joined the Fortune 500 companies. Given this international expansion, increased cross-cultural expertise is needed. Business anthropologists can expect that such requirements will provide future opportunities. (Jian 2009).

China is a large country transforming its traditional agricultural and preindustrial society into a postindustrial and commercial powerhouse. Therefore, the future of business anthropology in China is promising. Currently, business anthropology is being taught in China. And increasingly, a "localized" approach is being embraced to deal with the distinctiveness of the country and its regions.

The Chinese recognize that business anthropology is an important tool. As a result, the profession can be expected to grow. This progress will be spurred by governmental economic development policies, innovation, and advanced business research methods.

Although business anthropology has not yet fully matured, it has already demonstrated an ability to promote a postindustrial and commercial society in China. It is also helping devise ways to deal with ethnic minorities equitably. Combining business anthropology with distinctive Chinese characteristics will emerge as a vital strategic and tactical tool. By doing so, it will simultaneously make international and global contributions.

Summary and Conclusion

Business Anthropology is emerging as an important strategic and intellectual force in China. However, as Margaret Mead (1975 14) once observed, "We only apply anthropology if someone applies it." Thus, in China, applied and business anthropologists have conducted work that others commissioned and wanted to utilize. Due to this reality, it should not be a surprise that applied and business anthropologists focused on such topics in an era when industrialization was prioritized. Eventually, the government and other decision-makers became concerned with the lives and economic realities of rural peoples and ethnic minorities. This shift of emphasis has provided business anthropologists with the chance to deal with vital issues facing Western China and its ethnic minorities.

Today, business anthropologists conduct significant research and practitioner assignments involving indigenous people, ethnic groups, and rural communities. These efforts dovetail with much work in economic development and mesh with what some people have called "Tribal Management (Walle 2009)." The achievements of Chinese business anthropologists are significant, and anthropologists from around the world can learn from them.

A foundation for the field and its current advances was created by Fei Xiaotong (Fei Hsiao-tung) and Shi Zhengyi, among others (Tang and Chen 2017). They made significant contributions to Chinese anthropology and pointed the way toward developing business anthropology (Zhang, Zhou, and Lin 2003). They applied their research findings to various societal fields, including the development of ethnic minority areas, economic development of underdeveloped areas, business administration, etc.

In short, our studies provide Western scholars with some interesting information about the relationship between the Chinese government and its policies and researchers. We hope our discussion on the distinctions among business anthropology, economic anthropology and ethno-economics contributes to the overall field of anthropology in general and business anthropology in special. Business anthropology is a subfield for both anthropology and business. It is a worldwide study theme. Its growth in China will make great contributions to the development of business anthropology in the world.

Business anthropologists in China are thriving because China needs them. The research, analysis, and insights they bring to the decision-making process are vital and unique. Thus, they have a unique role when forging strategic and competitive choices. Because of the contributions business, anthropology is posed to make in China. It has a window of opportunity and a chance to grow and contribute. The number of business anthropologists can increase with their contributions, both domestically and globally (Pan 2016).

Chapter 2
Urban-Rural Relationships in China in the Context of COVID-19

Rural villages are the foundations of Chinese Society. City and the countryside, associated with the concept of the organic social cycle "falling tree leaves return to the ground,"[1] *have supported each other for thousands of years. However, Chinese history in modern times has not developed as it was imagined theoretically. While the city is advancing, the countryside is declining. The duality of urban and rural areas has eroded the countryside, and their relationship has undergone a fundamental transformation. This deformed social structure must be corrected. Therefore, since the founding of the People's Republic of China in 1949, the work to reconcile the contradictions between urban-rural relationships runs throughout China's socialist modernization. This provides the logical main line of urban-rural integration. A city is a consumption group,*[2] *and it does not have a production function, and the raw materials needed for urban development are all obtained from the countryside. Unlike cities, rural areas have always been production bases.*[3] *However, limited by the scarce economic structure of self-sufficiency, if a rural village wants to prosper, it must rely on the urban market. As a result, the dual nature of the interaction between urban and rural economic development has conditioned that the urban-rural relationship is an interdependent, mutually restrictive and inseparable*

---

[1] It means that the leaves of a tree fall to its roots on the ground. It is a metaphor that things have a certain destination. It mostly refers to that people who live in a foreign country will eventually return to their hometown.

[2] For the past 100 years, cities have been brokerage stations for foreign goods, and almost all local products used in exchange for foreign goods have been supplied by villages.

[3] Fei Xiaotong expressed this in Rural Recovery. The countryside is a traditional Chinese production base that places equal emphasis on agriculture and labor. They maintain a high degree of self-sufficiency in their daily lives. People in the countryside who are accustomed to lowering their lives to cope with the famine, apart from salt, can easily settle for a self-sufficient economy, although this economy is inevitably scarce.

balanced one. This also means that the fundamental essence of urban-rural integration is rebuilding the rural social pattern from a modern perspective. In the spring of 2020, COVID-19 disconnected China's rural and urban areas, which caused a major blow to cities and rural areas. When the organic cycle of the society is broken, the city will suffer first, and the countryside also cannot avoid economic losses. The cities and the countryside seem to have truly fallen into what Fei Xiaotong calls "the tragedy of urban bankruptcy and rural primitivization." Examining the urban-rural relationship under the epidemic, we see that the countryside has become a buffer for social distress and a refuge for urban crises. In the post-epidemic phase, rebuilding a more flexible and resilient organic cycle is the theme of urban-rural relations.

Introduction

During the Spring Festival of 2020, the outbreak of COVID-19 had caused China to suffer catastrophic losses in many aspects, including economic and social aspects. Wuhan was closed on January 23, and the next day all parts of the country launched a first-level crisis emergency response. Suspension of work and production and home isolation restricted the scope of people's activities to one foot centered at home. Except for a very small number of supermarkets needed to guarantee people's basic living needs were still operating normally, almost all factories, shops, offices, schools and urban buses were closed.[1] This has never happened before in more than 70 years in history. In the rural areas in China, to prevent the spread of the epidemic, the government took extreme measures to close villages and cut roads to restrict the entry of migrants. Airplanes, high-speed railways, highways, and even inter-city, urban-rural, and village traffic were all blocked.

---

[1]On January 23, 2020, the Wuhan government announced that the city's urban buses, subways, ferries, and long-distance passenger transportation will be suspended from 10 am on the same day; the airport and railway stations will be temporarily closed. Following this, provinces and cities in China adopted compulsory measures such as closing cities and villages to strictly control the movement of people. Until the end of March, China's epidemic eased significantly, and the country began to resume transportation and production in an orderly manner.

For thousands of years, the pattern of mutual dependence between urban and rural areas has been broken. All connections now relied on the Internet. The severance of commodity circulation and interpersonal communication has severely disconnected urban and rural areas. When urban people were consciously or forcibly closed by the grid management to dozens of square meters of home space in urban high-rise buildings, most rural villagers could breathe fresh air in their courtyards. The villages, which had been forgotten or abandoned for a long time, thus became desirable homes for people. The relationship between urban and rural areas has once again undergone profound changes. This makes us wonder about the relationship between China's urban and rural areas under a major epidemic. If the epidemic continues for a long time, how should we handle the relationship between urban and rural areas? How can the countryside become a solid base to face major disasters and urban development? How can cities treat and feed the countryside? Where is the future of rural development and rural revitalization?

New Meaning of the Urban-Rural Relationship

The ever-advancing cities and the gradually abandoned villages constitute the basic structure of Chinese society in modern times. Since the founding of the People's Republic of China in 1949, the urban-rural relationship has generally undergone a development process from urban-rural coordination to urban-rural integration. The government tried to tackle the dual contradiction problem between the urban and rural areas. Facing the tragedy of the duality of urban and rural areas accumulated over thousands of years, Fei Xiaotong (2019: 28) wrote in *Rural Recovery*: "The rural is still our base for revival." His remarks reveal that the fundamental essence of urban-rural integration lies in the modern rebuilding of the rural areas, including rebuilding the man-land connection indicated by the phase of falling leaves returning to the ground and rebuilding the organic cycle between urban and rural areas (ibid. 87). This epidemic has allowed us to see the dual contradiction between urban and rural areas more clearly and understand the comprehensive interaction between urban and rural areas. The rural areas are increasingly affected by cities. Small disturbances in cities may cause waves in the rural areas. The outbreak of the crisis has hit both the urban and rural areas. The transmission of crises in any public area will be faster, and at the same time, it will affect urban and rural development more comprehensively.

Urban-Rural Relationship is the Basic Issue of the Modernization Process

The development of the urban-rural relationship since the founding of the People's Republic of China in 1949 has always been in line with China's socialist modernization. The issues derived from the duality of urban-rural development have always been major issues in Chinese economic and social development. In the early days of the founding of the People's Republic of China, the government had many things to do. In response to the recovery of the national economy, the government set the development goal of establishing an advanced industrial country under the planned economy system and formulating a strategic framework to prioritize the development of heavy industry.

Mao Zedong (1956) pointed out in his "On the Ten Major Relationships" that the heavy industries are the focus of the country's construction, and we must prioritize the development of production materials. Therefore, to guarantee the supply of production materials and the accumulation of original capital needed for industrial development, the government had allocated many resources from the rural areas to cities through the unified purchase and sales and planned distribution of industrial and agricultural products. But in this economic exchange, the price of industrial products was higher than their value, and the agricultural product price was lower than their value. And the difference between the two products shows a scissors-like trend. This is an unequal exchange, and the consequence is that rural resources are plundered. In 1958, to improve the efficiency of unified purchasing and marketing, the government quickly established a people's commune system with the centralized operation, centralized labor, and unified distribution.

At the same time, the development of industry continued to increase the urban labor force, so that food was in short supply in urban areas and became a heavy burden. Therefore, to prevent urban overloading, the state government began to restrict the excessive flow of the rural population to cities. It promulgated the Regulations of the People's Republic of China on Household Registration, which stipulates the agricultural population and the non-agricultural population by law. Since then, household registration seemed to have become an implicit distribution clause in public services, capital, resources and other aspects of urban and rural lives. Cities had become rural parasites, grabbing rural resources excessively. The contradictions between accumulation and consumption, industry and agriculture, and cities and villages had become more prominent. Peasants were firmly imprisoned on the rural land. The urban-rural relationship was in a state of division, and the dual social structure of urban and rural areas had been formed since then.

The turning point was in 1978, marked by the red handprints of 18 farmers in Xiaogang Village, Fengyang, and Anhui.[1] The prelude to reform and opening-up was kicked off, and the third agricultural revolution represented by the Household Contract Responsibility System[2] was started. This changed the collective economy of the people's commune, liberated the land production and management rights, and greatly mobilized farmers' enthusiasm for production. But unfortunately, this system had not changed the urban-rural dualistic situation and even caused some secondary problems. The rights of migrant workers in cities could not be guaranteed, and a large number

---

[1]On November 24, 1978, 18 households of farmers in Xiaogang Village signed an agreement very tragically to divide the cultivated land. Everyone pressed a red handprint. This event was recorded in the annals of Chinese history and represented the beginning of the Chinese household contract responsibility system.

[2]The household production contract responsibility system is a form of agricultural production responsibility system in which farmers take the family as a unit and contract land and other production materials and production tasks to collective economic organizations (mainly villages and groups).

of surplus laborers generated in rural areas had to stay in the village for employment. Because of this, in the early 1990s, the state government successively promulgated various policies to support rural collectives and individual farmers to set up various enterprises, and the emergence of township and village enterprises had brought prosperity to the rural economy.

With the gradual relaxation of the household registration system and the establishment of the socialist market economy system, many rural surplus laborers moved to cities in the late 1990s. The process of urbanization proceeded rapidly. However, in contrast to this, production factors such as rural capital and labor once again began to flow one way to the cities. Township enterprises were also gradually declining. Entering the 21st century, with China's accession to the WTO, globalization kicked off, and the process of urbanization in China had further accelerated. Benefiting from the open policies, cheap labor and the vast market, China's manufacturing industries have rapidly developed and become the World Factory. [1] However, many impoverished villages, empty nest villages, widow villages, and villages with children left behind by parents have emerged in China's central and western regions. The rural decline continued to accelerate.

Confined to the decline of the countryside caused by the continuous urban-rural dualistic situation, the government has realized that the overall development of the urban and rural areas has become a vital issue for China's socialist modernization. In 2002, the government established the idea of coordinating urban and rural development for the first time. In October 2003, the Third Plenary Session of the 16th Central Committee of the Communist Party of China further clarified the development policies of "coordinating urban and rural development" and "solving the three rural issues as the top priority of the party's

---

[1]At the turn of the century, with China's accession to the WTO, China's reform and opening up continued to deepen. The broad market, cheap labor and preferential policies have attracted many multinational companies to choose to set up factories in China. For example, Coca-Cola, Unilever, Procter & Gamble, etc. all entered the Chinese market at this time.

work."[1] This declared that the urban-rural relations entered a turning point. In recent years, with the introduction and practice of the concepts such as new urbanization, targeted poverty alleviation, and beautiful rural construction, urban and rural coordination has continued to develop. In 2017, the report of the 19th National Congress of the Communist Party proposed the strategy of rural revitalization and regarded it as one of the seven national development strategies. Building the new urban-rural integrated relationship is the key to solving major social contradictions and realizing people's yearning for a better life in the new era.

The Contradiction of Urban-Rural Relationship Lies in Insufficient Development

The report of the 19th National Congress of the Communist Party of China pointed out that the main contradiction in current Chinese society is between the people's growing need for a better life and unbalanced and inadequate development. The main ones are unbalanced urban-rural development and insufficient rural development.

Since the reform and opening up, great progress has been made in China's urbanization construction, and great changes have taken place in the countryside. By 2019, China's rural poverty population has decreased from 250 million to 5.51 million, and the poverty incidence has dropped from 30% to 0.6%. However, although rural per capita disposable income in poor areas is increasing at an average annual rate of 9.7%, the gap between urban and rural areas is still large. According to the National Bureau of Statistics of China (NBSC 2020a), the disposable income of rural residents in 2019 was 16,021 yuan, which is only 38% of urban residents' disposable income. The income difference is only one aspect, and there are big gaps in transportation, communications, housing, medical care, education, and culture.

In particular, many young and middle-aged rural laborers flock to cities to work, which has caused rural development to lose vitality and motivation, and the contradiction between urban and rural imbalances

---

[1]Three Rural Issues means the issues of agriculture, farmer and rural area.

has become increasingly prominent. At the same time, about 290 million peasant workers were living in cities (NBSC 2020b). Although they bear a deep peasant brand, they are different from peasants in nature. This group has not engaged in agricultural production for a long time and has been out of rural life for a long time. They bring cheap labor to the city and contribute to urban development. But the reality is that the city does not accept them because they cannot enjoy the same treatment as urban residents in terms of labor and employment, social security, medical and health care, family education, housing, and transportation.

The lag in rural development caused by the dual urban-rural structure has a fundamental impact on the social and economic life of the entire country. There are currently 560 million people in the country's rural areas, accounting for 40% of the country's total population (NBSC 2020c). The social status of the peasants will not change with the process of urbanization. How to satisfy their yearning for a better life is a major issue to solve in Chinese society. The countryside is the place to remember the excellent Chinese traditional culture, the ecological wetland with a high-quality natural environment and the spiritual home in the memory of countless urban residents. While the urbanization rate continues to increase and the urban and rural economy continues to develop, the rural revitalization construction under the background of new urbanization needs to deeply explore the countryside's potential value and humanistic significance. In this way, people living in the countryside can be balanced and dignified both at the material and spiritual levels.

Modern Rebuilding of the Urban-Rural Social Structure

We can conclude from the above discussion that the city and the village themselves do not cause the duality split. From the regular pattern of economic operation, the city and the countryside are one body. From the perspective of urban evolution, cities are the products of the earth (Miller and Mumford 2016:1) and models of rural societies that are highly centralized and functionalized. So cities naturally inherit the genes of the countryside, just as Miller and Mumford (ibid.) described:

Every phase of life in the countryside contributes to the existence of cities. What the shepherd, the woodman, and the miner know become transformed and 'etherealized' through the city into durable elements.

Therefore, since the city was born, no matter how it develops, it has been inseparable from the supply of resources from the countryside. From the perspective of the synchronic stage of urban and rural development, the most distinctive urban-rural relationship lies in the interdependence of economic activities, that is, the "rural and city complement each other" (Fei 2019:21) (Figure 1). Villages' surplus agricultural products are continuously shipped to cities as the production bases. And the city, as an industrial center, acquires all its raw materials for industrial production needs from the countryside. At the same time, industrially manufactured goods are imported into the countryside. As a result, a circulation cycle is formed between the village and the city.

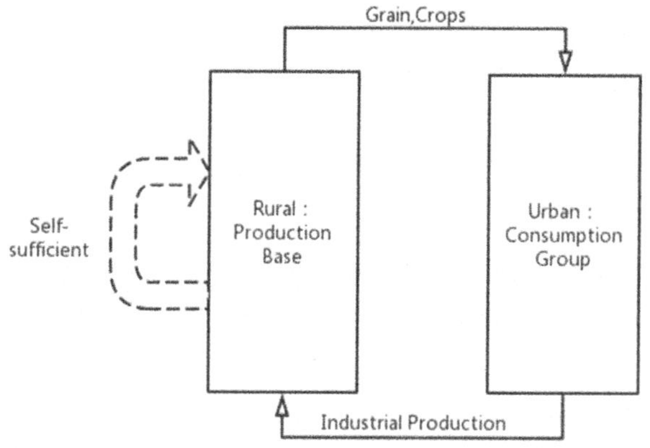

Figure 2.1. Rural-Urban Complement

However, as the two main bodies of the cycle, rural and urban areas are not equal. On the one hand, cities are more fragile than villages because villages have a self-sufficient self-circulation production base for agricultural products. In other words, the village's survival could have been independent of the city, but the city could only rely on the village. Once a crisis hinders this cycle, cities will first suffer and become "the cancer of the entire social organism" (Fei 2019:98). On the other hand, the countryside has also suffered huge losses. The intensification of the dual contradiction between urban and rural areas has caused the reduction of rural arable land and the loss of labor force, leading to the decline of rural production functions. The countryside is increasingly dependent on and constrained by circulation, and the crisis in the city has become a crisis in the countryside. Therefore, to rebuild the deeply integrated relationship between urban and rural areas, it is essential to reshape a more stable organic cycle and rebuild a more flexible and resilient social structure.

Urban and Rural Areas Affected by the Covid-19

On the eve of the Spring Festival in 2020, the COVID-19 epidemic suddenly hit Wuhan and spread rapidly. This is a major emergency with the fastest spread, the widest range of infections and the most difficult prevention in China. Many facts have proved that China's epidemic prevention measures have been effective, but the urban-rural relations exposed again under the pandemic are also worth pondering.

During the large-scale outbreak of COVID-19, cities and villages showed completely different life scenarios. Compared to rural areas, cities are more affected by the epidemic. This also shows that villages have stronger survival resilience than cities, and the resource and functional value of villages are further highlighted and revealed. However, in the context of the increasingly close urban-rural ties in the new era, measures such as closing cities and villages during the epidemic have brought a series of tests to urban-rural relations. The urban-rural division and the disconnection between urban and rural areas have made cities lose their dependence on daily life needs and prevented rural agricultural and sideline products from entering the urban markets. The daily industrial products needed by villages cannot be supplied, which is equivalent to an even worse disaster for the vast rural areas where the sanitation foundation is extremely weak.

Traffic Interruption Isolates the Urban and Rural Areas

Under special circumstances during the epidemic, although the travel bans like closing the city and the village prevented the spread of the epidemic effectively, they also blocked the urban-rural connections in traffic. Because cities are highly mobile, the epidemic's impact in cities is much greater than in rural areas. However, the epidemic's impact on urban and rural areas is all-around under the current background of close and frequent urban-rural ties.

The epidemic's impact on rural areas is more reflected in urban and rural production circulation. Cities are the front-end market for surplus products in rural areas. Still, due to the epidemic ban, many agricultural and sideline products cannot be transported to cities, resulting in poor market sales. The lack of export of raw materials resulted in a backlog of products that caused large-amount unsold sales. In particular, the obstruction of the production and marketing of fresh vegetables, fruits, and flowers has caused catastrophic economic losses in agriculture. Traffic obstruction and the reduction in employment caused by business shutdowns have also seriously affected migrant peasant workers. The unemployment rate of migrant workers in cities in June 2020 is 0.7% higher than in the same period last year (Zhang 2020). In the first quarter of 2020, the added value of Chinese primary industries fell by 3.2% (Zhao 2020).

The pandemic has had a huge impact on the employment of rural migrant workers, which were originally less stable. In the first half of 2020, the average monthly income of migrant workers fell by 6.7% year on year (NBSC 2020d). The living conditions of migrant workers stranded in the city are equally disturbing. The suspension of work and production in all walks of life makes it difficult for migrant workers in cities to guarantee their basic living income. The difficulty of returning home also made some migrant workers have to stay in the city. The original traffic control to prevent the spread of the epidemic lacked reasonable early warning and emergency arrangements. The social order problem hidden under the disconnection between urban and rural areas has become the biggest gray rhino crisis in urban and rural governance.

The circulation segment links both urban and rural supply and demand, and the epidemic's impact on circulation is bound to cause a chain reaction in cities. On the one hand, rural areas are the market for urban manufactured goods, and agricultural materials and industrial products related to cities cannot reach the countryside. On the other hand, rural products such as meat and eggs have become essential living materials for home epidemic prevention during the epidemic prevention and control period. However, due to the outbreak of the epidemic and the barriers to circulation, the supply to the urban areas is insufficient. In areas where the epidemic is more severe, there has even been a phenomenon of looting. The mismatch between production and sales, supply and demand, are out of line, and the widening price gap increases the living burden of the poor people. The normal life of urban citizens is disrupted, and the living necessities cannot be effectively guaranteed.

The epidemic's impact on urban and rural areas has moved from circulation to production, consumption and even social security. The transmission of crises in the public sphere is faster and more comprehensive in the new era of China's socialist modernization. The increasingly integrated and frequent urban-rural relationship promotes the flow of urban and rural production factors and improves the efficiency of resource allocation. At the same time, it also turns urban and rural areas into one living community. When the urban and rural areas that belong to the same life system face major public crisis events, no one can survive on an island and only protect themselves. The epidemic's impact on cities is also deeply felt in rural areas.

The Fragility of Urban Survivals and the Rural Values

The epidemic's impact on cities is greater than that on villages. In the consumer market mainly affected by COVID-19 in the first quarter, except for education, culture and entertainment, all consumption expenditures of urban residents have fallen significantly higher than those in rural areas (Figure 2) (NBSC 2020e). The high density and high mobility of cities have paved the way for the occurrence and spread of risk events. Although cities have better disaster prevention facilities, better medical conditions, and better emergency management systems, cities are more vulnerable than villages when faced with major public crisis events.

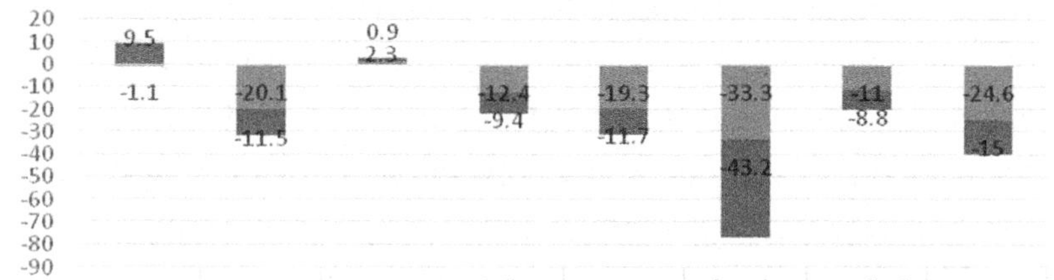

	Food	clothes	live	Daily necessities	transportation	education &culture	medical care	others
Rural	9.5	-11.5	0.9	-9.4	-11.7	-43.2	-8.8	-15
Urban	-1.1	-20.1	2.3	-12.4	-19.3	-33.3	-11	-24.6

Urban Rural

Figure 2.2 Per capita consumption expenditure of urban and rural residents in 2020 Q1

The individualization and independence of urban life make urban interpersonal relationships more indifferent and unfamiliar. The high density of the urban population also makes the virus easier to spread. The narrowness of personal living space in cities makes people who have been forced to stay at home for a long time physically and mentally more vulnerable. On the contrary, although the public infrastructure in rural areas is relatively weak and the control and governance capabilities are relatively insufficient, the social structure of the traditional rural community enables it to show stronger survival resilience than cities when a crisis comes.

The rural area is the stabilizer of social development. The stable traditional community structure in the village keeps its order and is stable for a long time to self-mediate in time under the impact of the crisis. The relatively abundant self-sufficient production enables the villages to maintain certain living needs during the epidemic. In the epidemic prevention and control work, the rural social structure that is close, tolerant and trusting can be concentrated on a high degree of cooperation based on the collective consciousness. Village cadres and village volunteers become the backbone of the rural basic level prevention and control workers during the epidemic. The low population density in the countryside and the relatively sufficient buffer space for disaster avoidance have also effectively prevented the spread of the epidemic. Low-carbon, healthy and friendly lifestyles and ecological environments have made the countryside a paradise outside the epidemic. Even due to the prevention and control management, the villages were forced to close, but the villagers could still live in peace.

The village is a buffer for social distress. The reason cities can withstand the cruelty of war and undertake the impact of disasters is the continuous supply of living materials from the countryside. "Cities always absorb fresh and pure life from rural areas. These people resurrect the cities with their flesh and blood and their eagerness" (Mumford 1961:53). Greek cities maintained a democratic style in the development process because of the village genes. Even in the most prosperous era of the Greek city-state, there were no abundant productive products and extravagant consumption that modern cities have. Still, plenty of leisure, freedom and unrestrained time were the most distinctive characteristics of the village, which was available adequately. During the epidemic control period, when cities were deeply affected by the spread of COVID-19 due to their high mobility, the villages accommodated many urban returnees. They reduced the possibility of secondary transmission with its small scale and low mobility. And in the post-epidemic phase, villages will also become energy storage pools for urban restoration and reconstruction after the disaster.

Reflecting on the urban-rural relationship under pneumonia, cities and villages have shown closer complementary functions, and the value of the countryside needs to be further emphasized. In the past, urban and rural construction promoted agriculture, whether agriculture was used to supplement industries or industries. Rural areas have long been marginalized. The integration of urban and rural areas in the new era is, in fact, a reshaping of the previous urban-rural relationship and functional roles. Suppose cities and villages want to maximize benefits through functional connection and difference. In that case, they have to re-focus on rural values and carefully consider the role of the villages in the social structure and function system. We can successfully cope with crises and risks by forming a resilient structure that integrates urban and rural areas.

Urban-Rural Integration Needs to Be Intensified

Although the epidemic's impact on rural areas is significantly less than in cities, there are many shortcomings and secondary risks in rural epidemic control work. Public health is the biggest shortcoming in preventing and controlling this rural epidemic. Compared with cities, rural public health infrastructure is relatively weak and medical and health care conditions are insufficient. Rural health institutions have insufficient diagnostic capabilities and insufficient stocks of epidemic prevention materials, and it is difficult to meet the emergency needs of sudden outbreaks. It is also difficult to support rural epidemics' health prevention and control if it is solely dependent on village-level clinics.

Problems such as weak farmers' health education and basic sanitation knowledge and farmers' inadequate attention to the pneumonia epidemic have made the prevention and control in rural areas more difficult. Approaching the Spring Festival of 2021, the epidemic broke out in Hebei, with 354 COVID-19 infection cases in 8 days. It is worth noting that this epidemic is mainly distributed in rural areas. The confirmed cases were mainly peasants, and many of them had participated in gatherings of people such as wedding banquets, funerals and other gathering activities. It indicates that peasants' weak awareness of individual protection, the peculiar acquaintance model and the close neighbor relationship in rural areas undoubtedly increase the difficulty of epidemic prevention and control. Compared with cities, rural areas have become China's main area to overcome COVID-19.

Social governance is also a major problem in rural epidemic prevention and control. Rural governance has its special forms and methods. For example, the "little horn"[1] played an important role in preventing and controlling the rural epidemic. However, rural governance is relatively independent and autonomous. Therefore, if the uploaded prevention and control tasks are truly implemented in the rural areas, it is faced with the problem of effective local transformation. Governments should formulate prevention and control measures based on local conditions. While giving rural entities a certain amount of initiative, they also need to regulate further and coordinate the relationship with rural grassroots. In addition, the lack of a horizontal joint prevention and control mechanism in rural areas makes communication unclear. It hinders the flow of inter-village resources and traffic, which are also problems in preventing and controlling rural epidemics. Unlike the city's convenient internal network linkage system, many natural villages often have one-way connections. The poor interaction and communication often result in the obstruction of material supply in remote villages, which undoubtedly increases the difficulty of governance for epidemic prevention and control.

From the SARS epidemic to the Wenchuan earthquake and the pandemic, the experience of many sudden public events has shown citizens' crisis awareness and response quality. The emergency response capabilities directly affect the loss situation and the efficiency of crisis management in crisis prevention and control. The general lack of knowledge to handle emergency crises among peasants can easily lead to misleading public opinion dissemination. As the front line of epidemic prevention and control in rural communities, shaping a good health culture and cultivating public spirit is important and powerful supports for epidemic prevention and control. Popularizing basic

---

[1]The little horn is kind of the broadcast used to convey news and notices to villagers in rural China .During the epidemic, the little horn played an important role in broadcasting the government notices and the health knowledge.

epidemic prevention and control knowledge, strengthening public health education, improving the people's public health emergency knowledge, and strengthening community coordination in the overall urban epidemic prevention and control are the top priorities in further preventing the spread of the epidemic (Hu and Long 2009).

Farmers are generally inadequate in emergency response literacy and are prone to panic due to the epidemic outbreak, making it often difficult to make correct judgments in the complex information environment shaped by the internet. Uncertainty in the development of the epidemic and unclear information can easily cause negative or false public opinion dissemination in public information sharing. Compared with the developed information network and timely information transmission in cities, the secondary disasters caused by public opinion dissemination undoubtedly increase the difficulty of preventing and controlling the epidemic in rural communities.

Cities have superior basic conditions and a more systematic prevention and control system in terms of public services, urban governance, and the transmission of public opinion than rural villages. Under the vision of urban-rural integration, building a new relationship requires deep interaction and coordinated development in multiple dimensions between urban and rural areas.

Rural Rebuilding in the Post-Epidemic Era

Rural villages are the foundations of Chinese Society (Fei 1992). The rural area is the solid foundation for urban development, and the city is an important support for rural revitalization. For thousands of years, urban and rural areas have been one entity, relying on each other. However, as urbanization continues to accelerate, the countryside as the matrix of urban development has gradually lost. This epidemic has continuously exposed the urban-rural relationship issues surrounding the dual urban-rural system. In the post-epidemic phase, the construction of a new urban-rural relationship should be based on the two strategic systems of new urbanization and rural revitalization to promote the flow and qualitative interaction of urban and rural elements, to cherish rural values more and focus on improving the overall resilience of urban and rural areas. This will be the most important task for the government for a long time in the future.

Promote the Organic Interaction of Urban and Rural Elements

The new urban-rural integration is not only a reshaping of the previous urban-rural relationship but also an inherent requirement of urbanization and rural revitalization strategies in the new era. The new urbanization has announced the historic end of the differentiation between urban and rural areas, represented by the household registration system and rectified the urban-rural division caused by the dual structure. Rural revitalization is a strategic deployment based on the integration of urban and rural areas and the comprehensive revitalization of the rural areas to achieve socialist modernization. There are various proofs that the core issue of the relationship between urban and rural areas is the free flow of production factors.

During the epidemic, the stagnant flow of production elements caused by traffic controlled a certain degree of disconnection between urban and rural areas, affecting cities and villages' economic and social development. Therefore, the key to urban-rural integration in the post-epidemic phase is to achieve qualitative interaction in industry, ecology, interpersonal, governance and culture based on the strategic integration of new urbanization and rural revitalization and promote the effective transformation of urban and rural resources.

Promote the Industrial Interaction in the Process of Modernization

Agricultural and rural modernization is essentially a process of exchanging and interacting with urban and rural elements. With the acceleration of new urbanization and the rural revitalization strategy, agriculture has been transformed from traditional self-sufficient small-scale farming to commercialized market-oriented modern agriculture. The revitalization of rural industries is an important starting point for fundamentally realizing agricultural modernization. It is also an important path to the marketization of the rural economy and a fundamental guarantee for increasing peasants' income.

With the vigorous promotion of rural cultural revitalization, the leisure economy represented by rural cultural tourism and sightseeing agriculture has risen, and cultivating land is no longer the only means of making a living for peasants. Agriculture has also begun to integrate deeply with industries such as tourism, health and elderly care, showing a diversified development trend. With the development of rural industries, the countryside has become a consumer market with huge potential, and the most important consumer group comes from the city. The resource capital, advanced technology and scientific management required for modern agricultural production also originate from cities. The construction of public infrastructure supporting the integrated development of rural industries also depends on cities. For large rural development projects promoted by rural revitalization, cities will become an important support for rural agricultural modernization.

Promote Low-Carbon, Healthy and Friendly Ecological Interaction

The huge impact of the epidemic has reawakened the importance of health and hygiene in social and economic development. It is very important to implement the concept of low-carbon, healthy and friendly green development into the urban-rural integrated development system. Establishing an ecological civilization view of urban and rural development is also an important part of ecological restoration and urban repair in the post-epidemic phase. To promote a good ecological interaction between urban and rural areas, it is necessary to strengthen the institutional integration and unification of urban and rural ecological governance, especially to prevent the shift and spread of industrial pollution to the countryside.

It is also necessary to transform the mode of industrial development so that the countryside can become an ecological wetland with conservation awareness and environmental consciousness. Through the pandemic test, people have become more clearly aware that a good rural ecological and livable environment is an important choice for urban residents to build a second residence in the future. The second residence, for urban residents, is an ideal place to realize a healthy and beautiful life. It is an effective breakthrough for enhancing vitality and upgrading the village.

Form an Open, Tolerant and Caring Interpersonal Interaction

In the new era, the social trend of urban and rural development is interpersonal interaction between urban and rural areas. It is also a new driving force for the overall rural revitalization. Groups of migrant workers working in cities play an important role in the urban-rural interaction. They bring the more avant-garde ideas and fashionable lifestyles in the city back to the countryside and, at the same time, provide a large amount of labor-capital for the operation of the city. The rural revitalization needs talented people from the cities and smart rural migrant workers returning to villages.

They bring the urban technology, capital and scientific construction concepts to the countryside, which is an important support for the overall revitalization of the countryside and the rescue of the countryside decline. The key to promoting interpersonal urban-rural interaction is to create an open, tolerant and humanistic development environment. Especially during the epidemic, the survival dilemma of migrant workers staying at railway stations and difficulty in resuming employment in cities requires further attention in the post-epidemic phase. To achieve true urban-rural integration in urbanization is to develop human interaction.

Shape a Cultural Identity of Trust and Harmony

Cultural identity and social governance are interlinked functional systems. Integrating urban and rural areas to achieve social governance depends on "Mechanical Solidarity" (Durkheim and Lukes 1984:57), social cohesion and centripetal force based on interdependence and cooperation. Building a cultural identity and a harmonious society based on tolerance and trust is necessary to form an organic social unity. The Chinese government has undergone role changes and power decentralization in recent years. At the same time, this practice has empowered multiple entities in the market to participate and has also tested the community's consciousness of society. The integration of urban and rural areas should be used to shape the collective cultural identity of urban and rural areas to condense the social participation forces of citizens, not only to achieve urban and rural coordination in the construction of public service facilities but to reconcile the contradictions between modern urban culture and rural culture. Governments need to integrate cultural concepts such as harmony in rural culture and harmony between man and nature into urban development and, at the same time, integrate modern values of urbanization into rural development.

Cherish Rural Values and Build a Flexible Functional System

The impact of the epidemic has made the value of villages more prominent. Even if there are no complete public facilities, sufficient material reserves, or a fairly complete disaster prevention system and emergency response mechanism, the villages have shown greater survival resilience and anti-risk capabilities than cities. In-depth analysis of the internal mechanism of rural prevention and control, to build a close functional system integrating urban and rural areas, and to embed the moral customs of the village into the concept of urban development and returning to the humanistic value goal of urban construction are topics that should be used for reference and reflection in the post-epidemic phase of urban integrated development.

There is a natural, cultural inheritance relationship between the city and the countryside. The village settlements of the Neolithic Age brought about a production economy that transformed nature and protected the proliferation of human offspring. The unity of man and nature, blood and land, constitute the most basic way of life in primitive villages. Humanity complies with the needs of survival and carries the humanistic ideal of the good romantic life, thus nurturing cities. The order and stability of the village, together with its mother-like protection and sense of comfort, are passed on to the city so that the city can remain vigorous for a long time and human civilization can be sustained (Mumford 1961).

Even though the city has produced a high degree of division of labor, social differentiation and power concentration in the cultural return and the pursuit of large-scale production, mechanization, and automated urban expansion have gradually shifted the city itself from pursuing the goal of humanistic value. But the village customs which remain in the urban communities and neighborhoods do not cause urbanites to evolve into a rabble of atomized individuals. When one side is in trouble, the neighbors support each other, and the urban society turns crises into opportunities time after time as it grows.

Realize Symbiotic Development with Complementary Functions

The most fundamental function of the village, as a maternal existence in urban evolution, is to nurture. In the new era, the village still practices this function. The countryside is cultural support for the continuous inheritance of Chinese excellent traditional culture (Chen 2019). However, the closed and static characteristics of primitive villages affect the transcendence of rural China and the overall revitalization of the countryside. Several wonderful civilization evolutions in history have occurred in cities. The city evolved from the countryside is a container that encompasses everything and a magnet with full gravity.

Especially since the Industrial Revolution, fast-growing cities have opened up closed and static traditional villages. However, the frequent flow of factors and expanded interpersonal communication have not created a closer functional integration of urban and rural areas. Instead, cities became crazy predators of rural resources, which led to a more serious decline in rural areas and caused urban crises. There is a dark side to both the countryside and the city. Although cities can tolerate the infinite expansion of the market and the infinite accumulation of production factors, they cannot provide and produce all kinds of production factors needed for industrial development. The production factors required for industrial development have always depended on the vast rural society. Although rural society is scattered, it is rich and diverse and can provide a steady stream of labor and production materials for urban industrial development (Li and Lv 2019).

The outbreak of the epidemic is a catalyst point, stimulating the original function of the village, making it play an important auxiliary and buffering role when an urban crisis occurs. Many of the problems presented by the villages also require cities to make up for their shortcomings in the post-epidemic phase of urban-rural integration. The complementarity of urban and rural functions is to offset the dark side of urban and rural development and achieve symbiotic and harmonious development.

Improve Overall Resilience and Shape the Interlinked Life Community

The concern over the rural areas and the ecological concern of rural people have become concepts that transcend “clan” and embody “kind” (Huang 2007). In the risky society created by the rapid flow of factors, urbanization, and globalization, cities and villages have become more and more united in life and share weal and woe. The loss of the countryside and the future development are closely related to the city. The cultural homesickness and social worries of the countryside have followed the cities. When crises occur, society develops, civilization sustains, and cities and villages need to share responsibilities and achieve flexible adaptation and resilient development.

Do a Good Job in Urban and Rural Planning under the Concept of Great Health

Rapid urbanization has undoubtedly caused high environmental costs in rural and urban areas. As a complex ecosystem, the development of a city follows certain objective laws and has certain complexity and uncertainty. Especially large cities often face many tricky problems with no ready-made or obvious solutions. They are often accompanied by various emergencies with huge impacts but are hard to predict (Zhang 2018). The source of risk is the structural social problem caused by cultural values hidden behind the social process

(Huang and Xia 2020). From the SARS epidemic in 2003 to the Ebola virus and Zika virus and the current outbreak of COVID-19, major events have revealed that if the harmonious relationship between man and nature is neglected in social development, heavy losses will be prevented be caused.

In particular, the prominent problems of population expansion, traffic congestion, and resource scarcity in large cities have brought huge social health costs. The future urban and rural construction should re-examine and reflect on the interdependence among man, nature and the city from the source of value. On the one hand, it is necessary to strengthen the ecological bottom-line constraints in urban and rural planning. The government needs to guide people to establish healthy life concepts and behaviors and shape a healthy environment for sustainable development. On the other hand, it is necessary to strengthen the disaster early warning, diagnosis and post-disaster repair mechanisms in urban and rural planning. Planners need to pay attention to the strategic blank of urban and rural planning and reserve flexible emergency space for the crisis.

Shape the Urban-Rural Living Circle under the Concept of Community

The long-term urban-rural dual system of an unbalanced distribution of urban and rural elements has led to social fragility. To realize the transition from social fragility to social ecology, it is necessary to allocate public elements in urban and rural spaces as needed and manage them intensively and efficiently. The living circle is a good method.[1] The living circle is a new urban planning concept adapted to the people's yearning for a better life.

From the 15-minute community living circle in Shanghai to the community-neighborhood-residential block three-level living service in the development plan of Xiong'an New District, the living circle

[1]The 15-minute community living circle has been widely used in China. As a measure of urban life planning, its basic meaning is that there are complete public facilities such as education, commercial transportation, cultural and sports, and elderly care within15-minute walk from the center of the home to make the city more livable.

promotes a more humane urban and rural planning and governance. Its essence lies in realizing the spatiotemporal production and reproduction of social capital through the overall planning of physical facilities in space to achieve sustainable development. Therefore, constructing a living circle integrating urban and rural areas is not simply allocating space resources in the construction of hard facilities but realizing the evolution from urban and rural public service living circles to cultural meaning.

The living circle promotes top-down collective management and control to the active participation of urban and rural citizens. It maximizes the rights and interests of citizens to realize the overall ecological livability of urban and rural areas. Maximizing citizens' rights and interests also realizes the overall ecological livability of urban and rural areas, activates the local inheritance of culture, cultivates literate cultural citizens, and enhances social cohesion and collective consciousness.

Conclusion

This chapter is first based on the historical perspective to analyze the relationship between urban and rural areas. It is not limited to tracing history but hopes to reflect the present situation. Secondly, the COVID-19 epidemic is a good perspective to consider the urban-rural relationship. Any major emergencies in history will make many social development problems more prominent and even change the entire social structure. For example, the Black Death in the Middle Ages created an era of extreme sin and darkness, giving birth to a new era of Renaissance.

Similarly, the Spanish flu of 1918 accelerated the end of the First World War to a certain extent. And back to the current Chinese urban and rural areas, SARS in 2003 exposed the public service imbalance in urban and rural development to the public's perspective. The COVID-19 epidemic has re-emphasized the important value of rural areas in the country's socialist modernization. The high degree of urban civilization is quite fragile in the face of the epidemic. However, despite the village's relatively backward economic and social development, it is like an ecological forest that can breathe. It preserves the organic circulation between urban and rural areas and makes disasters quiet here.

Over the 70 years since the founding of the People's Republic of China, the outlook of urban and rural has undergone major changes. Socio-economic development is also advancing by leaps and bounds, but the problem of urban-rural relationships has always existed. How solve this problem will accompany the entire process of China's socialist modernization. China has eliminated absolute poverty; 98.99 million rural poor people, 832 poor counties, and 128,000 poor villages have all been lifted out of poverty. There is no doubt that the solution to the problem of poverty alleviation in rural areas will become a turning point in the problem of urban-rural relations. In other words, overcoming the problem of poverty alleviation is not the end of China's urban and rural social development but the starting point for a new round of rural revitalization and a deep alleviation of poverty in industries, talents, culture, ecology, and organization.

Breaking the problem of the urban-rural dual system is still the top priority. The specific method is to take the rural revitalization strategy as an important starting point and continuously intensify the value connotation of urban-rural integration. We need to start with more cherishing the countryside. The subject of social participation, including the governments and the city planners, needs to truly stand from the perspective of human development and create space for future generations.

Chapter 3
Changes in Structures and Functions of Border Markets

The border areas of Yunnan show complex and diverse ecological environments and unique geographical locations, which make their rural markets bear typically ethnic, regional and open features of cross-border exchanges. The structures and functions of the border markets are undergoing a significant modern transformation with the development of the market economy, rapid urbanization and construction of towns in the border areas. This chapter explores how the space and time structures of the markets have been reshaped in modern changes; while as the traditional economic function of the markets has been gradually weakened, a trend of increasing social and cultural functions has emerged. This factor reflects that Yunnan's border markets, rural societies, and ethnic and cultural traditions undergo structural changes, bringing about diversity in the marketing system.

Introduction

In academic research, markets are often named "periodic markets" or "fairs," referring to buyers and sellers gathering at relatively fixed locations and periods for trades and exchanges. In the vast rural areas of China, since the markets always bear functions of trading and social interaction, the markets and their related studies have been focused in the fields of history, sociology, and anthropology for a long time.

In the 1930s, the Japanese scholar Kato F. (1973) first systematically analyzed and described the regular markets and their structures and functions in rural areas of North China with local Chinese records. Later, Yang Qingkun clarified the "internal function, structure and operation" of Zouping's traditional markets through a concentrated field survey of the Cheng-Guan-Ji, Ming-Jia-Ji, and Liu-Juqiao-Ji and other seven markets. He pointed out that when China's society was about to enter the industrial revolution and urbanization stage after Europe had done, the market reflected the changing economic structure and organization of rural areas in China (Yang, 1934).

In *Peasant Life of China*, Fei Xiaotong analyzes the rural markets, focusing on markets' economic and trading role in the rural community. He believes that the primary markets in the village community cannot meet the villagers' demands for social obligations, mutual reception, accommodation, mutual support, and gift exchange. Only a higher level—the intermediate market—can effectively satisfy the farmers' daily needs. Since the intermediate market is always located in a town, "the town is the center of exchanges between the farmers and the outside world" (Fei 2001:206-217). Farmers buy industrial products from the middle merchants in the town and sell the products to the acquiring specialists there. Yang Maochun (2001), in his study of the community of Taitou Village in Shandong, emphasizes the social and political functions of the markets apart from their economic and trading functions. Young's research shows that the markets provide the villagers with public places for communicating and are important joints of scattered villages.

In the first half of the 20th century, many studies were conducted on markets in China. They so were done on the social and economic conditions and trade in the southwestern region of China, especially in Yunnan's frontier regions. For example, Jiang Yingliang (2009: 167-169), based on the field surveys, discusses the market trade, commodity circulation, and currency in the "Baiyi" region. Li Youyi (2014: 75-85) makes a systematic analysis of the "Han-Yi" economic relations and changes in the Nanwei Village of Lunan in Yunnan in his book "The Economy of the Han-Yi Co-Inhabited Areas" and depicts the roles and status of grass-root markets, and how they affect the local villagers. Although the chapters of these works related to the markets are relatively simple, they laid the foundations for later research on trade in Yunnan's ethnic minority areas.

American anthropologist Skinner's "market system theory" indicates that the study of China's traditional township has entered a mature stage in the academic world outside China. He published the article titled *Marketing and Social Structure in Rural China* in The Journal of Asia Studies in 1964 and 1965. The article proposed a unique method to analyze China's grass-root society, namely the "Skinner Model." Adopting the "Central Place Theory" proposed by German geophysicist Christaller, Skinner put forward that the study of China's urban and rural economy and society is based on the structure of the markets. Skinner pointed out that based on the structure of the markets, the structure and operation of the Chinese economic system can be elucidated from a spatial point of view. The study of the structure of Chinese society can differ from those traditional studies based on the administrative system. Though at the lowest level in the market system, the rural market plays an extremely important role. It is not only a place for farmers to exchange goods but also a starting point for the rural surplus products to enter a higher-level market system. The rural market is also the end of goods provided to the villages.

Moreover, Skinner believed that the "farmer's actual social area is not determined by the narrow range of his village where he lives, but by the boundary of the grass-root market area where his village belongs" (Huang 1986:23). Thus, Skinner's analysis of the functions of the Chinese markets has reached an unprecedented level, leading to Skinner's comment, "a whole generation of American historians believes that Chinese villages are economically and socially highly integrated with the big trading system" (Huang 1986:23). In addition, influenced by Skinner's marketing theory, anthropologists who study China's problems are no longer constrained by small villages. Still, they pay more attention to the role of the markets in the social structure, expanding their research to marketing areas. When Eric R. Wolf was conducting his anthropological research in the Han Chinese society in Taiwan, he focused on the Sanxia marketing area. Since 1988, both foreign scholars such as Helen F. Siu, David Faure, Hamashima Atsutoshi, Okayama, etc. and Chinese scholars have focused on market towns in the Pearl River Delta region, such as Xiaolan, Shawan, Shatou, Lubao and Longjiang (Liu 1993).

In contrast, Chinese scholars' research on the Chinese markets remained low for a long time after establishing the People's Republic of China due to some complicated factors. Until the 1980s and 1990s, market research again won the attention of history, sociology, and anthropology. The research orientation and research focus of history are more consistent, focusing on the morphological structure and historical changes, like the rise and fall of the dynasties in various markets of different regions in China from the late Qing Dynasty to the Republic of China. Combined with empirical data, these historical studies launched academic discussions and theoretical dialogues among senior scholars like Skinner. For example, Bao Weimin (1998) conducted good research combining empirical research and theoretical analysis on Jiangnan Town and its rise and fall in modern times.

Fan Shuzhi (2005) adopted both macroscopic and microscopic approaches to explain the development of Jiangnan from the Ming and Qing Dynasties to the Republic of China. Wang Di (1993) applied "Skinner's model" to analyze regional trade. He studied the city system and market network in the upper reaches of the Yangtze River in the Qing Dynasty by discussing a series of issues such as the role and function of the market, market density and activity sphere, advanced markets and urban development.

Later, Wang Qingcheng made a detailed analysis of the markets and market circles in North China during the late Qing period based on the local records from dozens of counties in North China. He questioned Skinner's theory and formula on Chinese rural markets and social structure. Wang Qingcheng has made an elaborated study of the growth of regular markets in North China in the late Qing Dynasty. He put forward an innovative view that poverty resulted from the increase in trade volume, the number of markets, and the expansion of commodity circulation in northern rural markets in the late Qing Dynasty. Moreover,

Gong Guan (2001), Li Zhenghua (1998), Xu Tan (1998) and others have conducted some unique studies on North China markets, ranging from historical development and its characteristics, the transformation process and historic trends, the relationship between the railway and the town development to markets and commodity economy. The above researches fully demonstrate the important influence of "Skinner's Model" in this field.

Compared with historical research, research on the markets in sociology, anthropology, and other disciplines in this period was miscellaneous. However, much outstanding research was conducted on North China and Southwest China markets. Lu Yilong (2012) focused on temple fairs and markets in Dingzhou, Hebei Province. He drew a general conclusion based on the development and prosperity of the rural market in North China that the transformation and development of rural societies were brought about by the construction of modern markets for agricultural products and other products.

Huan Pingqing (2005) discussed the changes in the rural markets in Dingzhou, Hebei, the differences and reasons for the market transition between China and the West, and the difficulties and trends of rural social transformation in North China. He gave an innovative viewpoint about the transformation that urbanization was the only way to go out of the dilemma. In studying the markets in ethnic areas in Southwestern China, based on the ethnological and historical data, Wan Hong (2004) discussed the formation and evolution of the markets located in the southwestern ethnic areas of China. Wu Xiaoyan (2008) took Yuantong in eastern Sichuan as her research site and adopted microscopic empirical research methods that included rural markets in the historical process of modern country construction. Based on her research in the Nuosu (Yi) region in Liangshan, Sichuan Province, Liu Shaohua (2010) pointed out that the interaction between the traditional culture of Nuosu and the market system had caused great impacts on the local social life and social changes. Zhang Yue and Wang Xiaoyan (2010) took insight into the rich cultural connotation of the markets and their ties to the entire community network through a case study of markets in a Yi community in Yunnan. Most of the above research bears the features of facing the status quo and problems of contemporary Chinese markets from sociology and anthropology, expanding the views and dimensions of relevant market research.

However, though Skinner and other previous researchers on China's markets attached great importance to revealing and exploring the economic, political, and social functions of the markets, their studies were focused on traditional markets, which had existed for a long time before the establishment of the People's Republic of China. They paid more attention to such issues as the historical changes of the market, the rise and fall of the relationships, and the relationship between the rural society and the transformation, but less attention was given to the functions and roles of these markets at the modern times. Thus, in these studies, we cannot learn more about the changes in the function of the contemporary Chinese markets. Moreover, from the perspective of the regional study, the markets in the Northern part of China and Jiangnan regions have always been relatively prosperous with rich historical records, bearing clear historical development.

Therefore, market research in these areas seems to be a paradigm in the academic fields. Rural markets scattered in frontier areas, especially in the border areas of Yunnan, which are closely related to the production and livelihood of ethnic minorities, have received insufficient attention. Besides, research conducted in these regions is relevantly ignored. What is the space-time structure of markets in Yunnan's border areas? What role does it play? Are the functions of markets pointed out by modern researchers, including Skinner, continue being played in the border areas of Yunnan? Have any changes taken place in the structure and function of those markets that previous researchers have not noticed? To answer these questions, this chapter attempts to use a macroscopic approach based on historical literature and fieldwork to explore the continuation of the traditional structures and functions of the border markets in Yunnan province and to analyze the transformation of those border markets in the background of the contemporary market economy and urbanization process.

Traditional Structures and Functions of Markets in Yunnan

Yunnan is a province with the largest ethnic minority groups in China. The complex and diverse geography and ecological environment make this area inhabited by several ethnic groups, but each ethnic group relevantly lives together. Therefore, the scattered rural markets are not only an economic or cultural coordinate in the geographical space, but they also play important social and cultural roles. In particular, markets can be regarded as special areas extending across national borders and ethnic groups due to their geographical location. Since the appearance of markets in the Yunnan border areas, they have not only enriched the residents' material and cultural life because of their unique function of radiation and acculturation but, to some extent, have also formed a "marketing cultural circle" around the border markets, which has profoundly affected the lifestyle and even cultural traditions of the residents in border areas.

Continuation of Traditional Space-Time Structure

In the historical process, on the one hand, the development of markets in ethnic minority areas in Yunnan has been affected by many factors such as the local natural environment, folk traditions, livelihoods, and the pace of life; on the other hand, they have also been deeply influenced by the commercial culture of Han people. The time system is similar to Inland China based on "regularity," and some "regular markets" form a stable cyclic structure with a fixed time rhythm in a certain geographical area, which has continued to today.

In general, there are mainly five types of time systems for the trade markets in multi-ethnic areas on borders: (1) continuing to use the local traditional marketing system of 12 Earthly Branches; (2) adopting the old calendar or the lunar system; (3) adopting the calendar system; (4) adopting the week system; and (5) daily markets (Wan 2006). In addition, there are some markets in some areas without a fixed time.

Generally speaking, the local traditional marketing system of 12 Earthly Branches (represented by 12 animals) is adopted in some remote areas where transportation is not convenient. For example, there is a market for every dragon day, rat day, and monkey day in Chengguan Town of Yuanyang County in Honghe Hani and Yi Autonomous Prefecture in Yunnan Province. In Niujiaozhai Town, there is a market for every dog day, tiger day, and horse day; in Dunhou Town, there is a market for every dragon day, monkey day and rat day (Niu 2000:161-162). Markets are on every mouse day and horse day at Jinhe Town of Jinping Miao and Yao and Dai Prefecture County. Markets are on monkey days and tiger days in the town of Mengla (Niu 2000:161-162).

In these regions with the 12 earthly branches systems, the time system, rhythm, and folklore tradition differ from those in other regions. The names of the markets, such as "Horse Street," "Cattle Street," and "Chicken Street," actually reflect the 12 earthly branches of animals. Its formation is entirely related to the arrangements for agricultural production in different areas to avoid taking up too much production time to exchange goods conveniently. Therefore, the intervals of markets are neither too long nor too short and are roughly 5 to 7 days. Meanwhile, the periods of markets are overlapped so that people in different regions can exchange with each other and adjust to shortages (Ma 1987).

For example, according to the historical data, markets at Longchuan in Dehong Prefecture have transactions on five days. Villagers go to markets intricately. The market period calculated by the folk is that the fifth day is the market day after a four-day rest, except that the marketing day is the same day at the chieftain's residential place. During the Cultural Revolution, marketing for seven days or ten days was generally implemented the same day for the whole county. It was not until 1979 that it resumed marketing after five days. At present, the marketing time in townships is set by the overall planning office of the county, and the marketing in villages is arranged alternatively within the township (Wang 2012). Those who adopt the lunar calendar system are more often Han people living in agricultural areas, though some ethnic minorities also accept the lunar calendar system. Markets are set on every fifth to the tenth day or on every third, sixth and ninth day, or every fourth or ninth day, or every first, fourth or seventh day, etc. of each month according to the lunar calendar to form a periodic rotation in the region.

"Weekly" and "Gregorian calendar" marketing periods are more frequently adopted around the towns in the border areas. For the "weekly" system, every Thursday, Sunday, Wednesday, or Saturday can be the marketing day. In the "Gregorian calendar system," marketing days are on the 2nd, 5th, and 9th day of each month, on the 3rd, 6th, and 9th day of the month, or the even dates of the month, etc. Generally, the weekly calendar system's scope is relatively narrow, mostly confined to cities and towns' inner areas. The calendar system's scope is relatively large, which appears in some higher urbanized places where the Gregorian calendar system has long been established, and commodities are relatively developed. In areas where different ethnic groups live together, there are some cases where different time systems are used in a mixed way.

Daily marketing is often located in areas with high population density, rich products, convenient transportation, and high commercialization. In addition, it is easy to manage daily marketing or even large markets in some areas of raw material production or mining area at some fixed interval. Such regions haven't formed fixed markets is that these regions are distributed by ethnic groups located in remote mountainous areas. However, handicraftsmen and traders go to the villages from time to time to exchange daily necessities and food.

Thus, the contemporary markets in Yunnan border areas have a more complex time-space structure than in Inland China. The existing market network systems are determined by the markets' spatial and temporal distribution patterns, which reflect the overall situation of the markets in border areas in Yunnan to some extent. At the same time, the spatial arrangement and temporal system of various markets are formed in the course of long-term historical development, which is matched with their corresponding regions and populations. Such spatial arrangement and temporal system, on the one hand, reflect the close relationship between the complicated humanistic and geographical environment of the border areas in Yunnan and the diversity of cultural traditions. On the other hand, it also reflects their traditional agriculture and handicraft production, trading circles, and the interaction between settlement social relations and regional cultural identity in the long run. Above all, the continuation of historical development and distinctive regional cultural characteristics are embodied in the time-space structure of the markets.

Continuation of Traditional Economic Functions

As a primary form and place of commodity exchange, the rural market has lasted for thousands of years. As Braudel points out, "Exchanging has existed from the beginning of the human beings, and the historical research on the markets should be extended as far as possible. All the markets can testify that: several backward trading venues, which are rare, are at the first level, which are ancient species left before the Great Flood. The primary market is at the first stage of the economic ladder, which is the best form of exchange that is most direct, transparent, and supervised. 'First-hand' transactions are in the primary market. On the spot, the deal is made." (Braudel 1993:228) It can be said that the regular market determines the rhythm and pace of rural life. The market is a product of the peasant society, the peasant culture, and the peasant economy (Braudel 1993:103-105).

Commodity exchange in Yunnan's border areas has a long history, and it can even be traced back to the pre-Qin period. However, the real markets flourished in the Ming and Qing Dynasties, many of which still exist today. From the Qing Dynasty, the Republic of China to the present, the border markets have changed their forms from barter, "walking villages to exchange," and temporary markets along the roads, to the fixed market trading venues and market periods for exchanges, and even to rich commodity transactions like the daily marketing in big cities. Their development is similar to the evolution of the market trade in other parts of China. It has undergone a development process from a low-level, non-conventional market to an advanced fixed one. This historical change has not only been recorded in the literature and data but also has left a deep imprint in the historical memory and daily life of the ethnic people.

Markets in the Yunnan Border areas have been a material space with the main function of commodity exchange from the past to the present. It is characterized by the exchange of its surplus products, agricultural and sideline products, handicraft products, and special products among different ethnic groups in different trading circles, from mature rice farming and fishery products in the flatland to dryland crops and prey in mountainous areas; from the nomadic livestock and dairy farming products in the high mountains of western Yunnan to the local special products in the slash-and-burn mountainous regions of eastern and southern Yunnan; from subtropical fruits and vegetables of southernmost Yunnan to highland barley and blankets in the high mountain areas in northwestern Yunnan; from agricultural and sideline crops, poultry, livestock and regional specialties such as tea and salt in the Han people area to the ethnic handicraft textiles, handicrafts, medicinal materials, and mountainous property and other materials specially produced and collected by ethnic minorities.

As long as there are surplus products, they are sent to the market instantly. The scene is almost the same as the markets in Zouping in Shandong Province, written by Yang Qingyi in the 1930s. Today, the markets in the border areas in Yunnan are still the places for people living in the neighboring areas, especially for those cross-border peoples to sell their own primary agricultural and sideline products, handicrafts, and ethnic specialty products.

Moreover, the markets in border areas of Yunnan, as Fei Xiaotong (2001:206) said, "are the main places where every peasant gets the daily necessities that he does not produce." Although almost every village in the border area of Yunnan now has its grocery store, some daily necessities such as salt and candies can be bought in the village. However, more items needed by families still need to be got at the time of marketing in the town. For example, fresh pork, beef, and lamb are unavailable in the village canteens. They can only be bought at markets.

Many bulk oil and rice supplies or household appliances, such as rice cookers and electric teapots, household items, such as a hoe, sickle, or other agricultural tools or tables and chairs, and clothes are available at markets.

In addition, compared with the urban and rural markets depicted by C. K. Yang, Fei Xiaotong and Skinner in China before the middle of the last century, a unique trading way in the Yunnan border regions has continued: cross-border trading. Vietnam, Laos, and Myanmar border Yunnan Province. It is common for people (from different ethnic groups) to go across national borders. Therefore, cross-border markets have emerged. In the early stage, the bordering markets were only a form of transaction developed spontaneously by the people on both sides of the national borders. Its trading location and time are modeled on the traditional markets and set dates.

In the mid-1980s, the cross-border markets were gradually governed by the government's border trade management, allowing Chinese border residents to trade within 100 yuan per person per day. Since then, with the increase in trade amount in the border areas, the limit of borderline transactions has gradually increased to 8,000 yuan today. Also, the types of goods for trade have evolved from agricultural and sideline products to hardware, household appliances, building materials, daily necessities and sanitary wares, etc. As a result, the mutual exchanges on borders have also developed into a modern trade service industry that originally aimed to improve the bordering people's lives by bartering. For example, in the mutual exchanges in China and Vietnam border areas, people on the two countries' borders usually sell their unique native products in the markets and then buy some production and living goods at home. Even if it is not the marketing day, the phenomenon that Vietnamese go crossing the border to exchange goods is still common (Zhang and Gu 2012).

Another example is Ruili City on the border between China and Myanmar. Statistics show that the number of people participating in the border-marketing exchanges has reached millions each year. The types of mutual-traded goods have also increased from dozens in the early

1980s to the thousands. In the case of buyers and sellers, the Burmese sold overseas goods while the Chinese bought them in the early 1980s. However, the situation has developed to level off for both selling and buying (He 2011: 252).

In the areas like Hekou, Mengding, Mohan, Wanding, Daluo, etc., where there is a history of border trading, cross-border trade is an important source of income for local people. Even in the border areas where no ports are set, villagers and businessmen at home and abroad can enter each other's markets "conveniently" to do transactions. Such a "peaceful cross-border" trading model is a special way of economic exchange formed by the residents during historical development.

Skinner once predicted that China's rural markets would gradually disappear at the end of the 20th century with the development of modern society and the economy. However, the markets in the border areas of Yunnan remain an indispensable part of ethnic villagers' life. Compared with the urban and rural societies in Inland China, which have a relatively complete modern market system, the complicated geographical environment, the undeveloped economic foundation and the less urbanization in Yunnan's border areas have restricted the development of the social economy, the needs of people. Exchanges of necessities and commodities must be realized in rural markets. The small rural markets spontaneously formed in the past still play a role as an economical supplement to the production and life of various ethnic groups. In this sense," ethnic, economic exchanges are an important form of the ethnic economy. Economic exchanges are the first need to survive an ethnic group. They are the most important contacts" (Jin 2007:184). For all ethnic groups trading in the markets, the choices of commodities and transaction ways will be highlighted before their cultures and ethnic consciousness (Zhang and Wang 2010).

Continuation of Traditional Social and Cultural Functions

The market is one of the most dynamic places in rural society. In rural society, a market is undoubtedly a public space, reflecting a certain existing public nature within the society and the relatively fixed social association forms and interpersonal structures. As early as the 1960s, Skinner (1998) made it clear that since the market structure bears all the characteristics of the Chinese agricultural society, the market is a unique social system in traditional China. Later, Fairbank (2008: 26-28) further re-expressed the concept of "primary market," which was defined by Skinner as "market society," arguing that it is "the combination of an economic unit and a social world." "In a normal situation, the peasants' lives are not confined to a village, but to many villages that form a market community." Thus, since its birth, the market has borne a contact function that links goods and people, people and people.

Myanmar, Laos and Vietnam border Yunnan Province. The border markets in Yunnan have always been important places for many ethnic groups at home and abroad. First, the markets in such areas present peoples' transnational flows, radiating to the neighboring nations. Secondly, the ethnic minorities living in the border areas are mostly multinational, whose kinship, geographical relationships, etc., can be fully reflected in the markets where different nationalities gather. Economic activities weaken the boundaries of national differences. Language, commodity, and transaction are the main focus in the markets, while ethnic composition, consciousness, etc., are relegated to secondary positions. The ethnic symbols of the people in the markets are no longer the focus. For example, a researcher once did his research in the northwestern village of Ma Andi Township in Jinping County on the Sino-Vietnamese border. He found that the common languages in the local market were Hani, Chinese, and Hmong. Simple words such as sugar, cigarettes, alcohol, and needs can be helpful in the transaction. People who can't speak such marketing languages have to adopt gestures to communicate. Many vendors can speak several simple languages for trade (Li 2011).

Moreover, in the markets in Xishuangbanna, the Dai area, people can speak both the Han language and Dai language in marketing. Besides this, most Dai people there can speak other languages of neighboring ethnic groups. Bulang people have long-term economic and cultural exchanges with Dai people, deeply influenced by Dai's culture. Although Bulang people have their language, they expressed numbers in the Dai language except those from one to ten. Most Han residents living in the Wuyi "street" can speak Dai, Hani, and Yao languages (Wan 2006:83), not uncommon in other markets along the Yunnan border.

In the markets, contacts and exchanges based on geopolitical and kinship relations often constitute the most important "relationship" in the marketing area, which generally exists before the exchanges relationship in the markets. For example, in the traditional culture of the Jingpo people, it is extremely common to determine the relatives of the two sides through ethnic origins. The kinship is often expressed through a "practical way" in the market, such as drinking after the meeting, buying goods from relatives, or selling goods to their relatives cheaply or even for free. These seemingly contradictory marketing rules continually adjust family obligations in specific market areas. Bourdieu pointed out: "From a practical point of view, farmers' merchants strive to act following the rules and explain the rules according to their needs. All the strategies they have adopted remind us that the various phenomena, especially the classification of kinships, have a purely symbolic but still tangible effect" (Bourdieu 2003:269). Thus, the continuous consolidation and development of cross-border ethnic relations in this spatial structure are behind the market exchange and communicative activities.

In recent years, with the socialization of production, life, and contact, the needs for information, communication, and leisure have become increasingly diverse. The social space for farmers in border areas has been continuously expanded. However, the market is still a node in people's trade, entertainment, and communication networks. Many people still regard marketing as their world of life. As depicted by Fei Xiaotong and Yang Maochunin in the 30s and 40s of the last century, people get influenced by local social and cultural traditions in the inland markets.

Meanwhile, they connect their lives with the wider outside world by marketing, gaining information there and going out of the village even into the cities. Thus, markets in Yunnan's border areas are not only the fields of exchanging goods; they always provide space for people to socialize. Trading, gathering and communicating in the markets create a public space for the local society, which plays an important role in economic and trade exchanges, cultural exchanges, relationship adjustment and social integration.

Transformation of Structures and Functions of Markets

Although the markets in Yunnan's border areas have been following their traditional development trend for a long time, they take up a central position in rural societies' daily economic and socio-cultural life. However, what cannot be overlooked is that the rapid development of urbanization and social transformation has not only caused a series of changes in the structure of time and space in the markets in Yunnan's border areas since this century but has also gradually weakened the central role that the markets on the border used to play. At the same time, because the dual relationship between urban and rural societies in China still exists in the border areas of Yunnan, which still has a huge impact, the process of urbanization and socio-cultural transformation have not immediately brought about the modernization of urban and rural life in Yunnan's border areas as it did in inland areas of China. On the contrary, the different cultures of the urban and rural societies encounter in the markets. Therefore, the markets function as a social and cultural hub between urban and rural areas. It is becoming more prominent and will be bound to exist for a long time.

Reshaping Market's Space-Time Structure

Compared with the traditional markets, the most obvious change in contemporary markets in Yunnan border areas lies in their space-time structure, which reflects the reintegration of the markets and their marketing period systems. In the 1950s and 1970s, after the founding of the People's Republic of China, with the establishment of the planned economy system, the state incorporated market trade into the planning system, and the policy on the primary market was adjusted several times, which aimed at controlling the markets more strictly or even eliminating free markets. Until the early 1980s, the once-banned market trade was gradually restored. During this period, some traditional fairs and markets in Yunnan's border areas because of their being closed for many years, and changes in the population and society in the border areas could no longer be able to restore the vigorous scenes of the good old days and disappeared silently into history. With the market economy reform in the 1980s, the Yunnan border areas began their transition from a "traditional agricultural society" to a "modern industrial society." They entered a period of rapid economic development.

In particular, after implementing the strategy for the development of western China, many transportation infrastructures such as highways, secondary roads and rural roads have been built and renewed on a large scale in the border areas, which has greatly promoted the development of local urbanization. Small and medium-sized new towns have sprung up in the border areas. Furthermore, some traditional markets either faded or disappeared due to geographical reasons or had completely lost the time-space attributes of the traditional ones and transformed into the "modern trading centers," as called by Skinner. At the same time, due to the emergence of a large number of small and medium-sized towns in the border areas, a new batch of regular markets has emerged in these towns and their surrounding areas.

It needs to be pointed out that, whether it is a continuation of history or the new birth of regular markets on the border, the time systems of the marketing periods have also changed with time. There are about five types of Yunnan Border Fairs: the Chinese Zodiac system, the lunar calendar system, the Gregorian calendar system, the weekly marketing system, and the daily marketing system. Since the new century began, the Chinese Zodiac system and the lunar calendar system have gradually experienced a decrease in their usage. The Gregorian calendar and the weekly marketing system have been adopted more extensively in some cities and suburban areas. The markets have gradually developed into a daily marketing system in some highly-commercial towns. All four systems show that the period of marketing is becoming shorter and shorter. This trend has met the standard of Skinner's "modern trading center." Thus, the last type of market system no longer belongs to traditional ones.

In addition, the village as a center of rural society again has also profoundly demonstrated the changes in the temporal and spatial structure of Yunnan's border market. Space research has proposed two ideal states: formal and informal space. For the formal space, the power is mainly derived from external administrative forces, while the informal space gets its power from the village's traditions, habits, and demands. The formation of the latter one and the various activities in the village are determined by the local knowledge and the rational choice of the survival of the villagers, which bear a strong folk tune (Cao 2005). Therefore, villages with government administrative power belong to the formal public space; the formation of the market constrained by the environment of the villages belongs to an informal space.

In recent years, the state's strategies of modernization and reconstruction of rural society, such as "beautiful rural construction" and "new rural construction," have mainly focused on building settlements centered on villages and defining the space of public services. Such strategies make the resources of configuration and power continue to flow to the villages in the specific space-time relationships, which partially replaces some functions of markets, leading to changes in the original market spatial behavior and the relationship of market components to some extent.

Fading of the Role of the Market as Economic Hub

The market is a place to exchange commodities, and its economic regulations and rules have been determined by the village itself as well as by the construction of the country in different historical periods. In the first 30 years after establishing the People's Republic of China in

1949, the market's trade was greatly affected and withered due to the economic policies of unified purchasing and marketing and the People's Commune System. It was not until the 1980s, when China's Reform and Opening-up period came, that the market entered a new stage of historical development and returned to the daily life of farmers with policies to develop trade in the market and the acquisition of farmers' economic autonomy.

In recent years, with the continuous advancement of the market economy led by the government, farmers' social life has undergone great changes. The traditional "natural economy no longer covers the current economic activities of farmers in the market." In the process of modernity, the structure and function of the market changed quietly, but the relationship between farmers and markets has changed, which needs to be re-examined.

As far as the border areas of Yunnan province are concerned, with the improvement of traffic conditions and the rapid advancement of urbanization, the most obvious change is that market as an economic hub has been gradually weakened in people's production and life. Changes are particularly prominent in some areas that rely heavily on markets. For example, in the Gongshan Dulong Nationality Autonomous County of Nujiang Prefecture in Yunnan Province, five township markets are located at Cikai Town, Bingzhongluo Town, Pengdang Township, Puladi Township, and Dulongjiang Township. In the past, since these areas were remote in high mountains and deep valleys, transportation to these areas was inconvenient and dangerous.

Therefore, the local people of the Dulong, the Nu, and the Visual used to depend on the nearby markets to make a living for a long time. Particularly, the area centered on the markets of Dulongjiang Township, and the traffic to the outside world was extremely inconvenient. The local people were deeply dependent on the markets to handle their economic activities. With the completion of the Dulongjiang road in September 1999, the history of no roads to the last ethnic community among the 56 ethnic minorities was ended. By December 2014, the completion of the Dulongjiang road reconstruction project completely ended the history when vehicles could not pass from November to May because of snow blocking all the roads in the mountain. With the change in traffic conditions, ethnic people can now get to Gongshan County quickly for their economic activities. The old market's central position in production and life has been gradually replaced by the bigger markets in the county where more goods are offered.

Another example is the Awa Mountain area, located at Ximeng Wa Autonomous County in the west of Puer City in the southwest of Yunnan Province. After the county government moved from Ximeng Town to Mengsuo Town in 2000, the urbanization construction was pushed forward rapidly. A modern city has been built quickly in the last ten years. In the past, people of the Wa and Lahu who used to trade in open-air markets around Mengsuo Town, Mengka Town, and Lisuo Township now frequently go shopping in the modern supermarkets of Ximeng County. They are becoming more and more accustomed to selling their agricultural products and livestock in the urban markets for a better price.

From the perspective of society, the economic activities of the villagers in the border areas have increasingly centered on cities. Villagers' contact with the outside world is not necessarily by "administrative hierarchy system" or "market hierarchy system." However, they can communicate with external society directly through some distributed network systems. They contact each market level directly and participate in any level of the market system by-products. Such changes have already appeared in North China. Lu Yilong (2012) completed an investigation in Dingxian, Hebei Province. He suggested that "the rural marketing centers have been moved to a region's central city and even farther away. The markets in towns were no longer important cargo distribution centers." Huan Pingqing (2016) put forward that "in county Ding, Hebei Province, the market was no longer a center for distributing agricultural products or a place for surplus goods, but to a large extent it had become a mobile market where the external goods are sold to rural areas."

The modernization of transportation facilities and the rapid development of small and medium-sized cities make the economy in all ethnic communities on the border dependent on the local markets. With the popularization of information and communication networks, the traditional economic functions of the markets have been continuously weakening. So far, all the villages in Yunnan province have access to electricity and have been widely covered by television signals. Furthermore, almost every villager who has received a primary school education does have a cell phone. Surfing the internet, communicating with WeChat, and even paying bills online is common.

National and local policies, regulations, and service information used to be learned only in the markets but now can be gained instantly from news on TV and cell phones. The fees that used to be paid in the towns can be paid online now. Thus, to some extent, information resources, cultural resources, and even administrative resources which were only obtained in the markets in the past can be gained through information networks now. Although markets are still the nodes of transactions and contacts, the farmers' vision has now surpassed the boundaries of traditional markets. They can selectively participate in market activities rather than accept and adapt passively as they did in the past. It can be expected that the role of the market as an economic hub and a resource allocation center will be increasingly affected by the development of information network technology which has penetrated the rural society in China.

Constantly Enhancing the Social and Cultural Functions of the Market

There has always been a fallacy on the modern transformation of the functions of the border markets in Yunnan. As the traditional economic function of the market and its economic center role are gradually weakening, its social and cultural functions are constantly increasing. It is playing an increasingly important role in social interaction and cultural recreation.

First of all, as mentioned above, the modernization of transportation and the rapid advancement of urbanization in Yunnan have brought about tremendous social and economic development in the border areas. At the same time, cities' influence and radiation functions have increased, especially in cultural production and communication, ranging from popular culture to popular fashion, which is produced in the cities and then spread to the countryside. Even though the dual division of identity and treatment between urban and rural areas after the Reform and Opening-up has been eliminated, the gap between urban and rural areas in terms of social interaction and lifestyle still exists because of historical influence. Thus, markets have always played an important role in rural society, both in social interaction and cultural recreation. Urban culture and lifestyle, symbols of modernity, will radiate in relatively densely populated towns with high mobility. Such urban culture and lifestyle will reach their peak during the marketing periods.

Moreover, due to China's once boom of "small towns" in the 1980s and 1990s, and the flourishing prosperity of markets on Yunnan's borders, almost all the townships on the border that rely on the markets have unprecedentedly well developed. It can be expected that urbanization is still one of China's most important social processes for some time. The function of the markets on the Yunnan border as social and cultural hubs between urban and rural areas will exist for a long time ahead.

Secondly, from the view of the village, as more and more young and middle-aged villagers in the border villages flood into nearby counties, prefecture cities far away, or even provincial capitals, those who remain in the village are older adults, and women and children. The growing hollowing of the village population has made it difficult for villagers to engage in social interaction that used to be normal. At the same time, traditional village entertainment, such as visiting friends, playing cards, and playing games on plazas, have gradually disappeared with the loss of the population. Thus, the markets have become the most important communicative and entertaining places for the remaining villagers, and activities at markets have also become the most important social communication and cultural recreation. Even if they have nothing to buy or sell, the villagers who stay in the village are eagerly looking forward to going to the market during the marketing day so that they can chat more with villagers who come from other villages in the markets or get together to sing folk songs, listen to the local folk songs, and watch drama performances to kill time when the family members are out and to enjoy the leisure time in ways not available in the village.

Therefore, we can often see such scenes in the markets: energetic middle-aged young men and women come and go or chat, and the elderly play cards or chess, smoke, and sunbathe. For most of the remained ones, "arena" has become an indispensable part of their lives. Skinner (1998:49-50) said in the 20th century: "The standard marketing community is the relevant context of organized recreation for the peasantry. Standard and higher level markets constitute the arena of professional storytellers, theatrical troupes, blind singers, purveyors of games of chance, boxers, jugglers, performing machine sellers and magicians. Such professionals are absent from villages and minor markets in the usual case. Just as market day brings relief from the monotony of rural life through the provision of recreational opportunities, so the temple fair affords the high point in the villagers' recreational year."

In addition, the villagers who are working outside have difficulty integrating into the city life and becoming residents in the city, even if they have been working in the city for a long time, because of the urban-rural dual household registration system and the gap between urban and rural areas in terms of social security such as education, medical care and pensions, as well as the unstable factors such as housing and work. Such a gap cannot be eliminated immediately. However, because they have worked in the cities for a long time, they have been familiar with and accustomed to their social interaction, fashion, and lifestyle. When they decide to return to the countryside, they are reluctant to go back directly to the villages, and they are more willing to make a living in towns closer to urban social and cultural styles. Even those young and middle-aged laborers who return to their villages for a break are not accustomed to the relatively simple rural lifestyle.

On the contrary, they feel more comfortable in town, and they are more willing to go shopping there to seek spiritual comfort. The markets have become places where people, especially the young ones, get together, entertain, communicate and hang out. However, the market people are not passively integrated into the market operation system. They will shape the markets as suitable fields based on their cultural habits the geographical and temporal characteristics to carry out various social activities.

Above all, Yunnan border markets' ever-increasing social and cultural functions and their impacts on local societies have surpassed economic significance. The original social interaction model was largely governed by kinship networks, ethnic and cultural traditions, and the state political system. However, with the participation of new markets and the growth of non-government markets, the dominance mentioned above was changed. The traditional power and authority, interests and rules, relations and order structure were fundamentally shaken. Meanwhile, the social, cultural and entertainment functions of markets have been unprecedentedly released, which contribute to the conversion of the original functions and structures of the markets. In addition, the increasing social and cultural functions of the markets are also changing and shaping all aspects of people's daily lives, such as exchange mode and the way of communication, which even affect people's social concepts and economic concepts. Markets also affect people’s professional ethics, values, fashion style, desires, sexual relations, and imagination (Yuan 2017), reflecting that modern changes occur in traditional cultures behind the markets.

Discussion and Conclusion

The current markets on the border of Yunnan province are undergoing a modern transformation; their economic functions are gradually weakening while social and cultural functions are enhanced, and such transformation will continue for quite a long in the future.

What does this functional transformation mean for the markets in the border areas? Skinner (1998:48) pointed out that the market provides trading places for goods produced in the marketing community and constitutes a hub in the social structure of this community. Loads of economical and intensive cultural interactions are proceeding in the standard market area.

Undoubtedly, the grass-roots market theory provides us with a very effective analytical tool for understanding the border markets in Yunnan Province. The tool can be adopted to examine the markets' structures, functions, and historical development in border areas. However, what should be stressed is that Skinner pays more attention to the "economic" activities in the market system. He believes other factors are the derivatives of rational economic behaviors. Meanwhile, because of the limitations of the times and the environment, Skinner could not predict the trend of the development of the markets in Yunnan border areas, especially the modern transformation of the market function and its consequences. So far, the modern transformation of the border markets in Yunnan is ongoing. It clearly shows a series of structural contradictions in social development. Therefore, this chapter attempts to use the functionalist concepts of "manifest and latent function" to analyze this problem.

According to Merton, the so-called manifest function refers to "the function that contributes to systematic adaption or adjustment, whose objective consequence is the recognition and expectation of participants" (Merton 2006:153). The latent function refers to the "function that doesn't contribute to systematic adaption or adjustment, whose objective consequence is not the recognition and expectation of participants" (Merton 2006:153, 174). When Merton (2006:174) put forward the concept of latent functions, he also clearly realized that "the prominent contribution of sociologists lies in the unexpected postulate of social activities where latent functions are involved and the expected postulate where manifest function lies." From the definition of Merton and the researchers' expectations, we believe that the modern transformation of the border market in Yunnan is increasingly showing two important consequences.

First, from the perspective of “significant function,” the markets' increasingly prominent social and cultural functions as hubs promote the deep excavation of tourism resources in the border areas and drive the upsurge of cultural tourism. People recognize and accept markets as cultural tourism resources with rural tourism development. Particularly, the markets in the border areas maintain their “original ethnic ecology.” Markets are the stages for folk cultural performances. The border areas of Yunnan Province have rich resources for cultural tourism. For instance, the ethnic people’s festivals, such as the “Kuoshi Festival” of the Lisu people, the “Torch Festival” of the Yi people, the “Gexu Festival” of the Zhuang, the “Huashan Festival” of the Miao people, the “Panwang Festival” of the Yao people, and the “Dong Songkran Festival” of the Dai people, have been recorded in local county gazetteers since the Ming and Qing dynasties. During these traditional festivals, villagers used to kill pigs and slaughter sheep, set campfires, and sing and dance in different ways to celebrate the festivals, which showed their unique ethnic cultures.

However, the village culture has declined with the market economy sweeping through the villages in the late 1990s and villagers leaving to work in cities or towns. On a festive day, even if the marketing day can’t be as prosperous as it used to be. However, many marketing towns in the border areas have become socio-cultural hubs today. Most traditional festival activities held in the villages in the past have been completely moved into these towns. As time goes by, even though the function of traditional festivals to satisfy gods and entertain the people has not changed much, the needs for food, clothing, supplies, and other services have turned marketing into an essential part of the festivals. In some tourist hotspots with rich ethnic cultures and convenient transportation, native culture is closely integrated into rural market tourism and has become the attractive logo for local culture. On the whole, border marketing as a tourism resource is gradually becoming a new trend for the cultural tourism industry in Yunnan, which undoubtedly offers a new perspective on the modern transformation of traditional ethnic culture.

Secondly, from the perspective of "potential function," in the modern transformation of the economic and cultural functions, a series of unexpected social problems have occurred in the markets in the border areas and have increasingly become prominent. For instance, porn, gambling and drug phenomena are particularly prominent. The Yunnan border markets are not only important places for goods and social exchanges but also the cultural recreation that the local villagers enjoy and gathering places for the people from the neighboring countries. With the coming and going of people from foreign countries, people in business, tourists, and other kinds of persons, the markets have a population of high mobility and complexity.

Moreover, affected by the external environment, people in these areas bear fewer legal ideas. Loads of smuggled goods such as cigarettes and cosmetics and porno publications are often sold in the markets; porno performances are also occasionally offered in the remote districts. Gambling by cards or machines has become common in teahouses, plazas, or open spaces. The worst thing is that the number of drug users and drug traffickers depending on drugs from abroad increases in border towns. Some markets even become the hardest-hit areas where drugs and AIDS are rampant. In addition, the markets that lack self-regulation and integration capabilities due to their remote location have become distribution centers for fake and shoddy products. Sham marketing and fraud activities also occur in the markets. The socio-cultural management of the markets is becoming more and more difficult. In all, what is mentioned above reflects that the functions of the border markets in Yunnan province have undergone an extremely complex transformation in the modern era and are facing unprecedented opportunities and challenges.

Chapter 4
Impacts of Roads on Dulong People and Their Coping Strategies

With the construction of a 96.2-kilometer long mud road in 1999, the Dulong ethnic group living in the Dulong River Valley in Nujiang Prefecture, Yunnan Province, China, ended its history without roads. Then on April 10, 2014, a tunnel was completed that connects the beautiful valley with the outside world more closely. The construction of this road has had a big impact on the ethnic Dulong communities and the ecosystem in the valley. This chapter will discuss the history of road construction in the area, road and development, road and socio-cultural changes of the ethnic Dulong people, and road and social resilience.

Introduction

Dulong people are one of the smallest ethnic groups officially recognized as one of the 56 ethnic groups in China. They have a population of 6,500 (Statistical Bureau of Yunnan Province 2015:379). About 4,300 live in the Dulong Valley of Gongshan Dulong and Nu Autonomous County in the Nujiang Lisu Autonomous Prefecture of Yunnan in Southwest China (Lu 2014). About 10,000 Dulong people live in Kachin State in Northern Myanmar who migrated there from China (Gao 2015:15). The Dulong ethnic group in Myanmar called themselves Rwang and declared that they had a population of over 100,000 (Yang and Li 2010).

The Dulong people are well-known in China as face tattoo people. The history of the Dulong is not well documented because they have been living isolated in the Dulong Valley, which sits in the mountains bordering Tibet and Yunnan, one of the most remote regions of China. Until 2014, the Dulong Valley was often closed to external communication for half of the year (Li and Li 2015). There is scarce information about the Dulong people in the imperial histories and travelers' chronicles. Some scholars have traced the origin of the Dulong people to the Qiang people in ancient China who lived in the Qinghai and Gansu Plateau (Wang 1987, Zhang 2000). Some scholars believe that the Dulong people and the Nu people in Gongshan have the same ancestors (Hong 1994, Gao 2003).

The study of the Dulong people can be divided into three periods of time chronologically: (1). the pre-1911 period when the Dulong people were recorded in some classic Chinese literature and documents. The ancestors of the Dulong people were first recorded in the *Annals of Huayang* (written in 348—354 A.D.) as "people with painted faces." (2). the period of the Republic of China (1911-1949) when the serious investigation and academic study of the Dulong people started as a result of the government's border-area construction programs. The most famous study was conducted by anthropologist Tao Yunkui on the physical characteristics of the Dulong people in the 1930s. (3). the New China period (1950-) when the investigation of the social history of the Dulong people was conducted in the 1950s and the 1980s which produced lots of data on economic, socio-cultural and environmental aspects of the Dulong people. Among them, the most influential works include *Investigation on the Social History of Dulong Nationality* by the Editorial Committee of Yunnan Province (published in 1981), *Comprehensive Study on Dulong River and Dulong Nationality* by He Daming and Li Heng (published in 1996), and *The Transmission on the Social Structure and Cultural Conception of Dulong Ethnic Group* by Gao Zhiying (published in 2009) (Chen 2017).

In recent years, the Dulong people have become a hot research topic in China, especially those studying globalization or modernization and culture change. The Chinese government has invested heavily in constructing infrastructure, health and education facilities, and various poverty-reduction projects in the valley. These have brought about tremendous economic and socio-cultural changes to the Dulong people. This chapter will focus on constructing a road that connects the Dulong

Valley with the outside world and its impacts on the ethnic Dulong communities.

Research Site and Methods

The research was conducted in the summer of 2016 by a research team consisting of three teachers and two graduate students from the Center for Social and Economic Behavior Studies of Yunnan University of Finance and Economics. Before that, a research team member conducted fieldwork there in January and February 2015. The research team visited six villages in the Dulong Valley and finally chose Longyuan Village as the research site. It now has 135 households and 558 villagers. Among the villagers, there are 286 men and 272 women. Its territory is 210.20 square kilometers with only 409 *mu* (0.27km^2) arable land, and the rest is mountain land. The altitude of the village is 1,800 meters. The average temperature is 15.7° C, and the average annual rainfall ranges from 2930 to 3980 millimeters, appropriate for corn, potato, and other crops.[1]

As this research focused on the economic and socio-cultural changes of the Dulong people resulting from the construction of roads, we used participant observation to collect data about landscapes, crop cultivation, houses (outside and inside), meals, and people's daily activities in the village. This allowed us to incorporate more evidence about how the villagers live today. About 30 unstructured or conversational interviews were conducted with seniors, adult women and men, and the head of Longyuan Village to understand the villagers' lives and strategies to adapt to the changes in their lives. The main themes of the interviews included issues related to household income and expenses, crop cultivation, livestock-raising, financial situation, government subsidies and aid, construction of houses, purchase of cars or trucks and other expensive equipment, religious and festival activities, problems they faced and strategies to solve them. Official documents at

---

[1] The data came from Baidu Baike at https://baike.baidu.com/item/%E9%BE%99%E5%85%83%E6%9D%91/ 3038355, accessed December 30, 2021.

the county, township and village levels were collected to understand the village's economic, cultural, ecological, historical, and social backgrounds and the construction of roads there. Other secondary data were collected through Baidu, CNKI and other internet databases by looking for keywords in Chinese and English, including Dulong people, Dulong River Valley, and Dulong road construction. They provided different types of data that could complement or discredit one another.

The History of the Road Construction

The first road that connected Dulong Valley with the outside world was built in 1964, just one meter wide, only for people and horses to walk (Fu 2015). It would take two days and one night to move from Gongshan Town to Dulong Valley. Food and other living and production goods were carried into the valley by horses before snow closed the mountain. On July 1, 1995, the construction of a mud highway to connect the county town with the Dulong Valley was launched by China's Ministry of Transport. The length of the highway was just 96.2 kilometers, but it took over 4000 workers four years to complete and cost 98 million yuan.[1] However, it marked the end of history that the last region in China that ethnic peoples inhabited had no highway (Zhang et al. 2014). Due to the snow, this old highway had low carrying capacity and could not be used for half a year. It took about 9 hours to drive from Gongshan Town to the Dulong Valley.

On January 29, 2011, the reconstruction of the Dulong River Highway was officially started. The newly improved highway was completed on November 13, 2015. It has a tunnel of 6680 meters long, which shortens the length of the highway by 16 kilometers and the driving time from 9 hours to 3 hours (Figure 4.1). It ensures that the highway can be used all year round. The cost of its reconstruction is 780

[1] The data came from Baidu Baike at https://baike.baidu.com/item/%E7%8B%AC%E9%BE%99%E6%B1%9F%E5%85%AC%E8%B7%AF/12025793?fr=Aladdi, accessed December 30, 2021.

million yuan. It ends the history that snow would close up the Dulong valley for half a year.[1]

Figure 4.1 Dulong River Highway Tunnel

The construction of another highway that connects the Dulong Valley with Tibet was started in May 2015. This highway was 27.54 kilometers long and would take four years to build. The Dulong Township now has over 100-kilometer highways and five suspension bridges over the Dulong River that connect all the villages in the valley, thus forming a transportation network (Bao 2020). The heavy rain in 2017 had caused severe damage to the highways in the Dulong Valley.

[1] The data came from Baidu Baike at https://baike.baidu.com/item/%E7%8B%AC%E9%BE%99%E6%B1%9F%E5%85%AC%E8%B7%AF/12025793, accessed December 30, 2021.

On September 22, 2017, the county government declared that the Dulong Valley would be closed to tourists and visitors for two years (from October 1, 2017, to September 30, 2019) to improve its transportation and other infrastructure (Li 2017). It opened again on October 1, 2019, with access only to 500 tourists a day (Li 2019).

Road and Social-Cultural Changes

For thousands of years, the Dulong ethnic group lived in an isolated mountain valley. Their livelihood depended on agriculture, but their productivity remained very low. Slash-and-burn cultivation dominated the production, and crops grown there were limited to maize, buckwheat and beans. Since the founding of the People's Republic of China in 1949, their living conditions have improved dramatically with aid from the government. Today, with the construction of the Dulong River Highway and the government's poverty alleviation programs, the Dulong ethnic people have experienced tremendous changes in their lives. The government has set them up as an example of "*zhiguo minzu*" (people who have entered the socialist society from "primitive society"). All the villages in the Dulong Valley now have highways, electricity and water supply, telephone, 4G internet, and radio and television services. The Dulong Township has become a bordering town with sightseeing, scientific investigation, exploration, and tourism activities (Xi 2015:22).

The first obvious change that one notices when entering the Dulong Valley is the pattern of residential houses. The Dulong people used to build wooden or bamboo houses on the steep mountain slopes and along the river (Figure 4.2). These houses were scattered around with large spaces between them. Their houses were often two-storied, with the second floor as the living quarters for the family and the ground floor as the storage and accommodation for the livestock.

The open space was used as vegetable gardens or as grounds to raise chickens, pigs, goats, cattle and other domestic animals, or even as a burial ground for a deceased family member. It was common to bury the dead within 100 meters away from the house. The Dulong people

Figure 4.2 An Old Traditional House

believed that burying a deceased family member away from home was hard to bear. Now all the families at Longyuan Village (and other villages as well) have moved into brick houses with five bedrooms and a living designed and built with funds provided by the Shanghai municipal government (76.7 million yuan) on one flat ground by the Dulong River and on both sides of the highway (Figure 4.3). The houses form several blocks with limited spaces between them. Every family has a separate kitchen room with a traditional hearth that symbolizes a family unit and a pigpen at the back and side of the village.

Another change that our informants at Longyuan Village all mentioned is related to their livelihood. The Dulong people used to practice slash-and-burn cultivation. Hunting, fishing and gathering wild fruits and vegetables supplemented their agricultural production (Ling 2016). Today, the highway and houses construction and the government's efforts to return land from farming to forestry to protect the ecological environment have taken away lots of their arable lands. The government has been promoting and subsidizing farming cash crops such as *caoguo* (cardamom), *chonglou* (Rhizoma Paridis, a

Figure 4.3 A New House

Chinese medicine herb), and *huajia* (Sichuan pepper) there, raising pigs and other livestock and opening restaurants and hotels for tourists. The county government has designated the village as a tourism model village specialized in providing Dulong ethnic food.

Directly related to the construction of the highway is the rise in alcohol consumption. The Dulong people had the tradition of drinking homemade alcohol to prevent or treat various rheumatologic diseases resulting from the long raining season from March to September. The Dulong's low agricultural productivity and yield restricted the production of homemade alcohol. Today, trucks and trucks of factory-manufactured beers and low-quality alcohol are transported into the Dulong Valley through the highway. Drinking has become a social problem in the Dulong Valley. At Longyuan Village, we saw villagers drinking while working in the fields or the afternoon. We were told that drinking caused divorce, family violence, loss of labor, accidental death or even suicide in the village. This drinking phenomenon had happened in many ethnic communities worldwide when they encountered modernization and globalization processes that created a "cultural disrupt" that cut them off from their old traditions and had not yet adopted them well to the new era. To deal with this social problem, the Dulongjiang Township government issued a regulation to ban alcohol drinking on September 5, 2016.

Many of the Dulong people resort to Christianity to help them stop drinking. One study reveals that most Dulong people believe in Christianity (Zhou 2009). However, it has not been successfully put into practice. Being a Christian, one cannot drink alcohol or smoke cigarettes. The influence of Christianity is still rising in the valley, which now has quite a few modern-style churches from the lower valley to the upper valley (Figure 4.4). Traditionally the Dulong people are animists and believe that all living creatures have souls, and evil spirits exist everywhere and can bring calamities to people (Cai 2000).

Figure 4.4 A Christian Church

The change in the beliefs of the Dulong people is another major cultural change in the valley. It is not just related to religious beliefs. The coming of tourists from the outside world, the easy access to the internet, and the setup of a modern education system (primary school in the village, middle school in the township, high school in the county town) have all brought new values and ideas to the valley which affect the young generation of the Dulong people most.

Apart from these changes, we found changes in many socio-cultural aspects of the Dulong people. The hearth of a household used to be an important place where family members sat around chatting or listening to older adults' stories. But now, the family members sit in the living room watching TV programs or chatting on their smartphones. The hearth has become just a dining place and cannot perform the function of consolidating the family. The social relationship among the Dulong people has been changing. The Dulong people used to live scattered on the mountain slopes or by the riverside. Every family had its own living space. They live in the village compound with very limited space between their houses (Figure 4.5). We often heard them complain that the village was too crowded and too noisy at night to sleep. The relationship with the dead family members has undergone some changes. Now the dead are buried outside the village. Compared with the past, the ethnic identity of the Dulong people has been enhanced since the identity of the Dulong people is the important basis that the local government distributes material aid and enjoys preferential policies from the state (Zhang 2015).

Figure 4.5 A Block of Houses

Discussion and Conclusion

The construction of the Dulong River Highway in 1999 and the improvement of this highway with a tunnel in 2015 have freed the Dulong people from isolation and half a year of snow blockade. This highway has brought tremendous economic, social and cultural changes to the Dulong people. It has put the Dulong people into the turmoil of the process of modernization and globalization. All these have been completed under the state government's slogan that "no ethnic group will be left to fall behind" and with various sorts of aid programs. This shows the power of the state. Neo-Marxists ' critical theory (or philosophy) applies to socialist China. This critical theory claims that in Western bourgeois society, the elite classes maintain cultural hegemony through, aside from their control of the means of production, the dual forms of external political control in the form of state bureaucratic machinery-namely the legal system, the police, courts and the military, and internal moral persuasion through education, mass media, literature, arts and beliefs (Huang 1993:164).

The Dulong Valley lies in the Zomia region. Zomia is a geographical term coined by historian Willem van Schedel of the University of Amsterdam in 2002 to refer to the huge mass of mainland Southeast Asia, including the highlands of north Indochina, Thailand, the Shan Hills of Northern Myanmar, and the mountains of Southeast China. "These areas share a common elevated, rugged terrain, and have been the home of ethnic minorities that have preserved their local cultures by residing far from state control and influence."[5] Professor James C. Scott of Yale University used the concept of Zomia. He argued that the tribes in Zomia are conscious refugees from modernity itself, choosing to live in more primitive, locally-based economies and that they are "best understood as a runaway, fugitive, maroon communities who have, throughout two millennia, been fleeing the oppressions of state-making projects in the valleys"(Scott 2009:14-16).

His argument does not fit the Dulong people, at least the Dulong people since the 1950s. From our interviews with seniors and our observation, the Dulong people are sincerely grateful to the government to provide them with food and modern houses and to liberate them from the exploitation by the Tibetans coming down to the valley from the North to collect land rents and the oppression by the Lisu people coming into the valley from the East to capture the Dulong people as enslaved people and take away their valuable goods. They purposefully get engaged with the government, not run away from it. They even wrote to Xi Jinping, President of the People's Republic of China, in January 2014 to report their social and economic development and got in return Xi's meeting their delegates in Kunming in January 2015. They have been making the best use of the government's policies to survive and thrive in the valley.

The socio-cultural changes that the Dulong people have experienced fit the anthropological concept of culture that the culture is always changing and culture is adaptive. The highway's opening has connected the Dulong people with the outside world. As Zhou Yongming (2010) stated that roads promote the flow of people and goods, facilitate economic and trade development, and provide channels for people to enjoy public services and other social resources, the Dulong valley has taken on a new look. The change of the livelihood from subsistence farming to cash crop farming and tourism development has involved the Dulong people in the market economy. The facts that some Dulong people have failed to adapt to the new conditions by committing suicide, that some have been converted to Christianity, and that the Dulong people express emotional "love" to the Communist Party demonstrates that the Dulong people have been trying to adjust themselves and their cultures to the changing world which they are connected with by the Dulong River Highway.

Chapter 5
The Role of Ethnic Enterprises and Entrepreneurs

Over the past few decades, most researchers have focused on a comparative study of the economic performance of different migrant groups in cities or their economic participation patterns. In this chapter, we use the "ethnic enclave" and its economic circle theory, trying to illustrate various factors that have affected the formation of the ethnic economic-cultural pattern based on first-hand information from recent surveys in some cities of China. The most important and substantial roles are played by the ethnic enterprises and the ethnic entrepreneurs.

Introduction

Since China's Reform and Opening-up, the distribution pattern of ethnic groups in Chinese cities presented a "scattered" and "hybrid" trend, with a large-scale population floating across regions and ethnicities and its city-oriented direction as its basic motivation. Some scholars worry that the fast process of urbanization will generate "fragmentation" groups (Hao 2017). Will all the border ethnic minorities migrating to a city with higher population heterogeneity be "fragmented"? And what changes will it bring to different ethnicities?

Over the past few decades, most research focused on comparing the economic performance of different ethnic immigrant groups or their economic participation. Chan Kwok Bun & Claire Chiang （1994） wrote in their work *Stepping Out: The Making of Chinese Entrepreneurs*: "Immigration is not a new topic, but linking immigration with entrepreneurship to understand the process of how the immigrants transformed themselves into small business owners, businessmen, entrepreneurs and industrialists is quite novel." They got rid of the existing socio-economic structures and blocks, seized new development opportunities, and created a new socio-economic structure. We researched floating urban minorities (immigrants) with this issue.

Literature Review

During 1970-1980, several studies were conducted on the Chinese community (especially Chinatown). V. Nee and B. Nee (1973) conducted an investigation and research on the Chinese community in America. They mainly focus on various factors that affect the economy, and the economic success of Chinese immigrants gathered in the region. B.P. Wong's study found that the relation between entrepreneurs and migrant workers in Chinatown lies in that the entrepreneurs provide shelters and protection to the new immigrants and act as brokers for the immigrants. While assisting the Chinese immigrants, the entrepreneurs also derive large profits from the business (Wong 1988).

Peter Kwong organized empirical research on New York Chinatown's evolving process from the 1930s to the 1950s, in which in-depth analyses of the labor market and laborers' living conditions were revealed. He believes that in the immigrant gathering zone like the New York Chinatown, the forepersons utilize immigrants not familiar with the new environment to make huge profits through low wages, poor working conditions, extended working hours, and other means. Thus those foremen became the nouveau riche, while many migrant workers still live in poverty. In short, in Chinatown, these bigwigs took the cheap immigrants labor as their new wealth accumulation tool and a ladder to climb to a higher class in the United States (Kwong 1979). In a later follow-up study, Peter Kwong still insisted that, whether the old Chinatown or the new Chinatown, they all are places of exploitation of the Chinese immigrants. As members of the ethnic enclave, most Chinese live in poverty (Kwong 1987).

Alejandro Portes and Robert Bach proposed the "ethnic enclave" and its economic circle theory in 1985 or the "ethnic, socioeconomic enclave" theory (Portes and Bach 1985). Alejandro Portes and L. Jenson, 1989, conducted an empirical study on the theory. In the research on the Cuban immigrants' enclave in Miami, they found that, on the one hand, the Cuban enterprises of the enclave are more adept at taking advantage of the American economy to gain greater profits and gains than the enterprises outside of the enclave; the Cuban immigrants inside the enclave can better utilize their human labor resources to obtain higher pay and status in the low-end labor market than the Cuban migrants outside of enclave. On the other hand, the common cultural foundation, the sense of ethnic identity and the ethnic solidarity of the Cuban enclave both help the ethnic entrepreneurs and the migrant workers to get rid of the variety of adverse factors in the American community (such as racial discrimination, etc.) and to better integrate into the society, and to get a higher income and social status (Portes and Jenson 1989).

The formation and development of the ethnic and socioeconomic enclave mainly depend on three factors: economy, culture, and social networks. First, the ethnic enclave's economic structure is consistent with the mainstream economy. However, the development of the enclave's economy largely depends on its unique mode of operation and its labor market. Thus its function is different from the "big economy." The ethnic enclave's economy supports its ethnic industry and commerce and helps immigrants improve their surviving ability and social status.

Second, the immigrants in the enclave form its unique social network, consequently leading to the expansion of group scale and the enclave range. Meantime the social network also provides a wealth of labor, goods and services markets for the development of the enclave.

Third, the sense of ethnic identity and ethnic solidarity within immigrant groups effectively promote the development of ethnic industry and commerce, creating more employment opportunities. The development of the enclave's economy and the frequency of social interaction also stimulate the ethnic traditional culture to blossom. For example, the characteristic ethnic and cultural recreational industries quickly grow and are strengthened. The interaction and mutual promotion of these three aspects have brought the enclave vitality and improved the enclave's status in the big society.

Zhou Min is one of the major American scholars who studied the Chinese immigrants and their enclave area. Inspired by Portes's economic enclave theory, she was optimistic about New York's Chinatown. In the 1990s, she studied the history of Chinatown's development process, which involved the Chinese immigration history, compared the differences between the early settlers and the new immigrants, examined the structure and development of the economy of Chinatown, analyzed the characteristics of Chinatown's labor market and women's role and status in Chinatown, and finally made optimistic forecasts about the future development of Chinatown. Her research depicted New York's Chinatown development history, present, and future from a new angle. Although Chinatown once acted as a refugee camp, it later evolved into a major ethnic economy with great flexibility and vitality. She also noted that Chinatown is not like most immigrants' ghettos or slums, but it is truly an area for developing careers. The Chinese immigrants and their descendants have established many independent local small businesses in the town, which helped the Chinese immigrants become one of the most developed and affluent immigrant groups in the immigration history of the United States. This is not the result of scheming or carefully planning by the Chinese immigrant entrepreneurs but rather an adaptive response to the harsh realities of American society (Zhou 1992).

In recent years, the city's ethnic diversity has become more evident, and many scholars have begun to focus on intergroup relations in the ethnic business environment (Light and Gold 2000). One research path is to investigate the intergroup relations between buyers and sellers. The main concern of this kind of research is the intergroup interaction patterns of the Korean business owners, especially the conflicts in the black areas. Some scholars have compared the conflicts between the Koreans and the blacks in New York and Los Angeles and discovered that the local political groups (e.g., community associations) were the main cause of strengthening factors of conflicts (Joyce 2003). Some scholars have pointed out that the conflict between the black and Korean economies reflects the Korean businessmen's unique status as the middleman in the economic structure (Weitzer 1997). These studies show that Mexicans and Koreans regarded each other as commercial rivals because both groups have many immigrants.

Another line of research analyzes the differences between various ethnic groups and their problems. One scholar, who made field observations and interviewed some South Korean business owners in Chicago and Los Angeles, noted that South Korean business owners' prejudice against blacks is greater than Latinos'. Because before immigration, Koreans already held erroneous prejudices against blacks, and after immigration, this bias was further strengthened (Yoon 1997). Another scholar pointed out that the status difference, different cultural expectations of immigrant business owners and residents, and sometimes language barriers can lead to conflicts between groups (Lee 2002).

Through the comparative study of ethnic enterprises of Chinese, Japanese and blacks in the United States, Ivan Light (1972) found that the ethnic enterprises and their economic development are different from the mainstream capital economy. General capital companies rely on class resources, i.e., labor and financial capital. In contrast, ethnic enterprises rely on ethnic resources, such as close social relations and various ethnic and cultural resources in the community. The workforce, funding sources and markets of ethnic enterprises are connected with ethnic resources but are also affected by the ethnic culture values, customs and way of life, etc.

Theoretical Framework

In many regions of China, local resource allocation and economic-social development have presented a strong characteristic of an "umbrella society," that is, a major driving force of China's economic development is still like the "umbrella relation" between local governments and enterprises (Zhang 2016). What is common people's role in the Chinese huge market transformation? Are they beneficiaries or impaired parties? To discuss China's complicated economic and social structure transformation (especially market transformation), the sole concept of "umbrella society" is insufficient. As a broader concept of "umbrella society," common people's economic and social life is a "beehive society." The transition from a planned economy to a market economy allows common people to achieve higher beneficial opportunities and surplus allocation opportunities, which improves the labor enthusiasm; therefore, self-employed, vendors, private owners, blue-collar, white-collar workers, professional managers and freelancers are increasing. We depict these common people's high involvement in market development as a "beehive society," in other words. Every person builds their relationship network beehives through personal or family efforts (Zhang 2018).

Portes et al. (1985) believe that the mass existence of ethnic enterprises in North American cities provides job opportunities to the ethnic minority groups and accumulates wealth to improve ethnic, economic development and support. My above concept, "beehive society," is very similar to Portes's "ethnic enclave" or the "ethnic, socioeconomic enclave," which would possess certain reference value for further exploring the function of ethnic enterprises and entrepreneurs in the formation of a new economic-cultural pattern.

The Analysis of the Data

The main sources of statistical data in this chapter came from a priority project of the Chinese Academy of Social Sciences: Floating Urban Minorities and Its Scattering Dwelling Trend. The project was officially established in the second half of 2006, and fieldwork and data processing work was completed in the first half of 2008. We chose four representative cities: Hohhot in north China, Qingdao in east China, Shenzhen in southwest and Kunming in south China. Questionnaires and in-depth interviews were the two main methods we used during the study.

The Basic Conditions of Six Ethnic Groups

We visited the four cities (Qingdao, Kunming, Huhhot and Shenzhen) and found a livelihood strategy and economic power as the main ground factors. Our survey shows that among the six ethnic minorities, the primary means of access to the current work of the Korean, Mongolian, Hui and Bai is to "apply by themselves" (48.1% - 60.0%), while the other two ethnics Yi and Dai is "through friends and colleagues' recommendation" (26.7% -36.1%). Among the six ethnic groups, Dai, Hui, Bai, Yi and Mongolian respondents have a high proportion of monthly income below 1,000 yuan, and the Dai respondents have the highest proportion (50.0 %). Korean respondents' income level is relatively higher, with a monthly income of 3,001 yuan and above, accounting for 36.7% (Zhang 2009, Zhang 2012) .

The concentration of industries and the habitant aggregation are also very important factors, on which the ethnic, socioeconomic enclave theory is proposed accordingly. For example, in Kunming, about 10 thousand Huis migrated from Xinjie Town, Huize County. They set up nine cattle farms, holding 90% of Kunming's red meat market, of which the two biggest Huis enterprises are Mu Shengda and Mu Hongda. On December 28, 2007, we visited Mr. Mu Hongda, who owned 60-70 % of the cattle slaughtering business in Kunming. In terms of economic activity, the Hui migrants occupied most of the trade and slaughtering business of live cattle and beef, a mutton market in Kunming. In Kunming, Dai and the Bai ethnic groups are also trying to develop food services, ethnic handicrafts and cloth trade.

Our survey shows that in terms of industries they are currently engaged in, among the six ethnic groups surveyed in the four cities (Qingdao, Kunming, Huhhot and Shenzhen), Mongolian respondents possess the highest industry concentration (83.9%) in catering services; Hui, Bai and Dai's respondents also have high degree industry concentration (64-69%) in "catering services"; Korean respondents hold the lowest industry concentration (23.5%) in the manufacturing sector. Hui and Mongolian respondents are engaged in only one industry that concentrates more than 10% of their population, which is "catering services"; Bai and Yi's respondents are engaged in two industries, namely the "catering services" and the "entertainment services"; Dai respondents also have two industries, "catering services" and "domestic service"; Korean respondents have three sectors, namely "manufacturing sector," "commercial trade" and "catering service."

Our survey shows that the profession of the urban ethnic migrants mainly can be classified into three categories: (1) ordinary workers, most of them working in the construction sites, home-moving companies and labor-intensive industries, mainly from the Southwest and Central south, accounting for more than 83% of the flowing population; (2) minorities from Qinghai, Gansu, Xinjiang, Ningxia, such as Hui and Uygur, engaged in trade and commerce, mainly dealing with beef, mutton, noodles and raisins, accounting for more than 14% of the flowing population; (3) itinerant traders mainly from Sichuan, Qinghai, Guizhou, Xinjiang and Tibet, such as the Hui, Uygur, Tibetan, Miao and other ethnic groups, mostly selling knives, jewelry, leather goods, accounting for 3% of the floating population（Zhang and Yin 2013）.

Our survey also shows that among the six ethnic groups, the proportion of the Yi (63.9%) and Hui (64.3%) respondents working in private sectors is higher than the Bai, Mongolian and Dai respondents, far higher than the Korean respondents; the proportion of Korean respondents (35.4%) working in the "joint ventures" is much higher than the other five ethnic groups; the proportion of self-employed Mongolian respondents (46.0%) is higher than the other five ethnics. The first row of positions that the six ethnic groups' respondents hold is "general corporate staff," but with different proportions, in descending order the Yi (69.0%), Hui (58.5%), Mongolian (57.7%), Bai (52.2%), Dai (48.3%), Korean (23.1%). The position that held more than 10% of the four groups of respondents (Yi, Hui, Bai and Dai) is concentrated in the "corporate general staff" (48.3% -69.0%). Except for the position of "general corporate staff," there is a certain percentage of Mongolian respondents that assume the "self-employed individual commercial households" profession (11.7%) and Korean respondents that serve as the "enterprise mid-level cadres" (15.4%), "enterprise grassroots cadres"(14.1%), "private entrepreneurs" (14.1%) and "professional technical personnel "(11.5 percent)（Zhang 2014）.

Qingdao: Korean Ethnic Migrants and Entrepreneurs

According to our survey, more than 8,000 South Korean enterprises in Qingdao and nearly 100,000 Koreans work and live in Qingdao. Qingdao has become the city holding the largest number of Korean people. South Korea is one of the most important economic and trade partners of Qingdao. Therefore, 120,000 Korean minorities migrated from the Northeast (Yanji, Jilin) to Qingdao to work in South Korean enterprises. Our survey shows: that Korean minorities respondents have mainly been distributed in three sectors: the "manufacturing" (23.5%), the "foodservice industry" (15.3%) and "trade" (14.1%).

For example, Li Cang District, one of the four districts in Qingdao city, is the new administrative division officially established in June 1994, which consists of the original Li Cun of Laoshan district and most of Cang Kou District. According to incomplete statistics, there were 21 ethnic minorities with 4782 people in Licang District, including 3014 Korean ethnics, accounting for 63%. At the northern end of Qingdao, Chengyang District, as the business gates for South Korean companies in Qingdao, holds the largest number of Koreans and Korean ethnicities. In addition to the Korean factories, there are also more than 800 stores, of which more than 90% are hotels, KTVs and food shops and other service businesses. The Korean investment draws the Korean ethnic in Qingdao to migrate to Qingdao. Their lives mainly depend on South Korean enterprises.

Observing the whole society, how does Korean folk "beehive" society locate itself and play its role in governmental "umbrella society"? Government builds the stage, and capital plays a role in market transformation. A powerless Korean migrant worker can't build up his own "beehive" overnight. They couldn't even rely on any relatives or friends. Therefore the cost and risk are relatively high. In short, it is very unlikely for migrant workers to build up a "beehive" in the first stage. Until the second stage, these Korean forgoers become queen bees and bring worker bees (relatives and friends) to work in the cities, and it is qualified for them to build up their own chain "beehives." In the third stage, the network of Korean migrant workers is becoming wider and wider. The range has gone beyond the consanguinity or affinity, and it is qualified to become a net type "beehive." In a word, the main principle of Korean migrant workers' self-built "beehive" is mutual help; it has two types "chain type" and "net type." Korean folk "beehive" society becomes a supplement to Qingdao's official "umbrella" society. They exist side by side and play a part together (Zhang 2018).

A senior Korean man told us: The Korean minority people are mainly attracted by the South Korean enterprises due to convenience and language advantages. In 1993, the Korean enterprises began to recruit laborers from northeast China. Most Korean ethnics work in factories, many of whom were engaged in the shoe-making, clothing, toy and sport utility industries. The elders tend to be nurses or cleaners or work in the kitchen, while the younger ones work in the Korean factories, earning more than the Han people, with salaries up to 5000-6000 yuan. Even those with the lowest income can earn 1500-2000 per month. There are also some Korean ethnic people working in Japanese factories because many Korean ethnicities used to learn Japanese in high schools, providing them with an advantage in finding jobs. Jiaozhouwan was opened up later than Weihai.

The Koreans came to Chengyang, then Laoshan and finally, downtown Qingdao in Qingdao. Many Koreans in Chengyang, Jiaozhouwan, Jimo and Pingdu live in Lichen. There are many Korean enterprises here. Owing to the language advantage, our children work as interpreters in Korean companies, and many of us settle down here following our children. Chengyang holds the most ethnic Korean population. Other Koreans scattered in Xifu, Xiazhuang, Liuting and others. Many young men work in the manufacturing sector, and some in the trade companies.[1]

South Korean companies in Qingdao fell into stagnation or even decline, which greatly affected the foundation for the development of the Korean ethnic people. Due to severe pollution, poor management

[1]Source: from the interview at a church in Licang district, Qingdao. He was one of the earliest Korean immigrants here. In 1994, he used to work in a factory. Later the factory went bankrupt, he started to do some trade business. Now he retired and entered into the church, though the church stuff was hard to maintain, he tries his best to do the job.

and other reasons, coupled with the recent international financial turmoil, some South Korean-owned enterprises had to leave Qingdao. At present, for example, Chengyang receives the most Korean migrants, but many of them just come blindly and can't find a job.

On the one hand, many young Korean migrants work in South Korean companies in employment and management. After some time, they mastered the technology and craft. They would quit and start their own business. Some could even annex the original Korean-owned enterprises, particularly the handicraft processing industry. On the other hand, the Korean ethnic people have to solve the employment issue themselves because the government has no interest in doing that. The Han enterprises are generally unwilling to recruit Korean ethnics. If the South Korean companies leave, many Korean ethnicities will fall impoverished.[1]

Qingdao Korean ethnic immigrants are mainly employed in procurement, production, sales, service, and other economic areas or operate their businesses. Their economy is mainly transplanted from the Korean-owned export-oriented enterprises. The professionalism and business activities of the ethnics are necessary for the local economy. However, their social and cultural life still retains their cultural identity yet absorbs various new elements, such as South Korea's modern corporate culture.

In religious aspect, Qingdao's Korean ethnics accepted Christianity from South Korea. Originally there were no Korean churches in Qingdao. Starting in 1994, the first Korean ethnic church was established in Liuting by the Korean company S & K. From the second half of 1994. The Korean ethnics began to join the Korean church activities with the South Koreans. The Korean church did not have any priests, so the South Korean churches sent some.

However, the Chinese authorities are extremely unhappy about this. South Korean missionaries are willing to help, and now 80 percent of the *Bible* is from South Korea. The Korean churches also provide us

---

[1] Source: Cui Yongji's speech in a residential committee symposium on January 14, 2008.

with many learning materials, but we dare not accept them. Currently, the Korean ethnics have three churches in Qingdao[1] organizing worship activities for the believers, trying to form their own ethnic, religious culture. Our funding sources are Korean Christians. Following the provisions of the *Bible*, everyone should hand in 1/10 of personal income to the church.[2]

Our survey shows that 66.7% of Korean ethnic respondents said they own an apartment in Qingdao City. 55.3% of the Korean respondents said their dwelling space ranges from 71 to 100 square meters; 21.3% claim their dwelling space is more than 101 square meters. The origins of Qingdao's Korean minority are quite scattered, such as Harbin, Jiamusi, Qiqihar, Mudanjiang, Jixi, Ning, and Mishan of Heilongjiang province; Changchun, Yanji, Longjing, Hunchun, Jiaohe, Liuhe, etc. of Jilin province; Shenyang, Yingkou, Fushun of Liaoning province. No matter how scattered they were, now they voluntarily assembled to form a new community.

A Korean elder told us: that Qingdao is equivalent to the second Yanbian. In Qingdao, the Korean language and customs are retained and continuingly strengthened through children's education and the elders' community activities and other means. Baitong Community Elders Society has more than 60 members of the Korean ethnics. Baitong Community has more than 20 Korean residents and many others living in nearby districts. The Korean ethnic properly assembled, like Xita of Shenyang, where the Koreans live quite concentrated so that no matter learning language, or living environment, are all very convenient. If Koreans live dispersedly, the language and customs will soon be gone. Daily activities of our association include singing, dancing, playing cards, chess, mahjong, etc. Every Sunday afternoon, a

---

[1] Li Cang District has two churches: one is Wenchangge church, which has 110 Christians; the other one is Zhengdinglu church, about 100 people; Laoshan district has one Christian church, more than 200 people.

[2] Source: I intervivewed Cui Yongji twice, first time in the Wenchangge church on January 13, 2008 and on January 14 in Cui Yongji's home.

reading party will be held.[1] As can be seen, many Koreans are ready to settle down in Qingdao for long-term work and living.

There are a few primary and secondary schools teaching Korean in Qingdao. We surveyed Qingdao Bishan Korean Elementary School.[2] According to the principal, Xu Yushan, the school is a private one under the guidance of the Education Bureau of Lee Chang District, Qingdao City. The school implements trilingual education: Korean, English and Chinese. Bishan school boasts Korean language teaching among all the 31 elementary schools in the Li Chang district. English language teaching is also among the best, while math and Chinese are at the middle level. The school offers many after-class activities, such as Korean traditional country music, long drum, fan dance, etc. The main enrollment targets are Korean ethnic children. The enrollment numbers of Han students are tightly controlled, with each class shall not exceed three. Chinese, mathematics and English teaching apply the unified textbooks; Chinese, mathematics, and English are taught in Chinese by Han teachers; while Korean language, Morality, Art and Music are taught in Korean.

Overall, in terms of employment, management, marketing, finance, technology, customers, design, religion, international contacts and modern pop culture, the Korean ethnics depend on Korean companies and Christian churches. From several aspects, such as primary education, traditional cultural heritage, etc., we can deduce the "transplantation" characteristic of the Qingdao Korean ethnics. The Korean ethnic immigrants in Qingdao are forming a kind of "dependence-transplantation" economic-cultural pattern.

---

[1] During the survey in Qingdao, with the help of Baitongyuan residential commettee, a large commercial residential area, the survey team members held a symposium with the elderly association members (they are all Koreans) on January 14, 2008. The elderly association is in fact a Korean folk organization in Qingdao. The President of this organization is from Yingkou, liaoning province. He used to serve in the army for seven years and retired as a captain. Now he lives with his children. His has four children, two of them working in Qingdao.

[2] Source: I interviewed Xu Yushan, the principal of Bi Shan Korean Elementary School on January 10, 2008. The headmaster's office has a slogan: "dedicated in the ethnic education career, establish a environment for the 200000 Korean children in Qingdao to learn their native language".

Huhhot: Mongolian Ethnic Migrants and Entrepreneurs

In recent years, with the help of its advantaged natural pasture, the dairy industry of Hohhot has developed rapidly and become a famous "dairy capital." Along with the rapid development of the economy and the urban infrastructure, characteristic tourism also grows vigorously. There are many dining places (some are Mongolian Food Streets), and the Mongolian-style business and service industry grows swiftly.

Batusuhe, a restaurant owner from the Xilinguole (Ximeng), believes that the Mongolian catering industry in the cities has to innovate. The Mongolian meal should add pepper, aniseed and various spices to cater to the urban taste. Originally Mongolian food added just salt, and the flavor was good. But now, it must add some flavors of Han people to meet the market's needs. Another question is whether the development of the Mongolian catering industry is quite mussy. For example, there is no industry standard. Every place has its characteristics, and so, he suggests, the Mongolian catering industry should set up its standard.

Batusuhe said: "I have three restaurants in Xi Meng. Now I intend to open the fourth, which will be the largest, 2000 square meters. I do not want banks' loans, and I try to integrate all the ethnic specialties and the original ecology into the restaurants. My red meat and dairy products are from Xi Meng. Here on the market, there is a lot of fake stuff. Xi Meng has many original ecological products. But due to some conditions, a lot of things are limited. All kinds of animals' blood are mixed on the blood farm. However, on the prairie of Xi Meng, animals are all raised separately. The Mongolian food industry has to take root on the grasslands, where horses, camels, all kinds of meat and weeds are abundant. Here there were too many restrictions. We cannot find a lot of raw materials we need. And the meat flavor here is not good because the cattle and sheep are all raised in the countryside, where the environment is polluted. The meat of the prairie tastes far better. I want to start a slaughterhouse, and we slaughter and cook for immediate consumption. I think the business will be better."[1]

The general manager of Bayinwori, Ma Quanxi, told us: "In 2005, we established the Mongolian Meal Research Institute, which is a nonprofit, non-governmental organization. We invested a lot of money into researching and developing Mongolian food. I formed this idea in 2002. At that time, I solved the food and clothing problem and also made some money every year. So I hoped to make a new height in my business. Mongolian food is healthy and nutritious. The people on the grassland are all very healthy and strong. Mongolian meals can play a role in raising people's health and nutrition. Bayinwori must retain the tradition and innovate according to modern tastes. For example, based on innovation, we launched the Abalone Camel Palm as upscale dishes, each costing 40 yuan. We recently launched the hot pot and fresh lamb for the first-floor lobby. If you do not innovate, the grade and level will stay low. At the same time, we also have to consider the health and nutritional functions."

Ma Quanxi said: "This year (2008), we start a project led by the Mongolian Meal Research Institute to integrate the eastern, central and west Mongolian food with support from Bayinhaori. I will lead the team with the assistance of the Inner Mongolia Agricultural University. The regional government and the state should support this. Mongolia has a long history, many things we have to ask for the elderly's advice. Our main goal is to develop Mongolian Cuisines as a cuisine system this year. Mongolian cuisine is not among the 8 National Cuisine Systems. We hope to integrate and promote Inner Mongolian cuisines, making it the ninth-largest cuisine system."[2]

Whether can this "transplantation" pattern of economic and cultural changes in Hohhot Mongolian come to success mainly depends on whether the driving force of all levels of governments, entrepreneurs and consumers are strong enough or not and whether this transformation

[1] Source: from the interview of Mr. Batusuhe, the boss of Qingkeerhada, on January 17 and January 19, 2008.
[2] Source: From the interview of Mr. Ma, manager of Bayinhaoriwo on Jan.19,2008.

can meet the market demand innovatively in the process of migration. The migration and transformation did not cause local social and cultural conflicts. Although there are differences between the pastoral Mongolian and the urban Mongolian, no matter pastoral or urban, they are all Mongolian ethnic people, and the two do not have significant cultural differences. Thus, in migrating to the urban area, the pastoral Mongolian will naturally link the two areas, which leads to the "transplantation" of the Mongolian economic-cultural pattern. In other words, the origin and resettlement area will be connected.

Therefore, we can see, in Hohhot, a city known as "Green Town," the Mongolian migrants are gradually transplanting the distinctive Mongolian culture into modern life and trying to commercialize and marketize the Mongolian material and intangible cultural resources to establish a new Mongolian economic-cultural pattern in line with the modern metropolis. For example, the daily diet of the Mongolians is highly related to the ecological environment, natural resources, cultural characteristics, religious beliefs, etc. The Mongolian economic-cultural pattern is transformed from the original ecology to market-oriented, with its impetus coming from all levels of government, entrepreneurs and consumers.

Conclusion and Discussion

Based on my investigation and observation among the above six ethnic groups in the above four cities, I consider there are three types of business "beehives": (1) family "beehive": family-centered mutual benefit network, (2) value chain type of "beehive": win-win network centered by value chain, (3) ethnic "beehive": mutual benefit network based on minority groups. The growth of these private ethnic enterprises depends not only on economic ability but also on social-cultural background. Private ethnic enterprises and managers have ethnic resources like distinct ethnic culture, language, value concepts, kinship and community relations. These distinct characters help them build up various "beehives" to obtain entrepreneurship capital, low-cost labor, and business credit and develop them into business and management activities after they leave home. These various relation networks have something in common: the existence of the queen bee (leader). The leader is like the "King without crown," who serves as certain leading or directing functions inside the circle. They could be the head of a household, the elder with high prestige or sometimes very successful businessmen. More and more successful ethnic enterprises and managers are gathering together and becoming ethnic enterprise groups based on human relations of various family "beehives" and value-chain "beehives" (Zhang 2018).

Among all the factors that influence the forming of the economic-cultural patterns, the ethnic enterprises and entrepreneurs play the most important and substantial roles, which epitomize the ethnic minority's livelihood strategy and economic strength in the city. Ten years ago, we asked an officer who worked at the central government: "If we take an animal as a metaphor, what do the ethnic enterprises in China look like?" He replied: "Butterfly. Because they are fragile, people usually make them or treat them as specimens." I said: "This is one side of it. The other side is that the worm pupates into 'butterfly.'"

The growth of ethnic enterprises and entrepreneurship is not a castle in the air. They have certain ethnic resources, such as a significant cultural identity, national values, family, community, social networks, etc. These features and advantages guarantee the success of businesses after they migrate to the resettlement place (Aldrich & Roger 1990). Chan Kwok Bun pointed out that Chinese immigrants often use their kinship and social networks to raise funds, venture capital, and gain financial credit when facing the cruelty and hostility of reality in the host society. Chinese enterprises in the past were and still are, established among the same tribes, especially families and relatives (Chan 1991). For the cultural, economic and ethnic division of labor, the principal North American Chinese restaurants mainly use the Chinese workforce. Peter Li argues that Chinese restaurant owners often have to work as hard as their relatives- waiters, thus blurring the boundaries between the employers and employees (Li 1976).

Furthermore, in the process of transformation of ethnic migrants' economic-cultural pattern, the number, the economic strength and the industry concentration degree of the ethnic enterprises form inflexible standards judging the success of the transformation. Accordingly, entrepreneurial qualities, quantities, courage, economic strength and social influence are key factors in transforming the economic-cultural pattern. Conversely, if an ethnic migrant group scatters all over the city in various industries just as ordinary workers and has yet to set up their ethnic enterprises and does not have entrepreneurs, how does this ethnic group change or create their economic-cultural pattern?

In Qingdao, from the view of government policies, employment and business, education, religious life, community society, language and traditional cultural heritage and other aspects, although the Korean ethnics' economic-cultural pattern presents a new prototype, "dependent-transplantation," we cannot assert its true content and form. The most fundamental fact is that Qingdao's Korean ethnics are mostly professional managers or common employees in South Korean enterprises. Yet, many Korean ethnical enterprises or entrepreneurs did not appear. For example, in the religious aspect, Korean ethnic in Qingdao are merely spokespersons or agents of the Korean Christian. They have not formed their independent Christian organization. In other words, their influence and social organizing force are not strong enough to form a new type of economic-cultural pattern with ethnic characteristics.

Without innovation, the "transplantation" economic-cultural pattern is meant to wither. The pastoral Mongolian left the ranch to the city and innovatively established commercialized food service, ethnic handicrafts trade and other economic activities, which have been proved to be an innovative way to build a new prototype of the economic-cultural pattern. The economic-cultural pattern of Hohhot Mongolian migrants' "urbanization and marketization of prairie products" is the "innovation-transplantation" type. Hohhot Mongolian immigrants are forming relatively concentrated business areas. Mongolian ethnic enterprises and entrepreneurs in the urban economy are forming an out-looking economic model: on one end is the grassland and pasture. On the other end is the greater China inland and the international markets. In terms of their social and cultural life, on the one hand, it has a relatively closed nature with the development in their own independent space.

On the other hand, it shows certain compatibility. It becomes the "articulation" between the area of origin and the resettlement areas, between the urban and rural areas, the tradition and modernity. The dichotomy does not apply to them anymore. Their economic-social identity and cultural identity have reflected diversity in nature.

For ethnic entrepreneurs who originated from remote ethnic areas, the ethnic characteristic business is their major path. These ethnic people start their businesses alone or with partners. It increases the survival and development opportunity and brings unique ethnic culture to city life. Thus, we analogize that the ethnic migrants in China have to transform or create their economic-cultural patterns. An ethnic enterprise is a social organization and foundation for changing or creating ethnic economic-cultural patterns. Without such an entity as the structural basis, the new type of economic-cultural pattern will have no foothold. Depending on the enterprises, the ethnic entrepreneurs can utilize their own cultural identity, ethnic values, family and community social networks to venture capital, gain cheap labor and commercial credit, etc., creating a favorable environment for the development of the ethnic enterprises. "Ethnic character" is important for market access and a significant competitive advantage. The "ethnic character" shows a distinct personality, attracting customers' attention. These characteristic entrepreneurs exactly fill in the "blank" or "gap" of the market's diversification demand and build up a kind of ethnic "beehive society" with an "ethnic enclave" or the "ethnic, socioeconomic enclave."

Chapter 6
Tobacco Growing and Cultural Impacts on Minority Female Smokers

Tobacco growing is very popular in Yunnan, China, and be traced back hundreds of years. Smoking has been a serious threat to women's health. This chapter, based on data from anthropological fieldwork conducted on women smokers from Yi, Wa, Hani, Lahu, Miao, Zhuang, Dai, and Tibetan peoples living in the southeastern, northwestern and southern parts of Yunnan, points out that smoking is popular among ethnic minority women in mountainous areas, especially among older women. Factors affecting smoking include socio-cultural, environmental, religious, gender, educational, and healthcare causes considered when implementing smoking control policies.

Introduction

Smoking has been a serious threat to women's health. As China became a member country of the World Health Organization Framework Convention on Tobacco Control (FCTC), smoking and second-hand exposure have become major concerns for professional organizations and the public and reducing smoking-based disease. Premature death has become a pressing task for improving national health. However, effective implementation of FCTC standards depends on cigarette users and non-cigarette users regarding their support for and compliance with these standards.

Many anthropologists have discussed how people use cigarettes and respond to health promotion and how factors such as ethnicity, age, and gender influence one's exposure to smoking. Augmenting these streams have been ethnographic descriptions of cigarette smoking framed vis-à-vis views of wellness (Mock 2000), social exchange (Kohrman 2008), and the comparison between cigarette smoking and the use of other substances such as marijuana (Lipset 2006) and betel-nuts (Reid 1985, Strickland 2002). Research examining cigarette use has covered topics from social class (Stellman & Resnicow 1997), genetics (Swan et al. 2003) and the use of alcohol (Cameron & Jones 1985). Nearly all these studies emphasize that cigarette smoking is acutely addictive. Some consider how biological habituation is shaped by employment (Longo et al. 2001), norms (Hosking et al. 2009), and diverse cross-cultural expressions of dependency (Quintero & Nichter 1996, Shadel et al. 2000).

However, one needs to consider indigenous culture while regulating the implementation of smoking-control policies and providing smoking control education and related services. In this way, such policies might be carried out more effectively. Investigating smoking among ethnic minority women in Yunnan of China by anthropology fieldworkers, and providing an ethnographic account of the customs as well as the reasons for smoking among ethnic minority women, will thus not only improve our understanding of smoking among ethnic minority women but also provide us with some guidelines on the issues of regulating smoking.

Yunnan has a diversified natural environment. Tobacco growing is very popular and can be found in river valleys several hundred meters above sea level and mountainous areas two-thousand meters above sea level. Tobacco planting in Yunnan can be traced back a hundred years. As early as the end of the Ming dynasty and early Qing dynasty, tobacco grew all over the province. In addition to satisfying local needs, the surplus was sold at markets in Weishang and Teaching.

Nowadays, most of the 17 prefectures in Yunnan grow native tobacco (Lianshaiyan), mainly in Zhaotong, Qujing, Yuxi, Honghe, Dali, Wenshang, Baoshan, Puer, Dehong and Lijiang. With the spread of planting tobacco in Yunnan, native tobacco is grown sporadically and leisurely in the villagers' gardens or at the corners of their fields, even in front of their houses or around ponds. The villagers have practiced tobacco cultivation for self-consumption till now.

Methodology

The total population of Yunnan is 47 million. Women of 15 and older amount to 14 million, according to the Statistical Bulletin of the National Economic and Social Development in Yunnan Province (2014). To reduce health risks to women and girls childbearing, Yunnan Chaoyi Health Consultation Center (Chaoyi Center) developed a project called "Reduction of Health Risks of Childbearing-Age Women and Children Related to Smoking" (also known as the "women and children smoking-control project"), aimed at improving accessibility of information on the health hazards of smoking and secondhand exposure, and introducing policies on smoking control.

The smoking control project for women and children intends to research the culture of ethnic minority women smoking in Yunnan. It is believed that the results of such research could provide effective health education and intervention on women smokers and secondhand exposure, provide evidence for policy-making and implementation, and possibly contribute to research on this particular topic.

This research on ethnic minority women's smoking will answer the following questions: (1) Is smoking among ethnic minority women a popular phenomenon? (2) Against the background of smoking control in China, should we pay attention to this particular group? (3) What are the present factors influencing smoking or passive smoking among ethnic minority women?

Multi-disciplinary (such as history, anthropology, and sociology) research methods are needed to control and reduce smoking among ethnic minority women. Anthropological investigation methods and multi-point ethnological approaches are of great significance. These two important research methods are applied in this study. A semi-structured interview is used to communicate with the villagers to collect information.

The ethnic groups and research sites that the author picked up include Yi, Lahu and the Kucong people in Po village of Shuitang town in Xiping Yi and Dai Autonomous County; the Hani people in Hani, the new village in Gasa town of Xiping County; the Huayao Dai people in

Pingzhai Village of Gasa Town and the Lahu people in Xianlisuo Village of Ximeng Wa People's Autonomous County of Puer Municipality; the Wa People in Yingla Village of Ximeng Wa People's Autonomous County; the Chushuidong Village of Bamei Town of Guangnan County in Wenshang Prefecture; the Zhuang People in Fali Village; the Miao People in Jiuchen Village of Wenshang County; the Aozi of Wengang Village of Jiujia Town in Zhengyang County of Puer; and the Kucong People in Zhangpeng Village of Zhedong Town and Tibetan in Shangrila County of Diqing Tibet Autonomous Prefecture. The fieldwork was conducted at these sites in March, May, July and August 2016.

The ethnic groups selected are very representative, with rich cultures and long histories. The history and current situation of tobacco use among these ethnic groups can be used to study smoking among ethnic minority women in Yunnan. This research covers a large geographic area and focuses on small specific villages. At the same time, it helps to understand the context of smoking among different ethnic minority women.

This research targeted women of different age groups, including over 80, smoking women in their 40s, and non-smoking women 20–30. Meanwhile, some smoking men, village heads, and religious ritual organizers were interviewed. Most of the male villagers interviewed were over 60. They are quite familiar with the history of their villages and can describe their family history of smoking. They have experienced changes in times and tobacco use. This research has its limitations. Due to financial, time, and energy constraints, the author finished the fieldwork in Yunnan's southeast, northwest and southern parts. The northeast and southwest parts of Yunnan have not been covered. Therefore, cultural analysis of smoking, including chewing, was not made for the Jingpo, Achang, Deyang and Lisu people.

Cultural Impacts

Yunnan is home to many ethnic groups. In addition to the Han people, there are 25 different ethnic groups, among which 15 can be found only in Yunnan. The ethnic population makes up 33.5% of the total population in Yunnan. Five ethnic groups (Yi, Bai, Hani, Dai, and Zhuang) have over one million people. Nine ethnic groups (Miao, Lisu, Hui, Lahu, Wa, Naxi, Yao, Jinpo and Tibetan) have a population between 100,000 and 1 million, according to the Statistical Bureau of Yunnan Province (2015). Many ethnic groups in Yunnan are accustomed to smoking, for example, the Yi, Wa, Hani, Deang, Lahu, Achang and Lisu people. Many women from these ethnic groups smoke (Yuan 2008).

Smoking is closely linked to legends, songs, dances, marriage and even the value of medication. There are many different ways of smoking in Yunnan: chewing, water pipe, smoke pipe, and snuff. Therefore, smoking among ethnic minority women is mainly classified into smoking tobacco and non-smoking tobacco. Smoking tobacco refers to burning tobacco leaves, which produces smoke, while non-smoking tobacco refers to directly taking in tobacco either by mouth or nose. Non-smoking tobacco is mostly chewed or snuffed among ethnic groups in Yunnan, and snuff is mainly found among Tibetan and Mongolian people.

Smoking customs are gradually changing, social and aesthetic change, education impacts, modern cultural shock, and medical and health improvement. The data collected from the fieldwork show that among Hani, Dai, Miao, Zhuang and Tibetan women, most of those smoking in the past have already died, leaving only one or two elder ones aged between 70 to 80 still smoking. The rest of the women in these ethnic groups no longer smoke. However, among Yi, Lahu and Wa, women over 50 still smoke, while the women under 50 no longer do so.

As everybody knows, smoking is harmful to one's health. Smoking could result in various diseases, such as lung cancer. During the fieldwork, the author found cases of coughing brought about by smoking; the symptoms eventually disappeared when the patients quit smoking under the guidance of local doctors. Smoking does therefore cause harm to women's health among ethnic groups.

However, according to this research, although there are a few cases of smoking hurting women, most of the women interviewees still argued that smoking did not affect their health and was not even aware that smoking is harmful to health. They still insisted that water in the smoking pipe had already filtered hazardous substances. The shank and mouthpiece of a tobacco pipe had taken away the most hazardous substances. The tobacco used by women had low nicotine and tar because they were dried fermented.

Moreover, they claimed that local tobacco didn't contain chemicals. They used to make paper cigarettes, and when smoking, they usually did not inhale the smoke. The smoke produced by tobacco was only turned around and around in their mouth and was completely blown out when the smoke had fully enjoyed the fragrance of the tobacco. Therefore, they believed that there was no danger to their health. Thus, they believed that different ways of smoking could help avoid damaging their health.

Environmental Analysis

Different ethnic groups live in different geographic environments in Yunnan. Most of them live in mountainous or semi-mountainous areas, where living conditions are very bad because of the environment and climate. Hot summers and high humidity in the southern part of Yunnan, cold temperatures in the northwest and northeast of Yunnan, hot temperatures and heavy rain in the low altitude areas, which might cause malaria or other diseases, affect the Yunnan people's work and livelihood. Mosquitoes in tropical areas can accelerate the spread of diseases.

Tobacco has brought a lot of harm to people's health and is even labeled a "poisonous grass." Many countries and areas have issued laws that confine smoking, and the World Health Organization members have signed a "Tobacco Control Framework Agreement." However, as a medicinal plant with a long history, tobacco has a medical value that cannot be ignored despite its dangers (Tian Youqing, Ding Ping, Zhang Yunqing 2015).

From the study of ethnic smoking groups' perception of smoke and ashes, the author found that a major reason for smoking is the prevention of mosquito bites. For example, the Wa and Lahu people live in remote mountain areas with many mosquitoes. The smoke and smell of tobacco can disperse them and protect women from being hurt while working in the fields or staying at home. Miasma occurs in forests, and forests have many leeches. If someone mistakenly drinks water polluted by vapor, they will put some ash of smoking tobacco into the water and drink it, which removes the haze.

Furthermore, in the case of a mosquito or leech bite, smoking ash can diminish swelling when applied directly to the bite location. Both ethnic minority women, and other villagers, know that tobacco can be used to treat diseases since it is traditional local knowledge. All 76 interviewees knew it, and all smokers and nonsmokers understood it. And it is well known in all the villages the author visited. For example, in Jiuchen village, where Miao people live, the local doctor even showed the author that tobacco, among other Miao medicines, can cure diseases.

A healthcare center has been set up in every village due to the development of modern public infrastructure. Medical staff recruited to work in the healthcare center must be Medical School graduates and have a graduation certification or professional working permit. Equipment and facilities in the healthcare center might be simple, but they should be enough to treat minor problems such as mosquito bites, headaches, colds or fever and diminish inflammation. The healthcare center is usually located next to the village committee building. One administrative village often has 6 to 7 natural villages under its control which might be far from or close to the village committee building. Villagers living further away from the healthcare center are more likely to decide not to travel for only minor health problems.

Furthermore, costs are always incurred when seeing a medical doctor in the healthcare center. If traditional medicine is good enough to treat certain diseases in poor rural areas, villagers will take it rather than pay to see a doctor. So the reasons ethnic minority women smoke might be economically-based.

Social and Culture Analysis

Social and cultural factors influencing smoking among ethnic minority women include (1) Social interactions. The author found that many women learned to smoke while playing with others during the fieldwork. "You smoke, I smoke, we smoke together to have fun." This reflects a kind of social interaction among these ethnic minority women. Many ethnic girls interact with others through smoking. But why smoke rather than some other activity? Lighting up a cigarette for others is a friendly gesture that helps people get along quickly. It is true even between husband and wife. There are cases where the wife learned to smoke from her husband, and the love between the husband and wife was enhanced when smoking together.

(2) Parents' influence on children. The author found that parents of smoking women all smoke from the interviews. Living with their parents, these women were influenced by what they constantly saw and heard. In the Lahu village of Zhenyang, there is even a custom that when parents smoke, they will hand over tobacco to their children to have them smoke. To have their children work in their fields, the parents will allow their kids to smoke to prevent mosquito bites. Thus, many ethnic minority women have learned to smoke under the family's influence.

(3) Religious influence. It is believed that tobacco helps the living to communicate with the dead. Smoking tools are burned or sacrificed in front of the tombs of the dead so that they can continue to enjoy smoking in the other world. In ethnic villages nowadays, fire is used in worship rituals which creates a lot of smoke. Moreover, women burn incense sticks in all festivities throughout the year. Incense is made of cedar leaf, and when burned, smoke rises as a symbol of communication between the living and the dead. Around 4,000 to 5,000 years ago, Mayans prayed through smoking to be able to communicate with the Holy Spirit.

All the ethnic villages where the author conducted fieldwork have witches or sorcerers. Some of them are men, and they all smoke. The author interviewed the chief sorcerer in Luoshuidong Village of Bamei Town, Guangnan County, Wenshang Prefecture, 69 years old. He told the author that his title as a chief sorcerer was handed over to him by his ancestor. The chief sorcerer must be chosen from his family members because his family has a rich Taoist tradition. He is the 4th-generation chief sorcerer. When the author followed an interpreter to his house, he made a water pipe from bamboo for sale in the local market. He likes smoking through a water pipe. He told the author: "Smoking is not allowed when we chant Buddhist scripts."

However, incense sticks are burned as a sacrifice to our ancestors. The smoke from burning incense will let the ancestors hear what we chant." Lahu women's smoking is also linked to sacrificial rituals. When an elder one passes away, family members will put all her smoking pipes in front of her tomb. If her water-smoking pipe rotted away, a new one would be placed every year. The smoking pipe placed in front of the tomb is very strong and usually will not decay easily. When Grandma Li in Chushuidong Village died, the villagers burned her water pipe before her tomb.

4) Influence from clothing culture. Ethnic Wa interviewees mentioned that in the old days, women smoked because wearing traditional short skirts attracted mosquitoes. Today, Wa people wear Han people s-style clothes with long sleeves and long pants that can prevent mosquitoes from biting. So smoking is not needed to repel mosquitoes.

Yi people living in Xiaoliangshang of Ninglang County, Lijiang, believe that the front piece of a coat where people put smoke pipes is the place where the soul of a little child is to be found. Little children often try to grasp the smoke pipe, and as long as they have the smoke pipe in their hand, they will sleep quietly without crying.

Social Systems and Education Factors

As more and more people have realized the negative impacts of smoking, it is banned in places like schools and airports. In Yunnan, educational institutes, primary, junior and senior high schools have banned smoking on campus. However, in the mountainous areas of Yunnan, where ethnic-minority people live, a smoking ban can hardly be seen in public social systems, except for schools where the effects of smoking restriction can be found. In public buildings housing village committees, elders associations, and even village squares, signs of "No Smoking" are not seen. Most old villagers have never heard of the concept that "Smoking is harmful to one's health." The government has not set up a system to completely ban smoking. The concept that smoking is harmful to people's health has not penetrated public education.

Social Gender Analysis on Smoking among Ethnic Minority Women in Yunnan

There is great evidence linking smoking among ethnic women to their social gender. The author has found that social gender is a major cause of smoking among ethnic minority women. In a more patriarchal ethnic society, few women smoke, while in an ethnic society with comparatively more equal gender rights, smoking among women is very popular. Women sometimes undertake equal or even heavier intensive physical work than men in these societies.

In the ethnic villages investigated by the author, different ethnic groups hold different views on women smoking. The elders of the Wa and Yi people are used to women smoking. They believe that in the old times, both men and women smoked. Smoking is a natural thing, like eating and sleeping. There is no difference between men and women smoking in a gender sense. Men consider women smoking as a natural thing, and women also consider men smoking as a natural thing. However, young women with Wa and Yi ethnic backgrounds consider smoking a bad thing and dislike the smell of smoking.

For the Lahu people, only older people smoke, and young people consider elders smoking as their hobby without intervening, and sometimes even help older ones to buy tobacco leaves and smoke pipes in markets to show their respect. In a Lahu society, when a man smokes, he will share it with his wife. Therefore, in his wife's eyes, smoking among the Lahu is quite natural.

According to the author's investigation, Lahu women in Ximeng County usually get up early, at about 5 o'clock, eat breakfast at 6, and then take rice, salt, and pepper for lunch to the mountains to do agricultural work growing corn in fields. They will keep working in the fields until 6 pm and then go home, having dinner at around 8 or 9. The Lahu women's average time working in the fields is about 12 hours. Adding 2 to 3 extra working hours at home, their average hours are about 14 to 15 hours per day. The long working hours and intensive heavy labor work will make them feel very tired.

Therefore, those ethnic minority women who have a similar workload to Lahu women see smoking as relaxation. When finishing a day's work, they prefer to light up a smoke pipe while sitting on a ridge in the field, enjoying it before going back home slowly or smoking slowly on their way back home. In their opinion, smoking helps the body relax. That is also why ethnic women regard smoking as physical and spiritual comfort. When they suffer from sorrow or are physically tired, they depend on tobacco to give them some comfort and become what we term "addicted to smoking."

Moreover, when family misfortunes occur, women, as mothers, are naturally under more pressure than men. Different physiological structures or degree of emotions of men and women makes women more sensitive. When ethnic minority women encounter sufferings such as the death of children at an early age or quarrels with their husbands, or even when their husbands die, smoking is a way to release their sorrow. They believe that tobacco smoke rising into the air will take away their sorrows. With the sedating effect of nicotine, smoking makes them feel excited mentally. In his fieldwork at Xiping, the author found that for many Yi women, the direct reason for them smoking was the loss of a young child; they might not have smoked before that.

For Hani, Dai, Miao, Zhuang and Tibetan people, one or two older women sometimes smoke, and they are all well known around the villages. They are frequently mentioned as the only female ones in the village who smoke. The attitude of men there is that it is not proper behavior for women. In a woman's view, a man smoking is quite ordinary. Do they argue that if a man does not smoke, what else can he do? In both men's and women's views, smoking among women is not good. Almost no women smoke in these five ethnic minority groups in this context. The situations of Zhuang people and Miao living in the Chushuidong Village and Fali Village of Bamei Town of Guangnan County in Wrenching Prefecture are similar. One 35-year-old female interviewee from the Shazhi branch of the Zhuang people explained why no women in the village smoked. She said that Zhuang people had been deeply influenced by Han culture, believing that men were superior to women. If a woman smokes, they consider it destructive to her morals, and no man would marry her, and men would look down upon her. Miao women's social status is quite low in their society. After they get married and move to live at their husband's home, they can't even eat with their husband's family members and cannot go upstairs in their houses. One legend says that food is stored upstairs and that the mother-in-law is afraid that the daughter-in-law might go upstairs to steal food. So she prohibits her from going there. Only after the young daughter-in-law grows old and becomes a mother-in-law can she go upstairs.

Discussion and Conclusion

The behavior and cognition of ethnic minority women in Yunnan related to smoking have changed over time. Smoking is found among older women. Younger women rarely smoke nowadays. The reasons for these changes are complex.

First, information from the world outside their societies has had an impact. Here, the information refers to school education (including no smoking in school), medical doctors' advice or guidance, propaganda on radio and TV, etc. Taking the Wa people as an example, for those women 50 or over (born around 1960), when they first learned to smoke as children, their parents' attitudes were open and imposed no strict restrictions. This demonstrates that in Wa society, smoking used to be quite popular. However, Wa women of 20 or 30 (born around 1980) would be punished severely by their parents. This shows that the information from the outside has attacked the customs of smoking among ethnic minority women.

Secondly, the perception of smoking has changed along with their clothing. In other words, changes in clothing have resulted in young women giving up smoking. For Wa women, since their traditional short skirts have been changed into long ones, the function of smoking as a way to drive away mosquitoes has disappeared, and young Wa women no longer smoke. Lahu is somewhat different from the Wa people. When asking whether children are allowed to smoke, the author got two interesting answers. One is from some older women who opposed smoking and considered smoking no good for girls. But they had been smoking for years and were quite used to it. The other one is more related to farm work. Some parents wanted their children to work more in their fields, and to prevent mosquitoes from biting them, the parents allowed their children to smoke. However, with more and more modern information coming into ethnic villages and changes in clothing, most parents now prohibit their children from smoking.

Thirdly, this research found that influenced by the Confucian culture of the Han people. Men are superior to women, and young women do not smoke. The cases from the Zhuang and Miao people can fully explain this. In ethnic-minority villages, no advertising or promotion of smoking can be found today. Villagers who smoke still follow the old traditional ways of smoking.

With more and more women over 50 gradually passing away, the population of smoking women will shrink. However, this is not to say that the issue of smoking among ethnic minority women should be ignored. On the contrary, we should strengthen our efforts in health education and training scientific knowledge to control smoking, thus turning ethnic minority women away from smoking.

There are records of smoking in Yunnan before tobacco was introduced there. It is quite popular for ethnic minority women in border areas to smoke. This research has found that most smoking ethnic minority women in southern Yunnan are from Yi, Wa, and Lahu people over 50. They use smoke pipes or water pipes. For mosquitoes, haze, the death of parents, friends, or children, fighting with husbands, premature death of family members, religious and socio-cultural reasons, and factors of a social system or gender, ethnic minority women learned to smoke. However, in ethnic minority areas, only older women smoke; young women do not smoke.

The reasons for younger women not to smoke include school education, propaganda of scientific knowledge, information from the outside world, the influence of Confucian culture, and changes in women's clothing. Therefore, efforts to prevent, control, and prohibit smoking among ethnic minority women should consider environmental factors, culture, social systems, and gender. Public education on the harms of smoking to human health should be reinforced. Non-smoking systems should be fully established in ethnic areas. Good health-care systems should be constructed in border areas. Meanwhile, the lifestyle and spiritual health of ethnic minority women should be attended to. In this way, addiction to tobacco among ethnic minority women can be avoided, and efficient smoking control policy can be implemented, and more accurate education and services related to smoking control are provided.

Chapter 7
Foodservice Industry in Shantou

The revitalization of classic brands is an intriguing topic for scholars and professional marketers, and managers alike. While many Western scholars have different prescriptions for revitalizing classic brands, little exists in the English literature on classic Chinese brands, particularly how they adapt to the changing market conditions in China today. Based on an in-depth ethnographic study of five classic brands in the foodservice industry in Shantou, this chapter examines issues surrounding branding that are facing these classic brands and suggests concrete measures for these restaurants to modernize their brand management. This chapter contributes to the interdisciplinary study of classic brands management by providing an ethnographic case study of classic brands' (mal)adaptation to the market in a post-socialist economy.

Introduction

Classic brands are surviving historical brands (precise definition in next section). It is widely recognized that classic brands are valuable assets. Some scholars have noted that classic brand equity helps stabilize financial returns and reduce share price volatility (Li 2014; Johansson, Dimofte, and Mazvancheryl 2012). In addition to their economic value, classic brands also embody local, regional, or even national traditions and cultural legacy (Wang 2015; Xu, Du and Zhao 2015). Unlike new brands, classic brands have withstood the test of time, in the case of China, the tumultuous history of the contemporary period (Zhang 2016). In this process, classic brands have accumulated distinct artistry, knowledge of management, and acclaimed reputation among consumers. For both economic and cultural reasons, the continued success of classic brands is not only important to policymakers (in the case of China, these include officials in the

Ministries of Commerce and Culture as well as local government officials) but also of great interest to scholars and practitioners in the fields of marketing, business management, and economic anthropology (e.g., Brown, Kozinets and Sherry 2003; Dev and Keller 2014; Tian 2016; Zhang 2012).

The popularity of classic brands and retro brands (revived brands) has been an intriguing phenomenon for scholars and practitioners on different levels. Conceptually, modern marketing theories and practices always remind us that the market is in the process of segmentation and that product differentiation is needed to ensure market success (Aaker 1996). At the same time, classic brands and their imitations, retro brands, remain highly popular in today's market (Franklin 2002). Many scholars are interested in understanding what makes classic brands popular today (Brown, Kozinets and Sherry 2003) and, more importantly, how to successfully revitalize a classic brand (Dev and Keller 2014). This study follows a similar line of inquiry to examine how classic brands in the foodservice industry in Shantou operate and explore how these classic brands can modernize to better adapt to the market conditions in China today. By modernizing, we do not suggest any support for the much-criticized modernization theory in anthropology (Tipps 1973); instead, we simply mean to keep up with the changing market conditions. Because of the rapid shift of the Chinese economy from a socialist planned economy to a market-based one, which will be discussed further below, we argue that it is high time classic Chinese brands modernized their brand management. Moreover, we make a series of concrete recommendations for Shantou's classic brands to do so in the end.

We will briefly overview the literature on classic brand management, particularly the issues surrounding classic brands in China. Then, we will provide an in-depth examination of five classic-brand eateries in Shantou based on our ethnographic study, followed by a discussion of the issues of brand management facing these restaurants. Finally, we offer some suggestions to modernize the management of classic brands in Shantou.

Classic Brand Management

Classic brands are called laozihao, "old name brand," or time-honored brands in Chinese. The Ministry of Commerce of China defines "national *laozihao*" as "a product, technique, or service that enjoys longevity, maintains a good reputation through generations, and carries Chinese tradition and culture legacy."[1] To many Chinese people, the term *laozihao* conjures an image of old shops hidden in densely populated streets with faded, yellowish signs hanging outside (Kong 1998). However, such a stereotype does not do justice to the many successful Chinese classic brands, such as *tongrentang* and *Quanjude*, which have modernized in the last two to three decades. Neither does the term capture the rich meanings of classic brands. As Gong (2004) puts it, there are multiple dimensions to classic brands in the foodservice industry, which include: longevity (they can be running for generations), good quality (they have a unique recipe and consistent quality), and a good reputation, and cultural legacy. More importantly, the brand name of classic brands is highly valuable. Studies have demonstrated that classic brand equity positively contributes to share prices (O'Sullivan et al., 2009). Aaker (1991, 1996) further argues that the value of "brand equity" is beyond financial value. François and MacLachlan (1995) also distinguish "brand equity," which is largely financially measured, and "brand strength," which tends to be rooted in consumers' brand experiences and reactions. Differently put, classic brands are not only valuable economic objects but also valuable cultural objects (cf. Schroeder 2009).

While classic brands have enjoyed consistent, strong brand recognition throughout China's recent history, the Chinese economy has experienced tremendous changes in the past few decades. To put it briefly, after the founding of the People's Republic of China in 1949, the Chinese economy was gradually nationalized and turned into a state-owned, state-managed, and state-planned economy. With the passing of

---

[1] Cited from the website of the Ministry of Commerce of the People's Republic of China, http://ltfzs.mofcom.gov.cn/article/aw/201209/20120908348719.shtml, accessed on August 30, 2017.

Mao and the ascent of Deng in the late 1970s, China embarked on a market-oriented economic reform and increased participation in the global economy (Naughton 1995, 2007). However, the economic reform initially meant the emergence of new market participants, including private businesses and foreign-owned businesses, but not structural reform of the state-owned enterprises (SOEs), which did not begin until the 1990s.

Most Chinese classic brands were collectively owned (by local governments or state-owned enterprises) or state-owned (by provincial or national governments) before the 1990s. Thus, they are used to the culture of a planned economy, which generally includes a lack of competition and innovation, inefficiency, poor customer service, and boss-centered management. On the other hand, private businesses and foreign-owned companies (including joint ventures and wholly foreign-owned enterprises) are typically more efficient and competitive, especially in the 1980s and 1990s. The private sector's superior market performance was the impetus for China to reform the state-owned sector in the 1990s. For example, the growth and success of the private sector in the textile and apparel industry in the 1980s and 1990s essentially forced the state to reform the SOEs in the industry to avoid widespread bankruptcy and become more competitive against the private sector (Zhao 2013).

Because of the reform, large SOEs regained their competitiveness, owing to their increased efficiency and economy of scale. While most classic brands are not large SOEs, the shift from a planned economy to a market-based one did (and still does) similarly require classic brands to make timely and important adjustments suited to the current market environment. Classic brands that are not quick to adjust are consequently confronted with development bottlenecks or even survival crises (Li 2015). For example, "Wangmazi" scissors, a classic brand based in Beijing, went bankrupt in 2002, which brought the attention of Chinese policymakers and academics to issues surrounding classic brands as the continued success of classic brands is not only important for economic reasons (such as providing employment), but also for the preservation of Chinese cultural heritage.

According to *Blue Book of Classic Brands--A Report on the Development of Chinese Laozihao Enterprises No.1* (2011), produced by the Chinese Academy of Social Sciences, classic brands in China are facing serious challenges (Zhang 2011). Using SWOT analysis, Luo (2010) argues that classic brands in Zhengzhou are at risk of being weeded out by the market. Still, at the same time, there are abundant opportunities for these businesses to continue to grow and thrive. Zhang Jijiao and Li Yujun (2012) concur with Luo. They believe that classic Chinese brands can continue to thrive if they overcome the global and local competition and integrate their traditional advantage with modern management. The Chinese State Council also specifically pointed out that the fundamental problem of classic brands lies in their neglect of brand building and marketing (Song 2003).

In marketing, brands are frequently personified. They have identities and life cycles such as birth, growth, aging, and death (Keller 1999). A poorly managed brand is like a sick person, which could lead to a swift and untimely death if left untreated. Wansink and Gilmore (1999) also think that external factors such as changing consumer demand and intense market competition could drive the brand to caducity and death. At the same time, just like a sick person can be healed, aging brands can also be revitalized. There is extensive literature on brand revitalization (e.g., Aaker 1991; Berry 1998; Brown, Kozinets and Sherry 2003; Dev and Keller 2014). Some scholars even suggest concrete measures to revitalize brands (e.g., An and Li 2013; Berry 1998; He 2006; Zhang 2013; Zhu 2008). For example, Zhu (2008) suggests that the design of the brand logo and the promotion of the brand story are important ways to revitalize classic brands. An and Li (2013) point to enhancing customer experience management to give new meaning to classic brands.

While those measures serve as a good reference, they do not offer a direct formula that can be applied to classic-brand restaurants in Shantou because they are generally very small in size and have very few resources at their disposal. Furthermore, the literature on marketing and branding does not consider the entrepreneurs' backgrounds or the shift in the broader political economy of China. By utilizing ethnographic methods, our study highlights the specific issues facing classic-brand restaurants in Shantou. It examines the impact of both the broader political economy and the personal backgrounds of the entrepreneurs on their businesses. Our analysis thus brings together both the micro (data about the entrepreneurs and their restaurants) and the macro to argue that it is high time Shantou classic-brand restaurants modernize their brand management.

Moreover, we suggest concrete solutions that these restaurants can adopt. Our research enriches the interdisciplinary literature on classic brand management and marketing, which tends to solely focus on the firm or brand, with anthropological analysis of the personal, the firm, and the broader political economy of China. It also adds applied anthropological knowledge to address a pressing issue facing classic Chinese brands.

Research Site and Methods

Shantou is a mid-sized city in South China. It enjoys a rich cultural legacy and a long history and is known as "Coastal Zou-Lu" (meaning a city with a prosperous culture) and "Home to Gourmet Food." Facing the South China Sea, Shantou has a rich food culture with distinct regional characteristics. Due to its proximity to Chaozhou city, the area is known as the Chaoshan region. This region is also known for its diaspora worldwide, because of which "Chaoshan snack" (Chaoshan *Xiaochi*) is well-known among Chinese around the world. For older people in Shantou, "Chaoshan snack" represents nostalgic memories. On a macro level, the evolution of Chaoshan classic-brand eateries reflects that of Shantou as a "hundred-year commercial city." Among the Shantou classic-brand eateries, "Wing Heung O Lok" and "Aixi Dumplings and Noodles" have a history of over seventy years, bearing witness to the rise and fall of the old town of Shantou. Other famous Shantou classic brands include "Laomagong Rice Ball," "Aromatic

Bamboo Shoots Cake with Dried Shrimps," "Fuk Hap Shing Beef Ball," and "Taro Cake and Sweet Soup," and so on. These foods represent fine processing, boasting a perfect color, aroma and flavor. Some snacks have won state-recognized titles of "Renowned Snacks in China," such as the peach-rice cake with ground chestnuts from "Aroma Eatery," the Aixi dry noodle from "Aixi Dumplings and Noodles" and "Laomagong Rice Ball" (Zeng 2008).

There are twenty plus foodservice enterprises designated as "classic brands" in Shantou by the Shantou Municipal Association of Social Sciences and Shantou Bureau of Tourism. At the Shantou Bureau of Tourism recommendation, five classic-brand restaurants are selected for this study due to their relatively long history and favorable reputation. As a result, the sample is biased toward better-performing classic brands in Shantou. However, we also realize that without the authorization of local government agencies, we may not be able to study any sample of classic brands, representative or not. Furthermore, our goal is not to develop a representative description of all classic-brand restaurants but to assess how Shantou classic-brand restaurants are run through an ethnographic study and then suggest solutions to modernize them. The fact that we find that even these better-performing restaurants are in dire need to modernize their brand management suggests that our findings are widely applicable to classic-brand restaurants in Shantou.

The five restaurants are "Taro cake Sweet Soup," "Wing Heung O Lok," "Aroma Eatery," "Aixi Dumplings and Noodles," and "Laomagong Rice Ball." The last three were rated as "Classic Brands for Chaoshan" by Shantou Municipal Association of Social Sciences and Bureau of Tourism. The peach-rice cake with ground chestnuts from "Aroma Eatery," the Aixi dry noodle from "Aixi Dumplings and Noodles," and the rice ball from "Laomagong Rice Ball" was awarded the title of "Renowned Chinese Snacks" by the Ministry of Commerce of China. However, such celebrated titles are not matched with scale or financial success. While in business for decades, these restaurants are still very small in scale. Most of them only have one shop, employing a few dozens of workers at most, and they are all run by one entrepreneur (in some cases assisted by the spouse). These Shantou classic brands are the antithesis of modern capitalist corporations in very broad terms.

This project is based on firsthand data gathered through ethnographic methods, primarily observation and semi-structured interviews, by our team that consists of two faculty members and two graduate students (all listed co-authors) in the spring of 2012, as well as several follow-up interviews (Dr. Zhao joined the team at the later stage and mainly participated in data analysis and writing of this chapter). A total of fifty interviews were conducted, including five interviews with one owner and interviews with six employees and three customers from each restaurant. Our observations include the dining area, customers, and workers working on their different tasks in the kitchen. While IRB approval is not yet a part of social science research in China, our research was approved by relevant local government agencies and consented to by our research subjects. In addition, all our research subjects consented to use their real names in this chapter. However, we exercised caution and used a pseudonym (as noted in the text later) for one employee for fear of the potential negative impact on his employment. Our ethnographic methods in this study follow a long tradition of anthropological study of businesses, brand management, and marketing (Tian, Trotter, and Liu 2015; Kottak 2005). Ethnographic methods such as participant observation and semi-structured interviews are well suited to understand the nuances of the "culture" of a business or brand.

Five Classic Brands in the Foodservice Industry

While the five restaurants are not chosen as a random sample, there is diversity in ownership and scale among all classic-brand restaurants in Shantou. The following table summarizes the basic information of these five "classic brand" eateries.

Table 7.1: Basic information of five classic-brand restaurants in Shantou

Name	Location	Business Ownership	Founding Time	Scale of Shop	Main Products	Average consumption
Taro cake Sweet Soup	No.20 Fuping Road, Shantou; at a junction of 3 roads in the small park in the old town	Privately owned	1960, lay a stall on the street; 1978, opened in Xiangdong by Lin Shaowei; 1992, moved to a new store	One store, 10 m², a staff of 12 employees	All kinds of soup, rice products and sweet soup with taro cakes and taro soup being the most famous	5-10 *yuan* per person
Wing Heung O Lok	No.183 Outer Road, Jinping District, Shantou; at the crossroad in the old town	Privately owned	1930, Yang set up a stall in front of Jinxianmen in JieyangRongcheng	One store, 300 m², a staff of about 30 employees	O Lok, seafood, rice products, sausage with rice, beef ball soup	20-50 *yuan* per person
Aroma Eatery	At the center of the old town, No.39 Guoping Road, Small Garden. Branch in Coastal Garden in Business center in a new town	State-owned, managed by Shantou Foodservice Corporation, privately contracted	1965, set up by the government; 1989, contracted out to private entrepreneur Zheng Luhui	One main store, 150 m², a staff of 12; one branch, 80 m², a staff of 7	Specialties are Bamboo Shoot Cake with Dried Shrimp and Peach-Rice Cake with Ground Chestnuts	10-30 *yuan* per person
Aixi Dumplings and Noodles	The 13th store in the 13th block, East Sun Yat-sen Road, is in the small garden in the old town. One branch in Overseas Chinese Park by the boundary of the old town	State-owned, managed by Shantou Foodservice Corporation, privately contracted	1932, set up by Mr. Lu; 1949, turned collective; 1988, contracted out to Luo Yingyi	One store, 50 m², a staff of 10 employees; 2 branches, 80 m², a staff of 12 employees, respectively	A bowl of dry noodles with pork and chopped green onion and a bowl of soup with pig's internal organs, meatballs and fish balls.	10-20 *yuan* per person

Name	Location	Business Ownership	Founding Time	Scale of Shop	Main Products	Average consumption
Laomagong Rice Ball	No.57 Xinguan Street; in the small park in the old town	State-owned, managed by Shantou Foodservice Corporation, privately contracted	1920, Zhang Qiangde and his son set up a stall near Mazu Temple on Shengping Rd; later, the son rented a nearby storefront.	80 ㎡, a staff of 12. One branch that opened in Yuejin Road four years ago went bankrupt in 2010	Stuffed pig intestines; the horseshoe crab cake; double-cooked *Zongzi* (with stuffings); sweet *Zongzi*	5-10 *yuan* per person

While the above summary provides a brief overview of these five businesses, it is worthwhile to delve deeper into their history. After all, it is because of their (relative) longevity that they have earned the designation of "classic brands."

1) Taro Cake Sweet Soup

Before the Cultural Revolution (1966-76)[1], the father of the current boss Lin Shaowei set up a stall for selling taro cakes and sweet soup at the intersection of Xiandong Alley near its current location. He ran the business until the beginning of the Cultural Revolution, during which the business was closed. He reopened the eatery in 1978, about eighty meters away from the previous location. In 1992, they moved to the current location and ran their business for over eighteen years.

2) Wing Heung O Lok

Wing Heung O Lok originated in Jieyang Rongcheng, where current owner Cai Wuru's grandfather, Yang Zonglin, set up a stall to sell fried

[1] The Cultural Revolution is formally called "the Great Proletarian Cultural Revolution." It was launched by Chairman Mao Zedong in 1966 and spanned a whole decade. It was a tumultuous period that was characterized by political campaigns, during which millions of people, including intellectuals, artists, and former class enemies such as landlords and capitalists, were prosecuted. Young students, including college and middle school students, were sent to rural areas as "educated youth" (zhiqing) for reeducation.

O Lok under the brand name Wing Heung (locally means aroma) in the 1930s. Later, his son Yang Erbao moved to Shantou, selling O Lok as a peddler. In the 1950s, he joined "seventeen O Lok Stalls" near Taro Cake Sweet Soup to compete for best cooking skill and won the award. In 1982, Yang Erbao passed the restaurant to Cai Wuru, his son-in-law. After several moves, Wing Heung O Lok settled at No. 183 Outer Road about two years ago, and the owner invested a significant amount of money in remodeling the restaurant. Currently, the restaurant has an area of about 300 square meters, employing about thirty people.

3) Aroma Eatery

In 1965, Li Shaolin, the deputy mayor of Shantou, took the lead to establish the Aroma Eatery, where master chefs of traditional snacks in the Chaoshan area would offer a diverse menu of famous local dishes, especially to returning overseas Chinese from East Guangdong. During the Cultural Revolution, the restaurant was treated as a product of "feudalism, capitalism and revisionism" and suffered significant damage. In the reform period (post-1978), Aroma Eatery continued to operate as a collectively owned enterprise and lost its competitiveness. In the late 1980s, it went bankrupt. To save the brand, an employee named Zheng Luhui signed a lease with Aroma Eatery in 1989, and he has since been running the restaurant. In 2000, Zheng Luhui's brother, Zheng Lujun, became an equal-share investor in the restaurant.

4) Aixi Dumplings and Noodles

In the early 1930s, Lu, a migrant from Dapu County, established Aixi Dumplings and Noodles. In the very beginning, he only set up a temporary sidewalk stand on a pedestrian street in the southwestern part of the old town, selling dry noodles with sesame and dumplings. Owing to his business acumen, the restaurant proved to be rather popular.

After the end of the Anti-Japanese War in 1945, Mr. Lu rented a storefront at No.1 Guoping Road. Mr. Lu stopped selling dumplings due to their higher demand on time and complexity of ingredients and focused on dry noodles while maintaining "Aixi Dumplings and Noodles" as the name for the restaurant.

After the PRC was founded in 1949, Aixi Dumplings and Noodles became a part of the collectively owned Hengxing Company, a subsidiary of Shantou Foodservice Corporation. In the late 1980s, Luo Yingyi, a returned "educated youth" (*zhiqing*) from his "reeducation" in the countryside during the Cultural Revolution, was assigned by the government to work in Aixi Noodles. Later, the restaurant was contracted out to Luo and his partner Lin Yingqin, and they have been running it for over thirty years. In 2002, Hengxing Company registered "Aixi" as a trademark.

5) Laomagong Rice Ball

In 1920, Zhang Qiangde and his son Zhang Liangjie set up a stall near the old Mazu Temple on Shengping Road. Thanks to the busy street where it was located, the business was booming and, more importantly, their unique products. Their special "double-cooked *zongzi* (wrapped rice ball)" contained two kinds of stuffing, one salty and one sweet, all wrapped up with six edges and four angles, and they are three times the size of regular *zongzi*.

However, Zhang Qiangde thought it was too laborious to make *zongzi,* so he did not want his son to take over the business; instead, he tried to persuade him to learn how to make porcelain inlay. He said, "Once you have mastered the skill of the trowel, you would never have to worry about livelihood." The son, however, declined his father's suggestion; he rebutted, "Making porcelain inlay is a good skill for survival, but making small *zongzi* could lead to prosperity." After his father's death, Zhang Liangjie rented a storefront across from the old Mazu Temple on Xinguan Street with a sign that said: "Shi Ding Zheng Zhi" (meaning "the more you eat it, the tastier it becomes"). The tasty *zongzi* near the old Mazu Temple (Laomagong Rice Ball) became a household name.

In 1955, as a part of the nationalization movement, Laomagong Rice Ball became a collectively owned business controlled by Shantou

Foodservice Corporation while still being run by the Zhangs. Recently, Laomagong intended to trademark its name, only to discover that the name "Ma Gong" (literally means the Temple of Mazu Goddess) was already registered as a trademark by a Taiwanese company. As a result, even though Laomagong Rice Ball has a history of ninety years, it has lost the opportunity to trademark its name.

From the above descriptions of the five eateries in Shantou, it is clear that they enjoy a relatively long history, especially in the foodservice industry, and they all have very distinctive and popular products, which earned them the acclaimed designation of classic brands. At the same time, they are small in terms of scale, especially given their relatively long history. In the following, we will examine brand management issues in these restaurants in greater detail.

Issues of Brand Management in Classic-Brand Restaurants

The core value of classic foodservice brands has risen from function to effect. The so-called "functional value" refers to the designs or functions of the products or services, while the affective value is built on customers' psychological identification with the brands. For instance, the well-known Chinese classic brand Quanjude (a restaurant chain that sells Peking ducks) has a traditional Chinese loft design, featuring carved windows and doors, red-wood pillars, and furnished with a large traditional style square table, copper teapot, celadon candlestick, old-fashioned telephone, old account book, and so on.

The entire restaurant gives out a deeply cultural and historical aura and thus maps history and culture onto the brand and creates strong, effective value for the customers, which ultimately enhances the brand's value. At the same time, the restaurant has rapidly modernized its management and become a successful chain across China. Successful Chinese classic brands in the foodservice industry, such as Quanjude, are capitalizing on the trend that Chinese consumers are no longer just satisfied with the food that fills their stomachs. Still, they are also seeking the experience and the distinctive affective and social value that the restaurant provides.

However, classic brands in Shantou's foodservice industry are all very small in scale and are generally run by the owners (or contractors if they are leasing). They usually do not make any investments in the design of the logo, the interior design of the restaurant, or marketing. They maintain a belief that if the food is good, it will sell regardless of the dining environment. In other words, they are banking on their products and the reputation of being classic brands, ignoring the changing market conditions and market competition. To illustrate these issues clearly, we will focus on three management areas, namely brand positioning, brand marketing and promotion, and employee compensation, in the five classic-brand restaurants in Shantou.

Issues of Brand Positioning

Given that the five classic-brand restaurants are tightly controlled and run by private entrepreneurs (in some cases assisted by their spouses), the views and experiences of these entrepreneurs profoundly influence how these businesses are run. In the following, we will present ethnographic data obtained through in-depth interviews, specifically exploring how the entrepreneurs' personal life histories, health conditions, and religious beliefs shape the brand positioning of these classic brands.

Personal life history

There is one thing I will never forget. When I was a schoolboy, the Cultural Revolution broke out. One morning when I was sitting as usual under the image of Chairman Mao and the character "Zhong" (meaning loyalty), reading the remarks of Jiang Qing in the "Red Flag Magazine," I read four characters wrong, which was witnessed by my classmates and recorded by a teacher. As a punishment, I had to stand in front of the image of Chairman Mao at seven sharp every morning, bowing and reading a self-written confession, for half a month. As a sixth-grader, it was very embarrassing to face so many people. Fortunately, my family background was in line with the revolution but not of the anti-revolutionary elements (such as the landlords and capitalists). Otherwise, I would suffer even more. After that, I took my revenge on the teacher, making him "accidentally" fall into a pit full of shit.

When I was in middle school, my classmates and I were sent by the government to a rural village (as "educated youths") for reeducation. We ate, lived, and worked alongside the farmers. I did farm work on a tea plantation. There was a school called Sun Yat-sen Medical College, 50 meters away from the plantation. I saw the President of the College doing manual labor like a farmer. He was called all sorts of names. I couldn't believe that he was a well-educated person.

After eight years, I returned home without a job. In 1982, I was assigned to work at Aroma Eatery, a part of Shantou Foodservice Corporation. In 1989, I leased the eatery from the Corporation and have been running it ever since.

The above story was recounted to us by Mr. Zheng Luhui, the boss of Aroma Eatery. His life experience, particularly the experience of working with the farmers in a rural area during the Cultural Revolution, shaped his worldview and how he runs the restaurant. His motto for the restaurant is "simplicity on the outside, but honesty and superiority on the inside." He says he always tends to stay low-key and does things with a humble and prudent attitude in his everyday life. Similarly, Aroma Eatery is also rather down-to-earth in its decoration and dishes. Only those who have tasted the food know that the restaurant offers delicious dishes.

Table 7.2: Brand Positioning for Five Classic Foodservice Brands

Name	Owner/Manager	Age	Brand Positioning
Taro Cake Sweet Soup	Lin Shaowei	Age: 47 Inherited at age: 23	Proximity to a busy street, original flavor
Wing Heung O Lok	Cai Wuru	Age: 53 Inherited at age: 23	Moral responsibility
Aroma Eatery	Zheng Luhui	Age: 60 Leasing since: 37	Simplicity on the outside, honesty on the inside
Aixi Dumplings and Noodles	Luo Yingyi	Age: 50 Leasing since: 40	Authentic and superior quality
Laomagong Rice Ball	Zhang Yimin	Age: 46 Leasing since: 38	Unique skills and features

Mr. Zheng is not alone in his down-to-earth attitude toward life. As table 2 below indicates, all the current owners or managers of the five restaurants were born in the 1950s and 1960s, which means that they all went through the Cultural Revolution. Some even experienced hardship in the aftermath of the Great Leap Forward (1959-61), a period during which millions perished due to starvation. Such a life experience undoubtedly left its mark on the entrepreneurs' no-frills, no waste attitude displayed in their restaurants. They also have strong work ethics and perseverance. They usually work harder than their employees and do not complain. For them, today's hardship is nothing compared to that of the old days.

Part of the hard work of being the boss of a classic brand in Shantou has to do with the fact that the boss/owner is also the master chef. A case in point is the boss of Aixi Dumplings and Noodles, Luo Yingyi. He has been the master chef of the restaurant for thirty years. He rises at 5:30 in the morning to knead dough to make noodles, prepares a soupy stew and makes gravy for the noodles. The freshly made egg noodles require forceful and repeated pressing, kneading, and rolling, which gives the noodles a springy texture. He also prepares his sauce and gravy, made of sesame, BBQ sauce, fatty pork, and chopped green onion. When customers come, Luo cooks the noodles in boiled water, drains them, and adds slices of cooked meat, gravy or soup, and cilantro and other condiments in less than five minutes. Because of his keen emphasis on the "authentic and superior quality" of his food, Mr. Luo is always personally involved to ensure the quality at each step of food preparation even though he has trained staff working for him.

Health Conditions

The health condition of the boss is also a factor that impacts classic-brand restaurants. On average, the bosses/owners of the five restaurants have worked for over thirty years. Because of the small scale of these restaurants, the bosses have to do the hard work alongside the employees. Years of working in the kitchen, withstanding the heat and heavy fumes, jeopardize the bosses' health. Cai Wuru, for example, has developed a serious lung disease. Two times, he almost died and had to use an oxygen inhaler. For a time, he had to leave the restaurant to his wife while he was recuperating at a friend's place near a reservoir where there was a lot of vegetation and little pollution. He claimed that his health conditions had been a major impediment to his expansion plans for the restaurant. Lin Shaowei, the owner of Taro Cake Sweet Soup, came within inches of losing his life at thirty-nine due to a dangerous health condition. Zheng Luhui, the boss of Aroma Eatery, also said, "It [the job] is tiring, ceaseless work, no break at all!" Since 1989, he has risen at 5:30 every morning, regardless of the weather. Before the employees come in at 9:00, he does everything on his own to get the restaurant ready for the day.

In general, the long hours and hard work have a debilitating impact on the health conditions of the bosses/owners of the classic-brand restaurants, which in turn impacts the management of the restaurants. During our research, one thing that stands out is that none of the bosses has the vision or ambition to be number one in his sector, and they are mostly content with, or rather, resigned to keeping their current businesses afloat. Only Aixi Dumplings and Noodles opened two branches in addition to the main restaurant. There has been hardly any expansion for these businesses in several decades. As Cai Wuru states, personal health conditions have prevented the bosses from working on expansion plans.

Religious Beliefs

Buddhism is a dominant religion in Shantou, and many business owners in this area practice Buddhism. However, among all the owners/bosses of the five classic eateries, only Cai Wuru, owner of Wing Heung O Lok, practices Buddhism. Cai's belief in Buddhism began in 2003. He believes that Buddhism can change not only one's mind but also one's behavior. Indeed, his faith affects his personality and his business management. Faith plays an important part in his successful management of the business. Since 2005, he has been giving free food to beggars and people in need at 11 o'clock every day. Wing Heung O Lok has since been a "morally responsible" restaurant. Cai Wuru openly talks to us about his faith.

As my health got better, I returned to Shantou from the reservoir. My wife was running the business in my absence. I knew it was hard for her, so I went right back to the restaurant to help. I worked there day and night, almost like a never-stopping clock. A friend of mine said, 'You will burn out if you keep working like that.' I heeded his warning and decided to go to the park and exercise in the morning, practicing taichi (also called shadowboxing). Practicing taichi requires one to close the eyes and clear the mind before one starts. Everyone (in the park) could do that, but I couldn't even close my eyes for thirty seconds.

I thought to myself, 'There must be something wrong with my eyes; otherwise, why wouldn't I be able to close my eyes?' One day, I met a 70 -year-old man who could close his eyes for over two hours while sitting in meditation. Out of curiosity, I asked him how he could do it. To my surprise, he knew who I was, and he said to me, 'you are too busy and always thinking about money, and that is why you can't close your eyes. If you stopped worrying about money, you would be able to.' I thought to myself, 'my health was in such bad shape. What is the point of making money?' Realizing that my health was more important than the restaurant, I decided to join the older man to learn how to meditate every morning. I also took my tea set and offered tea and cigarettes to him. He never took my cigarettes, but I would take them whenever he offered. I wanted to get close to him whenever possible. I guess I wanted to learn his secrets for good health. (laugh)

For the past six years, I've known him. I have not only learned from his tips for good health but also much, much more. I learned from him that it was important to live by the rules and moral principles. Otherwise, misfortunes can befall your health, family, life, etc. The moral principles he has taught me are consistent with the Buddhist teachings, which include filial piety towards one's parent, loyalty towards friends, etc. I learned to feel at ease and be content with life, even when I suffer losses. He didn't just teach me with words, but more importantly, through his actions. He told me one hot summer, "Cai, it is hot, and here is some money for you to make cooling tea for passers-by. I will give six hundred yuan per month for three months to cover the cost of your tea." I listened to him, went out to buy several big buckets, and handed out free cooling tea to passers-by in the park. He paid me twenty-one hundred yuan, including the money I spent on the buckets. The next summer, he mentioned again handing out free tea. But my wife reminded me that he was over seventy years old and that we were younger and could afford to pay for the tea ourselves. Since then, we started to hand out free cooling tea in the summer using our funds. Inspired by him, I also started to hand out free meals to beggars and people in need in 2005. Initially, we handed out thirty meals each day, and the food ran out very quickly, and then we increased to fifty meals a day.

Mr. Cai's religious belief has changed him and his style of management. Since finding his faith, moral responsibility became the guiding principle of his business. He used his profits to give back to the community with free tea in the summer and free meals for the needy. He also changed his way of treating his employees—no longer the tyrant he used to be, but now a compassionate, caring boss. He installed ventilation equipment in the kitchen and provided financial support to the employees should they have emergencies in their lives, all of which are supported by our interviews with the restaurant employees.

In sum, the boss's personal life history, health conditions, and religious beliefs are important factors that influence the brand positioning of these restaurants. Aroma Eatery's motto of "simplicity on the outside, honesty on the inside" and Wing Heung O Lok's "moral responsibility" determine the bosses' character and belief. In other words, what's personal to the bosses determines what's public for the restaurants. The strategic brand positioning of Shantou's classic-brand restaurants reflects a top-down model, which is opposed to modern brand positioning philosophy and the Segmentation, Targeting, and Positioning (STP) model developed by Philip Kotler and Kevin Keller (2005). According to this model, a business should study the market and understand the different segments as determined by the needs and preferences of the consumers. Then the business should choose one or several segments as targets, positioning its brand accordingly. The STP model is a bottom-up model that considers first and foremost consumer needs and market conditions.

On the contrary, Shantou's classic-brand restaurants' brand positioning is primarily determined by the personal preferences and beliefs of the bosses. While some are beneficial to the business (e.g., Cai's religious belief), many (such as health conditions) limit their ability to expand and modernize. In general, the bosses of these Shantou restaurants focus on their food, but not so much on its presentation, the dining environment, or the consumer experience. This is a big departure from the approach of large successful chains such as Quanjude discussed previously. While Quanjude caters to changing consumer preferences and market conditions in China, the classic-brand restaurants in Shantou appear to be completely oblivious to these trends.

Issues of Marketing and Promotion

Brand marketing and promotion are important factors in increasing sales. Therefore, below we analyze the marketing and promotion strategies of the five restaurants, respectively.

Taro Cake Sweet Soup

The restaurant does not invest in marketing; instead, it relies on word of mouth. The owner claims that its customers are mostly repeating visitors. Old customers may bring new visitors along, and if these new customers like the food, they would come back again and bring more people with them. Because the restaurant has been around for a long time, most people in town know of it. Some people from nearby counties would even drive over to drink the sweet soup and eat the taro cakes because of their reputation. Sometimes, they would even bring their entire family.

Occasionally, the restaurant does receive media attention. For example, some special TV shows, including "Gourmet Tide" and "Perspective Today" from Shantou, as well as the Pearl River Station from Guangzhou and Asia Television (ATV) from Hong Kong, have been interviewed by the owner, Mr. Lin. But he sometimes hesitates to accept interview requests from the media. He believes that his customers do not come because of media exposure but because they are regulars and know the restaurant already. Furthermore, he thinks that even if the media exposure helped with the restaurant's publicity, there would be too many diners for the restaurant to accommodate.

Wing Heung O Lok

The restaurant does not spend money on advertisements in the media. However, since 2005, Mr. Cai has donated meals to the needy daily, which attracted attention from the media. News outlets such as "Dawa Net" and "Shantou Youth Daily" have reported on this good deed of Mr. Cai, who claimed that Buddhist teachings inspired him to do good. While it is not immediately clear how much these media reports have contributed to the restaurant's bottom line, they have benefited the reputation and image of the eatery.

Aroma Eatery

Mr. Zheng, the boss, ran some advertisements for the eatery some years ago, but it was not effective. He has not done any advertising or promotion for the restaurant since, and it mainly relies on repeat customers and word of mouth. However, the media have always been interested in restaurants. Years ago, even media outlets from Chaozhou, Guangzhou, Hong Kong, and Singapore came to report on the restaurant (including videos). In recent years, the restaurant received significant media coverage, and consequently, traffic to the restaurant started to pick up in 2007 because of this media attention.

Aixi Dumplings and Noodles

Among all the bosses of the five classic-brand restaurants, Mr. Luo of Aixi Dumplings and Noodles is perhaps the least interested in publicity and advertisement. In his view, his products would sell if their qualities were good. He also believes that Aixi is already widely known for its quality, so any brand promotion would hardly produce additional financial benefits. Once Hong Kong's ATV came with its local partner to shoot a short video without any advanced notification or appointment, Mr. Luo turned them down. He said he never even invited passers-by (who would provide direct financial benefits) to his restaurant to illustrate his principles further. He believed that customers would come in on their own accord as long as they liked the food. Mr. Luo also turned down the opportunity to participate in the annual Food Festival in Shantou because Mr. Luo could not guarantee the quality when food was made at the fair, and he did not want to raise prices just because it was the Food Festival (believing both actions could harm the reputation of the restaurant). He is fully confident in the quality of his food, which he believes is at the core of his brand.

Laomagong Rice Ball

In the early days, Zhang Qiangde and his son Zhang Liangjie set up a stall near the Mazu Temple to sell their food, and they did marketing by yelling out "rice ball for sale." Later, when it became a collective enterprise, no advertisements or promotions were made, even though the phrase "Shi Ding Zheng Zhi" had already been associated with the restaurant since its early days.

Today, Laomagong, while being privately run, still does not take any initiative to advertise through the media. Yet, the boss does not believe in the publicity in the media but thinks that making good products is the basis of success. However, because of the numerous awards it has won, many TV stations and newspapers, including Shantou TV Station, Shantou Daily, and Hong Kong's ATV, came to report on the restaurant.

While the business is usually good, it is especially good around Dragon Boat Festival (May fifth according to the lunar calendar), an occasion when *zongzi* is traditionally consumed. To curtail the demand, the restaurant would limit five *zongzi* per order. If one wishes to buy more, they would have to queue again to make another order. While this strategy of "deprivation marketing" may create more consumer desire, it does not help realize the full profit potential of the restaurant.

None of the five classic-brand restaurants currently have an advertisement in the media; neither do they actively seek to promote their brands, even though they all have received some positive publicity through free media. Their main marketing approach is through their points of sale—the restaurants, and through the word of mouth of their loyal customers. These restaurants' general lack of marketing efforts is perhaps due to the bosses' view that their brands are already well recognized in Shantou, which is probably true among the older generation. However, the same may not be true for the younger generation. The classic-brand restaurants risk declining name recognition and missed future growth opportunities by ignoring the younger generation and their consumption preferences. For example, the Internet is a part of daily life among the younger generation in

China. Yet, none of the classic-brand restaurants have an online marketing presence. Neither do they, individually or collectively, have a website that would allow for online purchases.

Issues of Employee Compensation

Employee compensation is a key way to incentivize performance. In our interviews with employees of the five classic-brand restaurants in Shantou, we find that employee compensation does not generally correlate with their performance at work; instead, it is closely tied to the position, duration of service, ownership type of the business, and the management style of the owner or boss.

Mr. Cao (pseudonym), an employee of Aroma Eatery, responded to our question about compensation in this way:

The longer you work in Aroma Eatery, the more you get paid, but no more than 1,600 yuan per month. There are no big pay gaps between employees; the difference is between 100 to 200 yuan. But master chefs get higher pay than others, of course. On holidays and festivals, we get double-paid, that is to say, you work for one day and get paid for two days' work. What's more, we have year-end bonuses, ranging from 1,000 to 2,000 yuan.

From Mr. Cao's response, we can learn that there is general pay equity among the employees. The biggest factors that impact employee compensation are the position, such as being a master chef, and duration of service (the longer the service, the higher the pay). Moreover, worker compensation and benefits are ultimately decided by the owner or boss of the restaurant. So, if somehow the boss changes his mind, employee compensation and benefits can also change. For example, after the boss of Wing Heung O Lok found his faith in Buddhism, the workers' overall working conditions and benefits also improved.

The other factor that influences worker compensation is the business owner type. There are two types of ownership structures among the five classic-brand restaurants: privately owned and collectively owned (specifically owned by the local government). In general, collectively-owned businesses have better salaries and benefits as they have to follow government regulations more closely, and their employees' salaries are usually adjusted for inflation. By contrast, workers in privately owned businesses have fewer benefits and usually do not have frequent pay raises like those in collectively or state-owned businesses.

Based on the above examination of worker compensation, employee compensation at Shantou's classic-brand restaurants does not directly correlate with working performance. Hence, it does not entirely reflect the principle of the market. As the primary producers of market value, the workers are not properly incentivized to deliver optimum results for these restaurants.

Discussions and Suggestions

The previous section described key issues in three management areas in the five classic brands in Shantou's foodservice industry. In China's changing economy and increased market competition from other Chinese food establishments and foreign fast-food chains, Shantou classic brands are at a critical moment. Should they not adapt and modernize, the chances are high that they would wither away. Given their current sizes, the economic cost of the demise of these classic brands is, in fact, quite low. However, the resultant loss of cultural legacy and generations of memories would be immeasurable. The success of classic brands transcends their economic value, which is largely treated as a means of livelihood by the entrepreneurs. It is particularly because of classic brands' broader social and cultural importance. We are offering solutions to modernize the management of the classic brands in the foodservice industry in Shantou.

In terms of brand positioning, individual owners or bosses make key decisions in Shantou's classic-brand restaurants. More importantly, because of the bosses' personal life histories, health conditions, and religious beliefs, they generally take a top-down approach to the management of their businesses, which focuses on the products, but invests very little in branding, including the design of a logo, the interior design of the restaurants, and the marketing and promotion of the brand. Also, the application for trademarks of the brands appeared to be an afterthought. However, branding undoubtedly contributes to a competitive advantage in today's market (Mercer 2010). The general lack of emphasis on branding by these Shantou entrepreneurs has to do with their personal life histories and the legacy of the socialist planned economy to which they were accustomed. Therefore, it is incumbent upon the entrepreneurs, perhaps with the help of relevant local government agencies, to realize the importance of branding in the current market environment in China. Until then, they would hire, as they need to, consultants to come up with a complete brand management solution. While the specific solution may vary from restaurant to restaurant, it needs to include four basic elements: brand story, brand essence, idealized community, and brand paradox (c.f., Brown, Kozinets and Sherry 2003). Specifically, they have to create an updated but consistent design for the brand logo and an updated interior design for the flagship restaurant (consistent designs should be maintained if branches exist). In other words, they have to come up with a consistent brand story and a marketing strategy to communicate the message to consumers.

It is well documented that innovation increases competitiveness (Silva and Duguid 2010; Galletto 2008; Wilkins 1992). Implementing a brand management solution requires investment, yet classic-brand restaurants are small businesses with limited resources. This does not mean they cannot implement a brand management solution because part of the cost of branding can be recouped from relatively cheap innovations and offset by increased sales. One such relatively inexpensive solution is to create online marketing and sales channels. The online channels have the potential to broaden the reach of the classic brands to younger consumers and thus increase revenue. The restaurants should also adopt a performance-based compensation scheme, which would provide the right incentives to increase productivity and efficiency, offsetting the cost of implementing a brand management solution.

Another cost-saving measure is to build a brand alliance among the classic-brand restaurants in Shantou. Llonch-Casanovas (2012) demonstrates that the consolidation of brands played an important role in the survival of the knitwear sector. Similarly, a hundred classic brands formed an alliance in Fuzhou under "the Association of Classic Brands," which developed a "Street of Classic Brands" in 2001. This measure helped classic brands to regain their competitiveness against modern restaurant chains (Zhang 2001). Another example is "Xiguan People," located at Liwan Square in Xiajiu Road in Guangzhou and consists of three classic brands that offer over three hundred kinds of traditional snacks and small eats. These successful brand alliances illustrate that they have the advantage of lowering the cost (through cost-sharing) while increasing the exposure of the brands (cf. Zhang and Lin 2007). Still another innovative strategy is to create new products and brands within the family (i.e., the restaurant). Of course, this assumes that these Shantou classic-brand restaurants have successfully implemented the initial phases of branding and marketing and are ready for the phase of brand extension and expansion to the management of a portfolio of multiple brands, each with its distinct positioning and target market (Aaker 1996, 2004; Keller and Lehmann 2006; Keller, Aperia, and Georgson 2008; LaForet and Saunders 1994).

We believe that such a phased brand management solution that contains both branding strategies and cost-saving measures is best suited to the classic-brand restaurants in Shantou because it takes into full consideration that these restaurants are small businesses that have limited resources, which idealized models to revitalize brands such as Berry's (1998) seven-step model do not account for. In other words, ethnographic data help yield a targeted approach that will be more likely adopted and be successful. Furthermore, our anthropological study of classic brands in Shantou reveals that adopting any brand management solution predates the entrepreneurs' realization of its necessity and urgency, which is the first leverage point for policymakers and entrepreneurs to ensure the continued success of classic brands. Therefore, anthropological methods as applied in this case study of Shantou classic brands contribute to marketing and brand management by offering grounded solutions based on detailed, nuanced ethnographic data and contextualized analysis of these businesses within the broader political economy. It also adds to anthropological knowledge by applying it to pressing issues confronting these culturally important small businesses.

Conclusion

This chapter provides an in-depth examination of branding issues, including brand design and marketing, facing classic brands in the foodservice industry in Shantou, China. Our ethnographic study finds that the five classic-brand eateries in Shantou enjoy good publicity. Their food has been consistently popular among consumers for a long time (many for over half a century), which earned them the designation of *laozihao* or classic brands. At the same time, we also find that despite their relatively long history, these classic-brand eateries are all small, closely-held businesses. This is common among all classic brands in the foodservice industry in Shantou. Also common is that the boss is deeply involved in the operation and management of the business. Thus, the entrepreneurs' personal life histories, health conditions, and religious beliefs directly and profoundly impact the management of the classic brands. The entrepreneur cares deeply about the quality of his food but invests very little in its presentation, the restaurant's interior design, the design of the brand logo, and the marketing of the brand. This pattern is, in fact, quite common in classic Chinese brands (Song 2003), and it reflects the influence of the personal life history of the entrepreneur and the lingering effect of the socialist planned economy, which solely focused on production but not the brand image and consumer experience of the brand.

However, since the late 1970s, China's planned economy has gradually given way to a market-oriented economy through state-initiated economic reforms. From a nearly closed economy in the 1950s and 1960s, China has become the world's second-largest economy that fully participates in the world market. China's market conditions have changed dramatically in the past few decades, entailing intense market competition and changing consumer preferences. Brand image and brand experience have become highly important in attracting consumers in this new market environment. In this context, some classic Chinese brands, such as Quanjude took measures to modernize their brand management and have become enormously successful, while others, such as Wangmazi, that failed to do so went bankrupt. Thus, we argue that it is imperative and urgent for classic brands in Shantou to follow in the footsteps of successful Chinese classic brands and modernize their brand management to ensure continued success.

Given that most of the owners/entrepreneurs of Shantou classic brands are facing retirement, a branding strategy is of utter importance to ensure the longevity of these classic brands. Given the specific circumstances of classic brands in the foodservice industry in Shantou, we suggest a series of concrete and relatively low-cost or cost-saving measures for them to gradually develop a brand design and marketing scheme that would place consumer preference and experience at the center (Yang and Ma 2015; Tao and Li 2012). Such branding measures will help increase the visibility of the brands and broaden their reach to younger consumers. In addition to branding measures, forming the brand alliance and portfolio are also suggested as viable strategies to enhance the management of classic brands (Aaker 1996, 2004; Keller and Lehmann 2006; Keller, Aperia, and Georgson 2008; LaForet and Saunders 1994). All such measures will help Shantou classic brands to focus on the brands and consumer experience while deemphasizing the owner/entrepreneur.

Our ethnographic case study of classic brands in Shantou is very limited. Still, a ground analysis offers viable and concrete solutions to an important and pressing issue in Chinese society today (Tian and Zhou 2013). Through an ethnographic case study of classic brands adjusting to a post-socialist market, our research contributes to the growing interdisciplinary literature on marketing and classic brands management by bringing together the micro-level examination of the entrepreneur and the firm and the macro analysis of the broader political economy of Chinese society. It also enriches anthropology by applying anthropological knowledge to an area that is rather understudied in the discipline.

Chapter 8
NGOs in Southwest China

This chapter discusses the origin and operations of a dozen indigenous Chinese NGOs working to promote the social welfare of the marginalized ethnic groups in southwest China's hilly regions bordering Yunnan, Guizhou and Sichuan provinces. Data from this report is based on the author's fieldwork in that region over the past decade (circa 2008-2017). Even though they have different specific goals—including poverty reduction, post-disaster reconstruction, community development, environmental conservation, cultural preservation, and so on—these NGOs exhibit several shared characteristics. They were all initiated by community elites with broad-based information networks and connections. Most of them also received initial inputs in funding, operation space, technical training, and advisory supervision from international NGOs. This study's findings confirm that despite the unique governance systems in China, Chinese NGOs in the Mainland are more akin to global NGOs owing to their shared charitable and philanthropic concerns.

Introduction

Will the reduction of the Party-State control in China give rise to a genuine civil society? How will grassroots democracy gain its foothold in this post-socialist society? As the state-society balance tips toward the latter, will we see the revival or formation of non-government organizations (NGOs) to fill in the void for humanitarian assistance to meet long- or short-term needs? Are these newly formed NGOs duplications of their pre-modern predecessors or imitations of modern Western counterparts? What roles have NGOs played in facilitating China's post-socialist democratic transition? How will China's transformation conform to (or diverge from) the civil society building process based on Euro-American experiences? This chapter addresses these issues and sorts out some of the controversies raised by researchers in recent years.

Recent research in China indicates the mushrooming of NGOs in China and the increasingly significant social roles they have played in dealing with practical problems since the 1980s. External researchers, in the meantime, have raised questions about the compatibility between what they observed and theories related to civil society building. Some questioned whether these newly developed NGOs in China might be called due to their official involvement. Others argued that Habermas' civil society theory is too narrowly confined to European experiences and must be expanded to accommodate non-European societies such as China. These conceptual problems need to be resolved before we gain any insight into China's current development.

This chapter argues that the current incremental reform in China has entailed a gradualist political liberalization process. Party-State rhetoric aside, the expanding civil liberty has given rise to a new sense of citizenship. With the burgeoning middle class in the mainland and their incorporation into the Communist Party, we can anticipate further growth of civil society building in China. Furthermore, China's continuous expansion in global affairs will have to abide by the accepted international rules regarding basic human rights and civil society practices. In a nutshell, the communist government will have to accept, even though reluctantly, the rise of NGOs as a supplement to the governing arms of modern civil society.

Social Welfare and Civil Society in Post-Socialist China

In the post-1978 reform decades, China went through a steady and broad-based societal transformation, appropriately called "the Second Revolution" by Harry Harding, instead of the 1949 revolution, which primarily liberated the allegedly oppressed rural peasantry and urban industrial proletarians (Harding 1987). Under the current reform agenda, the abolishment of the three-tiered rural communal organizations in the 1980s and the disengagement of the Party-State bureaucracy from urban industrial and commercial enterprises in the 1990s have gradually nudged the society towards the establishment (or re-establishment) of a more "rational bureaucracy" (in the Weberian sense of the term) and an open and competitive market economy (Huang 1994, 1998). The retrenchment of the Party-State control over people's day-to-day lives, and the ensuing increases in personal liberty, have galvanized Chinese citizens' vitality and creativity to produce sustained economic growth in recent decades (Bian 2000; Howell 1998).

The comprehensive social safety net established during the Maoist collective era, appropriately called "Communist Neo-Traditionalism" (Walder 1986), that was built with the 'iron-bowl' job security under a command economy, had been discarded, along with its protective garment (Chow 2000; Whiting 1991; See also Wong and Flynn 2001). As this neoclassical, laissez-faire socio-economic policy has gradually taken hold in China, the Party-State, with its curtailed power and resources, has encountered increasing difficulties to meet short- and long-term humanitarian needs at the grassroots level especially after natural calamities or human-made disasters. Under these conditions, Chinese authorities are increasingly paying attention to the formation and operation of civilian self-help organizations, popularly called non-governmental organizations (NGOs) in the West, as a measure to assist the government in shouldering these new demands (Bian 2000; Estes 1998; Howell 1994, 1995, 1998; Whiting 1991).

Will the reduction of the Party-State control provide the power vacuum that enables the citizens' grassroots mobilization and, hence, building a genuine civil society? How will grassroots democracy gain its foothold in this post-socialist society? When conditions compel citizens to take direct actions to defend their rights, will they appeal to the traditional (pre-modern) type of NGOs, or will they imitate their counterparts in the West? Will the formation of these self-helped NGOs facilitate attaining democratization in post-socialist China? How much has China's civil society building process conformed to (or diverged from) that of other societies? These questions have attracted tremendous scholarly attention because they point to China's possible future development directions and raise issues regarding the theories related to civil society-building and post-socialist social transformation (Estes 1998; Whiting 1991; Weller 1998).

To some extent, the problem seems to lay with the traditional Chinese social fabric that emphasizes interpersonal networks that often circumvent the supposedly impersonal and impartial rule of laws or market mechanisms, euphemistically called "social capital" by some (Chow 2000; Keane 2001; Redding 1998; Smart 1998). We may wonder whether it will require the development of a new citizenship concept and its new ethical commitments before ordinary Chinese consider taking part in such impersonal NGOs for common public goals.

However, the other half of the problem seems to have been derived from questions of Habermas's conceptualization of civil society building—a process largely based on European experiences where the church had played active social roles independent of the state-society dichotomy. Such tripartite social division was not significant in Chinese history and society (Whiting 1991). Furthermore, the state-society relationships in the Chinese cultural context may not be seen as oppositions but rather as one embedded in the other: the state is an indispensable part of the society and is expected to provide protection, guidance and order to it (Chow 2000; Hann and Dunn 1996; Keane 2001; Win 1998).

To understand the complexity of these issues, I begin by discussing the changing history and social significance of NGOs in the West. This will be followed by an analysis of the history of indigenous NGOs in pre-modern China and their current development under the reform and open policy. The next section points out some practical and conceptual controversies revolving around contemporary China's NGO growth. Some of these problems derived from pragmatic difficulties of promoting grassroots democracy in a nominally socialist society; others came from conceptual difficulties when transposing a European-based theory to China. The next section analyses a dozen NGOs I interviewed in Southwest China's hilly regions of Yunnan, Sichuan, and Guizhou from 2009 to 2015. Even though having different specific goals—including poverty reduction, post-disaster management, community development, environmental conservation, cultural preservation, and so on—these NGOs exhibit several shared characteristics. They were all initiated by community elites with broad-based information networks and connections. Most of them also received initial inputs in funding, operation space, technical training, and advisory supervision from international NGOs. This study's findings confirm that despite the unique governance systems in China, Chinese NGOs in the Mainland are more akin to global NGOs owing to their shared charitable and philanthropic concerns. Because of this type of international connection, the government has taken a jaundiced view of the growth and development of these grassroots organizations as foreign agents.

The Development of NGOs in the West

In Western social history, the development of NGOs is virtually synonymous with the development of civil society and democracy: the establishment of social groups or organizations by individual citizens based on shared needs and concerns outside the official nation-state domains. These voluntary, non-profit organizations serve a broad array of societal needs. For instance, in the United States, "Some 5% of the...Gross National Product is derived from this non-profit sector!" (Fox 1987). More specifically, "Most organizations existing before World War II were rooted in the Christian tradition and structure and were largely an outgrowth of missionary activities," such as the Salvation Army, Catholic Relief Services, and World Church Council (Fox 1987). Only after World War II did we find an increasingly large number of secular (non-church related) NGOs formed that provide relief assistance in developing countries. However, religious NGOs still play a dominant role in such efforts.

In the 1960s and 1970s, many western NGOs also began to devise development assistance in developing countries to eradicate the root causes of poverty and the shameful vestige of colonialism. By their grassroots nature, such groupings or organizations often provided timely assistance to needy citizens with more 'efficiency and efficacy' (Frantz 1987) than the state apparatus, thus strengthening people's sense of autonomy and independence and building civil society (Drabek 1987). In recent decades, such successes have increasingly attracted financial sponsorship and contributions from the private sectors and governments.

The rapid global expansion of NGOs in terms of number and size can be seen in a recent tally that "The NGO universe includes well over 15,000 recognizable NGOs that operate in three or more countries and draw their finances from sources in more than one country" (Gordenker & Weiss 1996). Another comprehensive survey of the non-profit sector in 22 North America, South America, Europe, Asia, and the Middle East indicates that it represents a $1.1 trillion industry and employs close to 19 million full-time equivalents paid workers (Salamon et al. 1999).

In Western history, the rise of such voluntary citizen groups is considered an indispensable part of the rise of democracy and civil society - the weakening of the autocratic, monarchical state. Furthermore, Jurgen Habermas's (1989) insightful discussion of the rise of the 'public sphere' in European history as an indicator of the rise of civil society has generated increased interest in the study of grassroots organizations beyond the official state machinery (e.g., Rankin 1993; Wakeman 1993). It can be regarded as a democratic forum where citizens congregate to pursue common goals and voice opinions to influence official policy-making.

NGOs' rising power and structural network across nation-state boundaries in the post-Cold War era have prompted many scholars to ponder the new roles they may play under the current abysmal conditions of the "crisis of the state" (Salamon *et al.* 1999). The critical relief assistance by NGOs in areas devastated by ethnic conflicts or civil wars prompted many international developers to urge the NGOs to serve the new roles as mediators or intermediaries in 'conflict management (Aall 1996; Fox 1987). The strengthening of grassroots civil society organizations directly challenges state bureaucracies and certainly implies the weakening of traditional nation-states in international politics (Ong 1999; Sassen 1996). Furthermore, the weakening of the traditional nation-state by transnational NGOs implies the emergence and formation of a 'global civil society (Hirst & Thompson 1999), which is ushering into a new 'global governance' (Weiss & Gordenker 1996) or "global associational revolution" era (Salamon et al. 1999).

NGOs in the Chinese Cultural Context

Researchers of Chinese history generally agree that pre-modern Chinese society enjoyed high levels of local autonomy (Hsiao 1960). To meet societal needs, the local elite engaged in "sponsorship or establishment of institutions for welfare, education, religious purposes, social betterment, or defense (*tang, yuan*, temples, schools, militia, etc.)" (Rankin, 1993). For instance, poor peasants in Southeast China's coastal provinces of Guangdong and Fujian provinces turned to kinship organizations, called 'patrilineal lineages' with corporate trust funds for financial assistance in funerals, famine relief, and even education advancement for the gifted and talented (Friedman 1958, 1966; see also Lam and Perry 2000). Merchants and artisans formed guilds and regional associations to assist each other as they traveled to distant cities—the predecessor of the Chambers of Commerce in modern times (Chen 2001; Golas, 1977; Ho 1966; Rowe 1993). Even though some scholars questioned whether such locally-oriented activities fit Western concepts of 'civil society (Wakeman 1993), they are genuine indigenous non-governmental organizations.

The three decades following the establishment of the People's Republic of China in 1949 had seen a rapid expansion of the Party-State power and controlling apparatus through collectivization. Since almost all social welfare needs were fulfilled by the hierarchically structured collectives or work units, virtually all traditional NGOs disappeared from official existence and actual operation, except for a few satellite organizations controlled by the Party-State as an extension of its arms to mobilize the masses, such as All-China Federation of Women, Chinese Association of Science and Technology, Chinese Writers' Association, and All-China Federation of Trade Unions (Whiting, 1991). It was not until the early 1980s when collectivization was formally abandoned, that we found the return of selected NGOs, such as the China Children and Teenagers' Fund, established in 1981, that provides social support, educational assistance and health services to poor children and their families (Estes 1998; Howell 1995a; Whiting 1991).

With the liberalization policy deepened throughout the decade 1980s, there was witnessed the explosive proliferation of NGOs in the form of professional associations (Howell 1995a; Chow 2000), philanthropic organizations and foundations (Estes 1998; Whiting 1991), as well as special interest organizations (Howell 1995b). It is estimated that "by October 1993, there were reportedly over 181,000 such organizations registered with the Ministry of Civil Affairs (Howell 1995a). Following the Wenchuan earthquake in 2008, the number of civilian organizations exploded to 431,000, including 238,700 mass organizations (*shehui Quanti*, defined below), 190,400 civilian organizations (*minban feiqiye danwei*), and 1,843 foundations (*Outlook Weekly,* September 12, 2010).

Researchers generally follow the nomenclature systems used by the Chinese government to breakdown these newly formed NGOs into three broad categories: mass organizations (*shehui tuanti* 社会团体), semi-official organizations (*banguan bamin tuanti* 半官半民团体) and popular organizations (*minjian tuanti* 民间团体) (Howell 1995b; Whiting 1991). A brief discussion of these different categories is needed to understand the complexity of the issues.

Mass organizations include satellite organizations established early by the Party-State as outreach arms to mobilize the masses, such as the Women's Federation, the Chinese Writers' Associations, All-China Federation of Trade Unions, and foundations professional associations established in the 1980s. The Party-State primarily funded these organizations, and their officials were transferred from state bureaucracies. Most of these organizations have government-assigned office space, and some even have regular publications to promote their works. While Party-State insisted that these organizations are not part of the state bureaucracy, and some of these organizations have been trying hard in recent years to project images that underscore their autonomy, external researchers have been debating whether they should be considered real NGOs (Howell 1995a; Whiting 1991).

Semi-official organizations include professional associations established in various regions or cities with formal encouragement, direct involvement, or initial funding from the Party-State. These voluntary associations have other revenue sources, such as membership dues and some elected officials and Party-State appointed representatives. They include organizations such as the Association of Individual Laborers, Association for Factory Directors and Company Managers, etc. The practical necessity of forming these professional organizations reflects the rapid pace of privatizing productive enterprises in China in the reform decades. As remarked by Chow in the following statement, "By 1997, there were 54,418,500 individual laborers, running 28,508,600 family-owned small business units (most of them were food stands, repair shops, and small restaurants)" (Chow 2000).

Similarly, the proliferation of private commercial enterprises such as chemical fertilizer retailers or landscape plants retailers also entails the establishment of new traders' organizations. The Party-State may provide startup funds and office facilities to encourage their establishment. Retired cadres may be assigned to assist their initial organization drives and, once established. However, these organizations may gradually shed their official connections by raising their membership fees and relocating to their own office space (Chow 2000).

The last type of NGO includes those popular organizations established through private initiatives without Party-State involvement. These include various hobby-oriented organizations, such as those involved in folk dances, calligraphy, meditation (e.g., *qigong*) and so on (Howell 1995a). These organizations would probably be considered genuine NGOs by the Western standard because of their financial and political independence. However, their narrowly defined goals and amorphous structures tend to be short-lived with limited influences. To gain official approval, these organizations must get registered with local authorities.

Among the above three types of NGOs, the first one has the best formal organization, nationwide network, official connections, and funding source, but the least autonomy. Researchers will be reluctant to accept them as true NGOs. My preliminary research in southwest China indicates that these state-sponsored organizations had been actively taking the lead in championing citizens' causes and rights. For instance, the Women's League promoted women's awareness against domestic violence and the Association for Professional Biologists. The latter advocated environmental conservation and anti-pollution issues through newspaper editorials and grassroots rallies.

The semi-official organizations tend to be closer to the "true" NGOs as we see them in the West, with higher political and financial autonomy. However, these organizations have a less social impact than the first type due to their localized nature. While resembling authentic NGOs in the West, the last type is probably the least significant in grassroots mobilization and civil society building. The issues will be further explored in the next section.

Practical and Conceptual Problems of NGOs in China

Several problems must be addressed to envisage the genuinely successful development of NGOs in China. There are two sources of such problems. The first set of problems is more pragmatic. It seems to revolve around the nature of the Chinese Party-State and its fundamental animosity towards any efforts to promote grassroots democracy. The second set of problems revolves around conceptual issues or theories related to civil society building. As the whole notion of civil society was originated from Europe's historical trajectory, its applicability in China might be questioned. I will discuss these two sets of problems separately.

The first set of pragmatic problems revolves around the intrinsic and seemingly inevitable contradictions between the authoritarian Party-State and the promotion of civil society. Based on heuristic foresight, we can almost predict the following three controversial issues in China as the NGO movements gain momentum at the expense of the Party-State. The first is the NGOs' religious affiliations. How can the Party-State reconcile that relief assistance provided by religious organizations has played increasingly important roles in China when the official Marxist doctrine is against religion? This issue could have involved both domestic and external NGOs. The second issue hinges on NGO leadership and organization structure. How can the Party State reconcile the rise of charismatic leaders in newly formed NGOs who can successfully mobilize the masses for particular goals outside the established Party-State structure? The third, closely parallel to the previous one, is NGOs' transnational nature and entanglement with state sovereignty issues. How can the Party-State reconcile the issue of having international organizations providing relief assistance to domestic needy without fearing the curtailment of its monopoly of power?

The most pressing problem for NGOs in China is their religious affiliations. As indicated above, most Western NGOs are rooted in Christian traditions. Today, church organizations such as World Church Council, CARE and Oxfam are active players in international relief assistance. Similarly, in Taiwan, lay Buddhist organizations, such as Ciji Compassionate Association, have taken active roles in providing philanthropic assistance in China after major disasters (Chang 1996; Huang & Weller 1998; Ting 1997). The fine line between relief work and proselytism can sometimes be extremely thin with the long-term presence of these religious NGOs. Given the Chinese official stance on anti-religiosity, how would the authorities respond when accepting assistance from NGOs with religious affiliations? Will permission be granted when such organizations seek to establish a long-term presence in offices, communication networks, and China warehouse warehouses? A related issue is: how would the government treat indigenous religious NGOs instead of foreign ones? Unless this issue is handled properly, perhaps through modification of existing laws that grant full legal status to religious organizations, there will potentially be causes of conflicts.

The second problem that needs to be addressed is NGO leadership and organization, especially indigenous ones. NGOs are often formed by individuals who share similar concerns and interests and are willing to work together to achieve common goals. These individual initiatives often provide fertile ground for the rise of charismatic leaders. By their persuasions, appeals, and convictions, these grass-root leaders successfully attract followers, command devotion and commitment, and mobilize volunteers and valuable resources to accomplish common goals. These goal-specific organizations often exhibit high levels of discipline and efficiency among the members and volunteers. Will the existence of such well-structured organizations be interpreted as frontal challenges to state authorities? Will NGOs' organizational efficiency and successful membership recruitment be covert efforts to undermine official Party-State power? What kind of communication should the NGOs and state apparatus establish that would neither undercut state authorities nor jeopardize NGOs' autonomy and independence?

Thirdly, we should consider the transnational nature of many global NGOs and their roles in China. Various international NGOs have been actively involved in promoting specific goals, such as the Carter Center's and International Republic Institute's involvements in China's grassroots democracy through village elections (Shelley 2000) and the Ford Foundation's poverty alleviation programs in southwest China that advocate greater local control of national forest (Saich 2000). Given China's sensitivity towards international interventions in her domestic affairs (Howell 1995a), it is initially difficult to know where and how to draw the line between providing international assistance in grassroots development or disaster relief on the one hand and interfering in domestic affairs on the other hand. To avoid potential confusion and conflict, some kind of mutually agreeable protocols and guidelines should be worked out between major international NGOs and Chinese authorities. We believe that only through open and frank discussions can all sides reach a workable forum in which joint efforts can be made to foster the development of democratic institutions in China through the growth of NGOs.

The second set of problems is conceptual and derived from the theoretical implications of civil society building as defined by Habermas. Are these predominantly government-sponsored NGOs in mainland China the true instruments of civil liberty? How should we consider them in light of democratic mobilization? And lastly, whether the civil society building process in the West, along with its democratization process, can be predicted by this model and be duplicated in China? I will elaborate on these issues below.

Most researchers who conducted empirical research in China argued against dismissing these government-sponsored NGOs as less than genuine. Howell argued that "The term civil society fails to capture the diversity of organizations that have emerged in China since reform" (Howell 1995b). In the same vein, Whiting pointed out that "Chinese NGOs may be characterized as existing in a transitional stage between complete dependence on the government and some degree of autonomy from it" (Whiting 1991; Howell 1995b). Furthermore, Howell suggested that "Foreign NGOs should not necessarily deplore the prospect of working closely with the Party/State or with some semi-official social organizations" (Howell 1995a) because of the all-permeating power of the Party-State. In light of these ambiguous conditions under which the NGOs developed in China, Estes coined the term GONGOs (i.e., government-organized non-government organizations) for China (Estes 1998).

Suppose the NGOs in China's reform era are not identical to NGOs in the West. In that case, the next logical question we may ask is: Can these organizations be regarded as facilitating agencies to accomplish civil society building predicted by Habermas' theory? In other words, Can we expect the successful duplication of the civil society building process in China even with less than ideal NGOs? Again, researchers who have conducted empirical research in China tended to be critical of Habermas' theory. Howell succinctly identified what he called "The Poverty of Civil Society" problems:

In applying the concept of civil society to China, we should also be aware of its particular history in Western political thought, its normative content and its multiplicity of meanings and usage. Civil society has been seen as a crucial ingredient for democratic life. Again, this historical and ideological baggage creates specific problems for the analyst studying China (Howell 1995b).

Similar reservation was also expressed by Chow, who argued, "One unique characteristic that needs to be specifically addressed is that the dichotomy of 'civil society and 'the state,' which is often used to analyze modern capitalist societies, cannot be simply transplanted to the study of China. In other words, there was no *a priori* state/society divide in China before the reform began" (Chow 2000).

Their viewpoints can be summarized into the following three arguments: 1. The state-society division in European history is different from that of pre-modern China, as seen in the absence of the church outside of the state-society dichotomy; 2. 'Citizens' expectation of their rights as well as the roles of the state played in protecting such rights is quite different between China and the West; 3. While useful in European cultural-historical contexts, Habermas' general theory of civil society building may not apply to understanding China's current societal transformation. These three arguments will undoubtedly be debated among researchers in the years to come. But, with increasingly more empirical research opportunities being possible, we might be able to put them to the test in the future.

NGOs in Hong Kong and Taiwan

While researchers have disagreements regarding the civil society-building roles played by China's NGOs, we may look at a similar development in Hong Kong and Taiwan. After all, all three societies share a similar cultural heritage and have gone through a rapid societal transformation in recent decades. The most salient features of Hong Kong and Taiwan are their rapid economic growth: Hong Kong in the 1960s and Taiwan in the 1970s. Improved living standards have seen the rise of the middle class in both societies, having formed the driving force behind their democratic movements and the building of civil societies (Hsiao and So 1999; Lam and Perry 2000; Win 1998).

Lam and Perry lamented that due to Hong Kong's great success in a market economy and *laissez-faire* government, even under the British colonial era before 1997, people seldom noticed the vibrant "third sector," i.e., the citizens' self-motivating, goal-oriented movements in the form of social services, political pressure groups and philanthropic activities that supplement government programs. For instance, one of Hong Kong's philanthropic organizations, called Community Chest, has coordinated activities of 125 member organizations, and, "In 1996, donations to the Community Chest were more than HK$177 million" (or US$22.7 million) (Lam and Perry 2000). Another interesting point about Hong Kong is that many NGOs are organized based on pre-modern Chinese indigenous organizations, such as lineages (called 'clans' by Lam and Perry) or regional organizations accounting for 15 percent of all registered non-profit organizations. Even more impressive is Oxfam International-Hong Kong. It established its first assistance office in Kunming, Yunnan, in 1992 and had committed over RMB$450,000,000 to various humanitarian assistance projects in China by 2007 (Oxfam International Hong Kong 2007). As will be seen in the next section, Oxfam International-Hong Kong has played a centrally critical role in China's current NGO development.

Similarly, in Taiwan in the 1980s, the rise of the middle class and large business conglomerates began to exert pressure on the authoritarian Nationalist government to launch political reforms that minimized some of its abusive state power. The reduction of state control witnessed the rapid growth of grassroots citizens' organizations based on various persuasions: consumers' rights movements, environmental protection movements, anti-nuclear movements, and women's rights movements. All these movements have been aggressive toward the authoritarian Nationalist government, further accelerating the demands for reform and democratization. Based on this, Hsiao and So coined the term "contentious civil society" to describe this process (Hsiao and So 1999). Regardless of what labels we use, Taiwan has been considered a successful transitional case to develop a full-fledged civil society with democratic governance.

NGOs in Southwest China

From 2010 to 2012, I carried out fieldwork in southwest China's hilly Yun-Gui Plateau, which includes the entire province of Yunnan, Guizhou, and southern Sichuan (See Map 1 below). To understand the organization and operation of the NGOs in this region, I

Map 8.1: Map of China and the Yungui Plateau

used the following research steps. The first one is to collect information about local NGOs through government registration and local news reports. This is followed by online visits to their official web pages to compile initial information about the nature and practices of each specific organization. Before I visited the organization, my assistant managed an appointment to verify the availability of the organization's responsible person for my interviews. I visited 66 NGOs in two years with wide stretches of organization formats and practices. In the following, I used information from 12 such NGOs to analyze these NGOs' nature and specific characteristics.

Spatially, these 12 NGOs have the following geographic distributions: four each from Yunnan and Guizhou, three from Sichuan, and the last one crosses Yunnan and Guizhou. In terms of time established, we have the following distribution:

Table 8.1: Time of NGOs' establishment

Time of Establishment	Before 1995	1996-2000	2001-2005	2006-2010
Number	1	1	5	5

The rise of NGOs in China was a post-2001 phenomenon when China's economic development reached a certain threshold level. Urban elites played a crucial role in China's post-socialist transformation. The rise of the urban middle class was a non-refutable social fact. In terms of the age of the 12 NGO founders, it also clearly showed its concentration among the younger and better-educated generations:

Table 8.2: Age of NGO founders at time of establishment

Age of NGO founder	**Below 29**	**30-39**	**40-49**	**Above 50**
Number	1	6	3	2

The elitist nature of China's newly risen NGOs can be seen in their founders' education levels. All 12 founders of the studied NGOs had attained college education degrees. Two even had post-graduate training and served as college professors. The other professionals included two livestock specialists, two government office workers, two middle school teachers, an architect, a news reporter, a retired government official, and a fresh college graduate.

When examining the origin of these 12 NGOs, we can divide them based on the organizer's initial inspiration: self-motivated individuals (9), government-initiated (2), and a branched-off from international organizations (1). It is interesting to note that the two government-initiated NGOs, or GONGOs, are the least active among the 12 and with the most complaints, even though they have stable and generous funding supports from various levels of the government (i.e., provincial and prefectural government both).

Table 8.3 Tasks and distribution of 12 NGOs

Work Category	Content of Activities	Number
Poverty Reduction	Community development projects; Small-scale loans; Improved animal breading; Promotion of indigenous handicrafts for tourists; Road building to facilitate trades.	7
Information Exchange	Internet information platforms for NGO projects and funding applications; Availability of volunteers; Post-disaster material needs.	4
Training	Short-term workshops for school teachers from poverty regions, future volunteers, and NGO workers.	3
Disaster Management	Post-disaster reconstruction; Mudslide prevention; Distribution of aid goods; Warehousing goods.	3
Cultural Preservation	Recording oral history, songs and dances, and handicraft production; Survey of temples.	3
Environmental Protection	Preserving biodiversity; Reforestation; Preventing soil erosion; Maintaining local indigenous species.	3
Life Improvement	Promoting a civilized 'urban' lifestyle; Proper social decorum for poor children; Enhancing people's devotion to socialism and social conscientiousness.	2
Fund Raising	Set up fundraising booths in shopping centers; Email fundraising; Recruitment of fixed monthly donors.	2
Education	Funding AIDs orphans' education; Building libraries in poverty regions; On job training for school teachers; Distribute sports packages for students in poor areas.	2
Health & Hygiene	Build latrines and drinking water tanks; Awareness of AIDs and other contagious diseases; Funding for cold-chain operations.	2

When looking at the financial resources of these 12 organizations, there is a clear cleavage between two broad categories. The GONGO (2) and the spinoff international organization (1) indicated no budgetary concerns. All three have sufficient structural backing from established institutions: the government and the church. The opposite is true for the other nine self-motivated organizations. Raising sufficient funds for operation seemed to be a major concern for all. Under this context, Oxfam International-Hong Kong (OI-HK, henceforth) played a crucial role in facilitating their birth and growth. All nine organizations had received assistance from OI-HK in one form or another during various stages of their development. The assistance may take the form of rented office space for an NGO during its incubation period. Or it may take the form of a grant to launch its maiden trial project. Or it may take the form of a workshop for its workers to learn how to recruit volunteers, raise funds, do bookkeeping, apply for external funds, and write annual reports. Since all of the 12 NGOs are multitasking, we can tabulate their involvements based on the specific tasks they are engaged in (see Table 8.3).

It is apparent from the above list that these NGOs have filled in major social welfare chasms that the government has been unable to handle. It falls on the shoulders of the newly risen urban middle class who, after gaining the material comfort of life, begin to search for the meaning of life through concerns over pan-human sufferings and humanitarian needs. The best example in our sample is an NGO called "A Ray of Sunshine" in this region. It was organized by an architect, Mr. Fan, who made a fortune through urban landscape designs and housing constructions in recent years before he even reached his 35th year of his age. Through a happenstance encounter, he discovered a poverty-stricken region in the hilly Miao minority area where elementary school students often have no shoes to wear or no money to pay school fees. He decided to do charity work. He organized his colleagues in the architecture firm in 2010 to form this organization.

They collected surplus goods from local manufacturers and warehouses through work connections and websites. In the hilly regions, the organization identified school teachers as contact persons to collect information on special requests from students. They used their all-wheel-drive vehicles to transport the goods to school teachers for distribution on weekends. All the volunteers paid for their meals and fuel costs when delivering goods to minimize expenses. Mr. Fan was very proud of his work and said, "When the provincial Red Cross found out about our work the following year, it proposed incorporating our NGO into the Red Cross system. Even though this move would have given us some legitimacy with the government and provided us with some logistic support, such as an accountant for our bookkeeping and capital liquidation, we decided not to accept it. This is so because we cherish our independence, and we dislike the kind of overhead charges Red Cross puts on every transaction." This NGO has blossomed into a vibrant social group with over 300 young volunteers participating in its various programs in 2017. Newly established projects such as repairing dilapidated classrooms and establishing scholarships for good students have been added to its recent activities.

Not all NGOs or their founders are successful. At a time of rapid social change, some young people are looking in vain for new aspirations and opportunities for self-elevation. In 2010 I met a new college graduate, Mr. He, who had just started an NGO. Having witnessed the abysmal chaos after the Wenchuan earthquake, he decided to take a new path in disaster management. He wanted to set up warehouses with a large capacity to provide emergency supplies, such as tents, clothing, instant foods, bottled water, electricity generators, first aid kits, etc., for future disaster relief. He and a co-worker went to shopping malls on weekends to collect donations to collect the necessary funding. They paid themselves only RMB$1,500 per month to conserve meager funding. They lived in cramped rooms for the low rents and purchased cheap foods late at night from the markets for their meals. Life was hard, but Mr. He was full of enthusiasm and energy. He proudly said to me, "With our capacity, the next time when a major disaster strikes, we will be better prepared." In 2011 when I visited this organization again, I was told that it had been folded and Mr. He had abandoned his goal. He was converted to Christianity, joined a missionary group, and went to Africa for his spiritual salvation.

Conclusion

Based on the previous discussion, we can draw a few concluding remarks about the growth of NGOs in China and their impact on civil society building. First, the proliferation of NGOs has been astronomical, and the trend will continue along with the current economic growth and the rising middle class. During the past three decades, sustained economic growth in China has contributed to the improved living standard, especially among urban dwellers along the coast. Enhanced education levels over the same period have also contributed to a new sense of citizens' awareness. The rise of the middle class, albeit small in the percentage of the entire population, signals a fundamental structural change in Chinese society.

Demands for legal rights and protections, such as consumers' rights, environmental conservation, and industrial workers' protection from work-related injuries, will generate more grassroots movements that accelerate the civil society building processes. The announcement of incorporating entrepreneurs into the Communist Party by then-President Jiang Zemin in 2000 signals the awareness of the top echelon of the Party-State that change is inevitable, and democratization will become China's mainstream development in the years to come.

Second, in considering the relationships between NGOs and civil society building in China, we should include the organizations initiated by the Party-State as genuine NGOs. Both the Chinese Communist Party and Chinese society are going through rapid changes. Owing to the all-encompassing and permeating nature of the Communist Party before the reform era, it would be next to impossible to expect the automatic formation of citizens' voluntary associations after 40 years of oppressive rules. Under this condition, it would not be unusual to find the best organized and best operated social groups outside of the Party-State bureaucracies established by the Party-State as fronts to appease certain segments of the society. The increased liberty given to citizens from the top has underscored a new dialogical relationship between the Party-State and society. Under this condition, we will find members of the Party-State-initiated NGOs deciding to disassociate themselves from the Party-State apparatus and transform their organizations into genuine NGOs to serve societal goals.

Along the same vein, we can conclude that while Habermas' general theory of civil society building seems appropriate in explaining China's civil society building processes, there are also discrepancies that must have been considered about the unique history and cultural heritage in China. The major difference is the lack of a religious institution outside the state-society dichotomy. Without an institutional alternative or mediator, the state-society division may become more sharpened and contentious, as seen in political riots in Taiwan in the 1970s and China in the 1980s. However, the shortened feedback loops between state and society make their changing balances more direct and observable. In other words, the reduction of the state power will entail the dramatic increase of grassroots organizations, even when such organizational formats are newly imported from the outside and not a part of the cultural tradition.

Furthermore, while we know something about the sudden plethora of newly established modern NGOs, either those formally established by the Party-State or those linked to special interest groups in the form of voluntary associations, we know virtually nothing about traditional NGOs and their revival in contemporary China's social landscape. Ethnographic reports have indicated lineage halls or regional associations (Huang 1998; Jing 1996), but these reports are sporadic and incidental. Other traditional self-helped organizations, such as religious cults and credit associations, are probably quietly making a comeback to fill in the void created under the current reform. However, there has been little information about them due to their sensitive nature. These organizations would not have been registered with Party-State authorities due to their uncertain legal status, thus making their existence virtually under researchers' radars. Unfortunately, this will remain so until democratization is fully established in China and all citizens' organizations are protected equally under the rule of laws that we will possibly have a clear count of all NGOs, both modern and indigenous, that operate in building the civil society in China.

The love-hate relationship between the Party-State and the proliferating NGOs is quite evident. The tangible material benefit provided by NGOs has fulfilled needs that the entrenched Party-State bureaucracy has been unable to meet. Furthermore, many NGOs have introduced efficient management systems that provide alternative governing models for local bureaucrats. But the negative implications of these are equally obvious. Any NGO's success in alleviating social suffering is a public indictment of the failed Party-State and its local bureaucracy. Even more troublesome are new ideas that NGOs introduce to the general public from the West. Concepts such as "participatory management," "transparent governance," "grassroots democracy," "open society," "gender equality," "sustainable development," and certain others often appear in NGOs' brochures and instructional programs. They have become common parlance among NGO workers.

This ambivalence hampers government efforts to lay out a clear set of policies for the mushrooming NGOs. One way to control them is by the registration practice mentioned above. This immediately puts many international and some local NGOs in legal limbo. Most international NGOs are not formally registered because of the unlikelihood that they would be taken under the wing of any government office. Hence, they are forced to operate in a legally gray area.

Will a financially secure Chinese state simply kick out the international NGOs and replace them with government-operated ones? I do not believe this scenario will take place. Under the current development trajectory, the Chinese state is eager to participate in international sociopolitical arenas in more sophisticated and responsible ways. The presence of international NGOs is a clear signal that China is a full-fledged member of the international community and abides by its common rules. In conclusion, the development of NGOs in China mirrors the country's reality and possibilities. It indicates both the international community's expectation of China's participation in global game plans and China's potential roles in a global future, given its distinct social development experience. These concerns are both Chinese and global.

Chapter 9
Unsuccessful Factory Project by a Sino-Botswana Joint Venture

This chapter is based on a long-term and in-depth fieldwork on a glass factory project owned by a Sino-Botswana joint venture. Firstly, the background of bilateral relations between China and Botswana will be introduced from diachronic perspectives. This will provide the context for discussing the origin of the project. Then the paper reveals the cooperative and conflictive aspects embedded in the construction of the factory from synchronic perspectives through data obtained from participant observation. These include operation mode, Chinese company's adaption to Botswana local laws and regulations, gaming between the partners, industrial diversification of Botswana, impacts from the political struggle in Botswana to the project, etc. This chapter further juxtaposes the discourse generated by the media with in-depth interviews with all parties involved in the projects to show the tremendous differences between these two cultures, two systems, and two ideologies.

Introduction

Political, economic, and cultural cooperation and exchange between China and Africa have increased. At the same time, Sino-African relations, particularly in education, politics, and business, have received more attention globally. The issues raised during this process include China's investment and economic activities in Africa and the influences on the development of Africa and Chinese migration to Africa (Alden 2007; Raine 2009; Hofstedt 2009; Yoon and Chen 2009). According to incomplete statistics, over one million Chinese people live on the continent.

China's "going out" strategy is not only largely responsible for the growing interest of Chinese enterprises but also for the increasing presence of Chinese people in Africa, a continent viewed with significant economic growth potential. The activities of these Chinese people vary, ranging from construction to wholesale and retail of small commodities and manufacturing. They establish their future in a Chinese style in this strange land and experience glories and hardships. This chapter focuses on some of the issues, including suspicions and doubts that lead to misunderstandings and conflicts between Chinese and Africans when the two peoples come together. As Sino-African relations develop with time, we can observe how the differences, misunderstandings, and disputes between Chinese and African actors have become more complicated. Making Sino-African relations more complicated are the Western powers' responses to China's growing economic strength and presence in Africa. These include the West's claim that China is a neocolonial power on the continent, neglecting its own and African countries' human rights abuses and allowing the sale of poor-quality goods to Africa.

In Africa, public opinion seems to follow the West, condemning China for its exploitation of Africa and Africans and, in some countries, displaying signs of anti-Chinese sentiments. However, in this chapter, I aim to show that the relationship between African and Chinese actors on the ground is more complex than how it has been represented and discussed in the media. I argue that many rumors, suspicions, and misunderstandings have resulted from a lack of fieldwork and in-depth investigations. This chapter, which relies heavily on fieldwork in Botswana and engagement with actors involved in a project to construct a Sino-Botswana glass factory, discusses the living conditions of Chinese people in Africa and their activities. More broadly, it examines the cooperation process between a group of Chinese actors and local people, which is complicated and confusing. Through interviews and analyses of local documents, this chapter aims to reveal some of the sources of doubts, misunderstandings, and conflicts, including cultural differences, between Chinese and Africans involved in a relatively large collaborative project.

As a sub-discipline of Applied Anthropology, Business Anthropology is still an emerging inter-discipline marginalized in China. It mainly focuses on solving practical problems in business by applying the theories and methodologies of anthropology. The research methodology applied is ethnography, the most common one in anthropology. However, its theoretical features are not distinct. At present, except for "Business Anthropology" and "Introduction to Business Anthropology" (Tian and Zhou 2012; Tian and Zhou 2013), two works were written jointly by Professor Tian Guang and Professor Zhou Daming, other theoretical works about this field can scarcely be found in China. Furthermore, almost all the research topics involved in the case studies are traditional ones, such as ethnic groups, religions and family clans. Research on Chinese companies' institutional management and culture is seldom carried out, especially those exploring how Chinese companies cooperate with foreign companies and foreign cultures during their internationalization (Chen and Guo 2015; Tian 2010).

Professor Tian Guang stresses that the Chinese company will meet the foreign culture and customs during internationalization. Therefore, anthropologists specializing in Business Anthropology research are needed to provide "cultural suggestions" for companies to carry out their business activities successfully, thus helping Chinese workers integrate their cultural background with the "local culture" of a foreign country and further promote the long-lasting development of the company (Tian 2012). The case study in this chapter is an unsuccessful glass factory project owned by a Sino-Botswana joint venture. It discusses the cultural differences and conflicts faced by both parties during the construction of this glass factory. This study explores the root reasons behind the differences and conflicts from the cultural perspective, such as different social systems and concepts.

The anthropological field study and case study methodologies are applied in this chapter. From January 2012 to January 2013, I moved to and lived in Gaborone with my spouse, but I also took on a visiting scholar position at the University of Botswana. This study largely benefits my spouse's role in the glass factory construction project. This connection has allowed me to visit the work site for long periods to observe how Chinese and Africans relate and give me access to the board and other staff members to interview. I have obtained objective and genuine information through my connection that is rarely available to researchers.

My relocation to the country allowed me to do research and collect first-hand information about the conditions in Botswana and investigate the living conditions of the Chinese people who have migrated to the country. The data collection included reports from the local media, namely popular newspapers, on the presence of Chinese people and the glass factory project itself. Through the study of the discourse in the popular media, the function and influence of the glass factory on the local area have been examined and elaborated. Nearly a hundred related news reports have been collected and analyzed.

China and Botswana

Since establishing diplomatic relations between China and Botswana in 1975, the two countries have continuously exchanged high-level visits, strengthened mutual political trust, supported state sovereignty and territorial integrity, and shared many experiences exploring new state governance and development methods. As far as economic cooperation is concerned, bilateral trade between the two countries has increasingly expanded based on equality, mutual trust, and mutual respect. Sino-Botswana trade has reached 266 million US dollars. The investment of China in Botswana also achieved a leap in growth. In particular, the direct investment in the non-financial sectors reached 402 million US dollars in 2016. (CMFA 2018) The Botswana Central Bureau of Statistics data shows that in the first quarter of 2012, the total value of bilateral trade between China and Botswana had reached 101.3 million US dollars (ECCOEPRC 2012).

Besides economic cooperation, the two countries have very close cooperation in the cultural field. In 2008, Shanghai Normal University established a Confucius Institute in Botswana. Since its establishment, two to three hundred local students have enrolled to study the Chinese language and culture each year, and the number has continued to grow. On the other hand, students from Botswana have been sent to China to study. In 2016, while 396 students went abroad to study in China, 632 professional and technical personnel had completed their training in China. Since China sent its first medical team to Botswana in 1981, 12 teams with 327 members have been sent there. There are 46 medical team members in Botswana (CMFA 2018).

The relatively long-term, steady relationship between the two countries has encouraged many Chinese people to invest and create new businesses in Botswana. It is estimated that more than 30,000 Chinese people are working in Botswana. While some Chinese people are originally from Jiangxi and Hubei Provinces, Northeast China, and Shanghai, the majority, 60 to 70 percent, are from Fujian Province.

People from Fujian Province primarily engage in small commodity wholesale and retail businesses. Their businesses are spread across urban and rural areas. Chinese businesses have made it more convenient for local people to consume daily needed goods in rural areas. Besides the traders, there are also those Chinese who came to Botswana to assist China's construction projects in the 1980s. Some foresaw Botswana's vast market and development opportunities and chose to stay in the country to develop independently. After more than ten years of persistent hard work, they not only have settled down in Botswana but have also encouraged many relatives and friends to come to the country to pursue new opportunities. Other Chinese people in Botswana have come from neighboring countries like South Africa and Zimbabwe. They are also attracted here by the stable social environment and China's continual economic interests in Botswana.

It is estimated that the Chinese companies in Botswana have created over 20,000 employment opportunities and made lots of contributions to Botswana’s construction and development. However, due to language and cultural differences between the two peoples, local Botswanians view the Chinese people as mysterious and separated from the local society. Extant stereotypes are gradually changing with time. Younger Chinese who are knowledgeable of technology, proficient in English, and experienced with management are leading the way towards dismantling some of the misunderstandings of Chinese people among the locals. They cooperate and communicate directly with local governments and develop friendships with many local people. Some Chinese companies pay great attention to their social responsibility. Every year, they make donations to local charity organizations and offer scholarships to local students with outstanding academic achievements to study in China.

Generally speaking, the living condition of Chinese people in Botswana is better than those in most other African countries. Botswana is universally acknowledged as a country with the least corruption and a relatively lower crime rate. It enjoys a stable political environment and constant development of the economy, which has provided a favorable living and developing environment for the Chinese. However, with the revision of related policies in Botswana, the Chinese have started to come across many difficulties and problems. According to some Chinese businessmen, the business operation now is getting increasingly harder, which is largely affected by the local policies towards the Chinese.

Former President Festus Mogae held a friendlier attitude towards China than President Ian Khama. This change in leadership with the leader having a less positive attitude towards his Chinese partner has been one of the key factors in changing the available opportunities to the Chinese who are doing business or investing in Botswana. Undoubtedly, changes such as this, which are influential on policies, would impact whether the Chinese businessmen remain or leave Botswana shortly. I shall further discuss this transformation below.

Background of the Sino-Botswana Glass Factory Project

The diamond industry and cattle farming have been the two major industries in Botswana's economy for a long time. Although Botswana has a wealth of mineral resources, the shortage of professionals and modern equipment makes it extremely difficult to develop new manufacturing. As a result, daily living and industrial products still rely on imports. Therefore, it has become the major goal for Botswana to develop a diversified economy. This goal has become more urgent since the world financial crisis in 2007. This crisis dramatically reduced the global demand for diamonds, severely damaging Botswana's economy--half of the country's financial income and two-thirds of its foreign exchange income relied heavily on the diamond industry. Against these backdrops, the manufacturing of glass, which entails silica sand, coal, sodium carbonate, and many other raw materials, has gained importance to the Botswana government. The government has made great efforts to attract foreign investment in glass manufacturing. The former president, Fsetus Mogae, vigorously promoted a Sino-Botswana glass factory project when he went to China for the Beijing Summit and Third Ministerial Conference of the Forum on China-Africa Cooperation in November 2006.

According to Tomas, a board member of the glass factory, "As early as 2004, the board had intended to build a glass factory in South Africa. We have done many feasibility types of research and found that South Africa has a wide market. This country has a population of forty to fifty million people. But for a long time, it only has one glass factory, namely PG Glass, which supplies glass to the 200 million people in 14 countries in the whole southern Africa region and enjoys generous profit alone. In 2006, during the period when Botswana President Fsetus Mogae visited Beijing, he graciously invited our board members to meet him in Beijing after learning our plan through the Botswana ambassador in China. President Mogae expressed his eager wish that we could build the glass factory in Botswana. However, Botswana is not an ideal place. The small population, the inland geographical location, and the lack of coastline increase production and sales costs. But President

Mogae was very persistent. He said that building a glass factory in Botswana had long been his dream for many years, and Botswana had all the raw materials needed for manufacturing glass. If we were willing to build our glass factory in Botswana, he would give support and cooperation in all aspects. The president's sincerity touched our board members, and at last, we decided to build the glass factory in Botswana."

When the Beijing Summit concluded, President Mogae sent his Finance Minister to investigate the project. At the same time, he traveled with the board members of the glass factory to Shanghai to discuss the terms of their contract. It was decided that the glass factory construction project would be pursued jointly by Botswana Development Corporation Limited (BDC) and Shanghai Fengyue Glass Company Limited (FYG). Since Botswana had no experience in constructing a glass factory or available human resources, President Mogae insisted that FYG be the larger shareholder of the project to provide technical support on design, civil engineering, installation, and production. BDC would simply provide financial support for the project. In this manner, the Sino-Botswana joint venture was agreed upon.

By mid-2007, the two parties signed a shareholders' agreement and the formal EPC（the Engineering, Procurement and Construction services）contract agreement in mid-2008. FYG is both the bigger shareholder and EPC contractor. The project should have started immediately once the EPC contract was signed. While the entire budget for the project was confirmed and everything was ready to begin, the Botswana government's fund and the BDC's credit were not ready until the beginning of 2010.

The latter was mainly due to the outbreak of the global financial crisis from 2008 to 2010. The financial crisis greatly crippled Botswana's economic structure, which depended heavily on the export of diamonds. During this period, FYG also suffered great economic losses: on the one hand, it suffered from the devaluation of the Pula to US dollars and the increased value of the Chinese yuan to US dollars; and, on the other hand, FYG had to face higher costs of raw materials, physical distribution, and labor recourse. These damages are important reasons for the funding shortage in the later stage of the construction project.

While the sluggish economic environment in Botswana affected the construction process of the glass factory, the change in the political environment also affected the factory's fate. The departure of the two most important figures that initiated and supported the glass factory project in Botswana led the project's fate to an uncertain condition. In April 2008, President Mogae stepped down, and the new President Khama came into power immediately. Unlike the former president, President Ian Khama did not show such a strong passion for the glass factory project. Unfortunately, the former Minister of the Ministry of Finance, whom the former president once appointed to promote this project vigorously, died of cancer in 2011, negatively influencing the construction of this project.

After three years of preparation and waiting, the construction of the glass factory finally started in Palapye, an emerging industrial town in southeast Botswana, in July 2010. Palapye was chosen for two reasons: first, it is a strategic place, and second, it is the hometown of former President Mogae. Palapye is not only where the only coal colliery is located, but it also has the largest power station and soda ash manufacturer. This meant that the place could provide ample electricity and raw materials for glass manufacturing. The glass factory was supposed to have been completed by 2011 and put into production. Moreover, it was supposed to provide more than 400 employment opportunities for Botswana and produce 450 tons of float glass each day.

However, the construction was forced to suspend at the end of 2011 due to a funding shortage and the unpreparedness of water, electricity, and other supporting resources. The suspension brought great repercussions in Botswana, and rumors were afloat. Some said that BDC corrupted funds and others said that the Chinese people were liars. How did this shift happen? This chapter will go in-depth to discuss and analyze the cooperation and difference between the two parties during the construction of the glass factory.

Cooperation and Difference during the Construction of the Glass Factory

Although China and Botswana are developing countries, they differ greatly in political and cultural systems. Therefore, it should be unsurprising that differences and disagreements would emerge during the cooperation process. A lack of communication between Africans and Chinese who choose to cooperate on a project further contributes to misunderstandings and distrust that could negatively affect the project. Here, I shall discuss several problems that have emerged in the glass factory project due to political and cultural differences and the lack of proper communication between the two shareholders of the project.

The difference in Operation and Management between FYG and BDC

Registered in the British Virgin Island in 2007, FYG is an offshore company with its office headquarters in Shanghai. The board members are all Chinese and have ten to twenty years' experience setting up factories and doing business in Africa. According to the contracts, FYG is the major shareholder and EPC contractor. It is fully responsible for the design, construction and management of the whole glass factory. When the contract was signed in 2007, FYG immediately began recruiting skilled and experienced engineers, technicians and management professionals in the glass industry in China. Following existing norms and standards in China, it completed the engineering design, manufacturing of equipment and materials and a full set of export through the advanced technology of Luoyang float glass. FYG is also a typical Chinese private company with all the major features and problems of a private company: its several top directors have absolute powers; it does not have a management system and culture of a western enterprise; individual personalities run its management and operation more than by law. However, high-level directors are not almighty. When they make decisions, they do not understand some business rules, project issues, or the local legal systems, thus often leading the company into unnecessary problems and financial losses.

BDC (Botswana Development Corporation Limited) is a state-owned company founded in 1970. It is devoted to state commercial and industrial development and mainly provides financial support and supervision for projects. A board guides BDC, and board members are appointed and dismissed by the Minister of Finance and Development Planning. The Managing Director manages the company with the assistance of two General Managers. BDC is a state-owned investment company that invests in many projects playing the role of a fundraising institution and a partner. The glass factory is one of those invested projects. However, since Botswana is almost inexperienced in the manufacturing sector and BDC has no technological and managerial personnel in the glass industry, BDC can't supervise and cooperate effectively. BDC does not have a technology basis and management capacity in many mass projects. As a result, many supporting facilities like water and electricity and visa services could not meet the demand. So the project process was delayed.

As outlined here, it should be obvious that FYG is a private company organized and driven by profit-making, while BDC is a state-owned investment entity set up to serve the country's aim, especially to develop a diversified economy. Both are fundamentally different in operation and management styles, making gaming during the cooperation process possible.

Gaming between the Two Cooperation Parties

The total investment capital of the glass factory project is 500 million Pula, consisting of the injection of equity capital from the two cooperating parties and a loan from the Botswana Government. As the Botswana government is the main funding source, the BDC not only has the responsibility to monitor the quality of the project and its progress but also to regulate FYG's use of funds. However, as mentioned before, since BDC has neither experience nor personnel in the glass industry, it cannot have an effective regulation. Therefore, BDC commissioned G4, a local structural engineering consultant, to regulate the glass factory project. Here began the gaming between the two parties. According to

Simon's statements, the FYG Executive Director noted that G4 was also inexperienced in the glass industry. It not only failed to monitor the project effectively but was also exploited by the commercial and political struggle that had emerged.

As a result, G4 attracted negative attention to the glass factory project. In particular, the project was implicated in a corruption scandal. As the local newspaper reported, in May 2011, G4 made a copy of the audit report, noting that BDC paid an extra 100 million, Pula, to FYG and accused the glass factory project of its slower progress than expected. G4 also claimed that corruption might exist inside BDC regarding this project (Mogapi 2011). Soon, all the major media reported the glass factory project. Clamorous rumors and suspicions put BDC and the glass factory project at the forefront (Balise 2011). The DCEC (Directorate on Corruption and Economic Crime), the anti-corruption agency of Botswana, investigated BDC (Balise 2011), and many related members were accused of corruption and dismissed (Ramadubu 2011). The Ministry of Finance and Development Planning of Botswana reappointed the members of the BDC Board of Directors and said that "The new board would be required to resolve any outstanding issues threatening the successful completion and implementation of the Float Glass Manufacturing project under construction in Palapye." (Baleseng 2011) BDC no longer employed G4. Instead, it hired a consultant firm with rich experience in the glass industry from the United Kingdom to evaluate and supervise the glass factory project. According to Simon, after two day's visit, experts from the United Kingdom positively affirmed the engineering quality and design art.

BDC and FYG are both collaborators and competitors in pursuing their interests. Economic interest is the main goal of the competition. To supervise the project, BDC firstly employed G4 and later hired a consulting firm from the United Kingdom. But unexpectedly, G4 put BDC into a corruption scandal. It is more than simply for economic interests. The little-known economic war and the necessity of political struggle are important hidden causes.

Influence of Political Struggle on the Glass Factory Project

From May 2011 to the end of that year, the news about BDC and the glass factory project dominated Botswana's major newspapers' headlines. It was reported that FYG would be sold by auction because it fell behind with the material funding and could not submit the performance bond (Morula 2011). This report made many people believe that this project would fail. The Chinese could not understand why such an industrial project would draw so much public attention based on rumors. No local media investigated FYG to verify whether the reports were true. Instead, BDC, a state-owned company and the Chinese cooperation partner, became the spotlight. After all, the political struggle is the root cause.

In 1966 when Botswana declared its independence from the United Kingdom, the new national government implemented a Multiparty Parliamentary Democracy and Presidential Cabinet. The Botswana Democratic Party (BDP) has always been the ruling party, and the major oppositional parties include the Botswana National Front (BNF) and the Botswana Congress Party (BCP). Since independence, Botswana has remained politically stable, realized rapid economic development, and improved people's living standards. Thus, Botswana is hailed as a model of democracy and development in Africa. However, in recent years, the support rate of the Botswana Democratic Party has begun to fall, especially due to the fierce competition within BDP. In 2010, some politicians who held different political views from the Present Khama split from BDP and formed a new party with some members of the Parliament. This party is called Botswana Movement for Democracy (BMD), the first political party split from the ruling party. BMD is known as being committed to protecting and developing the power of the people, removing the current undemocratic phenomenon in government, and fighting against dictatorship.

The year 2013 was the election year in Botswana. As a new political party, BMD sought every opportunity to expand its influence, gained seats in the Parliament, and competed with BDP for power. The glass factory project would inevitably be a tool of political struggle in the country, with the media paying close attention. On December 1, 2011, BMD sent a report to BDP titled "Botswana Movement for Democracy Makes History in Botswana ----Botswana Development Corporation (Fengyue Glass Project) Motion." Its main intention was to promote the establishment of a Special Selected Committee in Parliament to investigate BDC and the glass factory project (Modise 2011). At the same time, the reports about BDC corruption and the tricks in the glass factory project reached a climax, as some media reported (Kavahematui 2011). However, there were little-known political purposes and struggles hidden behind these reports.

I cannot know the internal political struggle in Botswana, but the influence of political struggle on the glass factory project is obvious. First, the project in Botswana is well known to all, and most comments are negative. BDC is trapped in scandal swirls and has no time to care about this project. Second, the cooperation between the project and the local departments and suppliers is increasingly difficult since those negative reports discredited the project. Last, many people lose their confidence in the glass factory, and even the internal employees become anxious. All of these facts greatly influence and further delay the construction process of the glass factory. Eventually, the project was suspended at the end of 2011 because of a funding shortage.

Cultural Differences Between China and Botswana

After describing the project background and differences in the cooperation, this chapter tries to make a deeper analysis from the cultural and anthropology perspectives. All human activities are deeply rooted in culture. What is culture? As British anthropologist Tylor put it in 1871, "Culture or civilization, from a broad ethnology perspective, is a compound, including knowledge, belief, art, morality, law, custom and all the other abilities and habits acquired by social members." (Tylor 1871) This definition defines culture as a general term for all the human creations during social development, including material and technology, social system and human creations.

In the transnational glass factory, the employees come from different countries and have different cultural backgrounds, and the cultures are deeply rooted in real life. A transnational enterprise can succeed only by understanding and recognizing cultural differences and establishing a friendly work atmosphere. The "cultural differences" not only can be used to question the managers' assumptions of the "right" ways of doing things but also can encourage them to study new methods to solve the problems (Tian 2013). This chapter will focus on the social system and concept of spirit to analyze the cultural difference between China and Botswana.

Chinese Socialism Meets with Botswana's Democracy

The establishment of a social system is shaped by its special history, customs and values. China and Botswana have different social systems, but both have come out of poverty and become relatively wealthy countries during the rapid development of the last forty years. Botswana's democracy is praised as a model among African countries. With a system of socialism with Chinese characteristics, China's GDP has grown by 10 percent per year and developed into the world's second-largest economy, following America in 2008. But why do these two countries encounter so many difficulties and differences in the joint venture of the glass factory project?

On the premise of a state-controlled economic lifeline, China has undertaken radical changes in the last thirty years by developing a non-state-owned economy and introducing a market economy system. The theory of "socialism with Chinese characteristics" was put forward by Deng Xiaoping, the chief designer of China's reform and opening-up policy. It stresses that "poverty is not socialism," "making our economic development as our central task, liberating and developing productive forces," "Black or white: the good cat is mouse-catching," and "learning as we go." Even the capitalist system can be referred to, learned from and introduced as long as it is conducive to improving the productive force, national strength, and people's living standards. China's reform started with these policies.

But China's political system is still characterized by socialism. It adheres to the constitution that has inscribed the Communist Party as the only ruling party in the country and adheres to the system of multi-party cooperation and political consultation under the leadership of the Communist Party of China. Under this situation, economic interests become the ultimate goal. The improvement of all the aspects of the social system and rules is overlooked. This leads to a lack of power constraints and capital supervision. As a result, the Chinese people have developed a flexible ideology and practices to achieve the abovementioned objectives, including fair and foul means in pursuing economic interests.

The Chinese business activities in Botswana reflect Chinese characteristics, namely being unruly and flexible, taking the pursuit of interests as the sole objective, etc. These features lead to the local people's distrust of the Chinese. They take it for granted that there are tricks in whatever projects with Chinese participation, and so are their opinions and attitudes towards the glass factory project.

On the African continent, democratic systems have failed in many countries. People live in extreme poverty. Under this condition, the democracy in Botswana is particularly valuable and successful. According to the democracy index rankings of the Economist Intelligence Unit in 2011, Botswana ranked 33rd with a score of 7.63, ranking the third among the African countries（EIU 2011）. The per capita income in Botswana has always ranked the top among African countries, and the World Bank has already added Botswana to the "high and mid-income countries" list. Since 1998, Botswana has been chosen as the country with the least corruption in Africa by "Transparency International" many times. According to its latest statistics in 2011, the Corruption Perceptions Index of Botswana ranked 32nd in the world, still ranking 1st in Africa (China ranked the 75th in the world).

Why is it that Botswana can achieve such outstanding success? One of the factors is the country's social system. Botswana has developed and implemented a constitution that combines modern with traditional civilization and aligns with national situations. The constitution provides for the implementation of Multiparty Parliamentary Democracy and Presidential Cabinet. Meanwhile, it established the Council of Chiefs, whereby the status and powers of chiefs are retained at the grassroots, and disparate clans are integrated to create stability and unity. In tradition, the chieftain system in Botswana heavily emphasizes democracy. When tribal disputes or insignificant events occur, the chiefs hold tribal meetings where everyone is involved in the discussions and decision-making. It can be referred to as deliberative democracy. Until today, this tradition remains in the village.

However, this kind of deliberative democracy also has its negative aspect. Since whoever can speak in the decision-making, the power is too decentralized to concentrate and make quick decisions. This situation also occurs in the practical work of various government departments. In the Sino-Botswana glass factory project, Botswana could not keep up with the construction pace of the Chinese party. It could not provide supporting services such as water or electricity promptly, resulting in delays in the project. In short, although Botswana has a complete and sound system, it often demonstrates a lack of execution and low efficiency subject to the low educational levels of the nation and weak ability to adapt to the industrial society.

When "Time is Money" Meets "There Is No Hurry in Botswana"

Anthropologists frequently discuss different socio-cognitive attitudes towards time. Time is often viewed as a social construct rather than a natural existence. As Jack Goody (1991) says, "Although all societies have some time reckoning system, some idea of sequence and duration, the mode of reckoning varies with the political organization." Since China and Botswana have different natural and social environments, the modes of time reckoning in these two countries inevitably vary from each other.

Due to a large population of 1.3 billion people, China has very limited per capita resources despite being an industrial power. To achieve the goals of industrialization and modernization, the Chinese people work overtime from dawn to dust as if running against time. As a result, the time has come to be equated with money in Chinese culture. This is the attitude towards time in all industrial societies. However, African people's concept of time is still based on the requirements of the traditional society. As such, "African time" means that things happened when they happened, not when your timetable said they should or would happen.

In Africa, there is a saying, "Africans do not wait for time. Rather, time waits for Africans." People here always say that "There is no hurry in Botswana." there is no other pillar industry project in Botswana except for the diamond industry. Besides, it only has a small population of 2 million people who live comfortably with no threats from natural disasters, enjoying high welfare, free education and free medical care.

When China and Botswana cooperated to build the glass factory, there were a lot of conflicts in the attitudes towards time between the two parties. To the Chinese, time is money. But the Batswana are often unpunctual. Funding is delayed; supporting services cannot be kept up with; the appointments are always delayed or breached. These are closely related to the local people's concept of time. The Chinese people often complain that a similar glass factory project could be completed within one year in China, but it is still under construction after three years in Botswana. The loss of funding and rising costs during this period are immeasurable. Still, the Botswana people do not care or understand the importance of efficiency to industrial development.

Conclusion

Although the construction was suspended at the end of 2011 because of a funding shortage, the two parties renewed the agreement for additional funding at the beginning of 2012. The Botswana government does not want to give up this project because it is vitally important to develop a diversified economy and change the economic structure, which merely depends on exporting diamonds. President Khama promises the nation that the glass factory project will go ahead as planned and the government will guarantee its successful completion (Sefhako 2012). His promise helped stop the media hype that lasted for more than half a year.

Also, the Chinese seem to be relieved and see signs of hope for the project. Although both the Chinese and Botswana people are continuously adjusting themselves to bridge the gap between them – the Chinese, in particular, are trying their best to learn and meet rules and regulations in Botswana, the differences still exist between the two parties. Therefore, people cannot help wondering: can the glass factory be completed and produced? This project was again suspended in the middle of 2012 for lacking funding. The salaries of Chinese workers defaulted for a long time. The project was suspended. A large collection of equipment and materials were left unused. All the Chinese workers withdrew, leaving the whole company in dead silence. The local media also stopped their advocacy for this project.

The glass company started to clear the procedures for the coming two years, but the process was quite slow since Botswana wanted to find other investors to take over the company. According to the report on February 24, 2016, in "Overseas Chinese in Africa Weekly," a Chinese newspaper in Botswana, "The Sino-Botswana glass factory project that has cost over 500 million pula will be sold by auction this week. All the efforts for this project will be gone with the wind by then." (Piet 2016) This announced that the nine-year-old Sino-Botswana glass factory, which had been prepared for three years, constructed for three years and suspended for three years, was a complete failure.

What has been described as the glass factory project in this chapter is only the tip of the iceberg. The project has gone through so many setbacks and tests since the signing of the contract. Furthermore, one paper is far from enough to explicitly demonstrate the two parties' problems' complexity. Therefore, it does not mean much to overemphasize the result of the project. The awareness of differences the two parties face during the cooperation process matters. The key to the success of such a cross-boundary, cross-cultural and cross-social economic cooperative project is to find the mutual rules and implement them firmly. But the premise is to transcend the communicative barriers caused by language.

This chapter explicitly explored a failed investment of a Chinese company in Africa. The purpose is to show that Chinese companies should not be overconfident and over-optimistic in the backdrop of the "Going Out" strategy and "One Belt and One Road" initiatives. It should also be realized that money can't solve all the problems. After experiencing so many setbacks and failures overseas, Chinese companies need to face the conflicts of different institutions and cultures in different countries. These conflicts show that China's investment in Africa should be based on mutual benefit and trust and find the balance of bilateral interest rather than be based on individual interests. The Chinese should also not just work hard blindly. It is more important for them to learn the local rules and policies, culture and customs, pay attention to the cultural differences and reach a balance between the two cultures. The two parties can eliminate misunderstandings and conflicts and achieve common goals by balancing interests and cultural differences.

Chapter 10
Commercialization of Stone Pot Chicken in Klu-Nang of Tibet

From "Medog stone pot" to "Klu-Nang stone pot chicken," a geographically iconic restaurant has been formed in Nyingchi in Tibet. This article investigates and analyzes the commercialization process of Stone Pot Chicken and reveals that the commercialization of Stone Pot Chicken is the result of the integration of the local catering culture in Tibet and the inland catering cultures. This process shows that the formation of a catering culture is related to the local ecology. Religion, economy and other factors are inseparable from each other. The formation of Stone Pot Chicken culture integrates Tibetan and Han culture elements, revealing the historical logic of the formation of specific ethnic cultures. At the same time, the commercialization of Stone Pot Chicken shows the process of Tibet's economic modernization from one aspect. This process reflects the complex interaction of many social actors.

Introduction

While walking in Klu-Nang Town of Ninychi, Tibet, you can feel that Stone Pot Chicken is a unique restaurant here, which is difficult to be seen elsewhere in China. More than 30 specializing Stone Pot Chicken restaurants in the town alone. In addition to them, hundreds of inns are also operated as Stone Pot Chicken, which entertains a stream of visitors waiting outside. As a cooking tool, the stone pot was originally produced in Medog, and later it was introduced to Klu-Nang. It was combined with hot pot cooking from Chongqing, and the local ingredients in Nyingchi, forming a Stone Pot Chicken. From "Medog stone pot" to "Klu-Nang stone pot chicken," it undoubtedly demonstrates its commercialization process that is regarded as a success. It has become a local geographical indicator product of Klu-Nang, and the local competitive industry. Many stone pot chicken or other meat restaurants in other parts of China, far away from Klu-Nang, are branches of Stone Pot Chicken of Klu-Nang, or they could have been inspired by it. However, like food, its emerging and commercialization reflect the marketization process of a commodity and its cultural development. As Professor Waston of Harvard University pointed out, through the "lens" of food, almost all aspects of social and cultural characteristics and their changes can be observed (Guo 2006). From the perspective of the historical background of Tibet, with a strong traditional culture moving towards modernization, it is not difficult to see that the commercialization of "Stone Pot Chicken" of Klu-Nang is the epitome of Tibet's economic modernization. So what is the commercialization process of Stone Pot Chicken? As a "lens," can we observe the process of Tibet's modernization from its commercialization process? Is the commercialization of Stone Pot Chicken a process of adapting to local ecology, culture and economy? These are the questions that this article will address.

Chinese anthropological research focused on the food and beverage culture in the 1990s. It initially focused on food and beverage in a cultural sense, such as Wang Zhusheng (1998) on the Jingpo people's food and culture (Wang 1998). And then, the social significance of food and beverage was explored. For example, Zhang Zhanhong (2001) focused on the changes in traditional food against the impact of globalization and the changes in Hong Kong's lifestyle reflected in the production and sales of local traditional food represented by Hakka restaurants after World War II (Zhang 2001). Later there are regional historical researches that trace foods, such as research on salt (Huang 2006; Su 2009), sugar (Mu 2009), and tea (Xiao 2009). In recent years, research has focused on the use of food to explain regional cultural and social changes, such as Bouyei festival food and rice culture (Wei and Zhang 2018), roasted meat for ghosts used in Liangshan Yi religious rituals, and newly emerging barbecue banquet that reflects the process of homogenization and heterogeneity of the Yi people's dietary culture

(Wu 2017). Zhao Ya (2011) studied the cultural changes and development of Tibetan rural areas from the diet by field ethnography approach (Zhao 2001). Liu Zhiyang (2012) took the diet structure and customs of Tibetan rural communities as the starting point to explore the relationship between traditional culture and modernization that emerged in Tibetan rural communities in multicultural interaction and modernization. Qiang Ge (2015) explored the process of modernization of Tibet and changes in Tibetan food culture from the phenomenon that wheat gradually occupied the position of the staple food at dinner. However, as a product of cultural fusion, Klu-Nang Stone Pot Chicken, which has developed into a new symbol of local food culture, has not yet been studied. The commercialization of Klu-Nang Stone Pot Chicken is an important research topic from an anthropological perspective.

To fully understand the detailed process of the emergence and commercialization of Klu-Nang Stone Pot Chicken, the authors visited Klu-Nang Town in Nyingchi in June 2019. The field survey work was conducted in three ways. The first way is to interview operators of Stone Pot Chicken. The operators are the main market players that promote the commercialization of Stone Pot Chicken. They could better understand the needs and market trends of customers in the commercial circle and grasp the various economic and non-economic factors aggregated around Stone Pot Chicken to the customer's table. These factors are the key factors for us to understand the commercialization of Stone Pot Chicken. These interviewees mainly came from Klu-Nang Town and the nearby villages of Tsahisgang Village, Norbu Village, and DumpaTshal Village. The second way is to visit local officials, including local cadres and aid Tibet cadres and technical personnel. The former has his own experience and observations of the whole process of commercialization of Stone Pot Chicken, while the latter came from inland provinces of China and was dispatched to Tibet to work on a one- to three-year rotation and observed various local commercial activities and other economic activities from "others'" perspective. . The third way is to interview personnel engaged in tourism, transportation and other activities in the local area. Although they are not directly involved in the commercialization of Stone Pot Chicken, they have heard the story of Stone Pot Chicken or have tasted Stone Pot Chicken as customers, and sometimes they are more capable of conveying real information. From 2015 to 2018, the authors conducted surveys in Klu-Nang and accumulated a lot of first-hand information on the commercialization of Stone Pot Chicken.

The Origin and Commercialization Stages

Generally speaking, utensils, cooking methods, and ingredients are the three basic elements in food making. Stone Pot Chicken was firstly named after "Medog Stone Pot." As a starting point, the "Medog stone pot" was used for cooking local food ingredients with specific cooking methods. There was a very long history of using a stone pot as a cooking utensil in Medog.

The Origin of Stone Pot Chicken and Its Emerging Commercialization

According to the "Ethnic Dictionary," the stone pot is "a kind of cooking utensil commonly used by the Monba people, which is hand-chiseled. It is generally 20-30 cm high and 20-40 cm in diameter. The highest can reach 50 cm. It is approximately barrel-shaped, white and clean on the outside and hollow inside. The stewed food is delicious and is kept warm. The cauldron is mostly used for steaming and filtering wine." (Editorial Board of Ethnic Dictionary 1987). The stone pot is made of Medog's unique soapstone. This type of soapstone is mainly found in the three towns of Bangxin, Reesa, and Being in Medog County. In these three towns, the cliffs on both sides of the Yarlung Zangbo Basin have soapstones from 400 meters to 2000 meters. It is off-white, with a soft texture and strong plasticity. So it is fit for making living utensils. Although archaeologists discovered Neolithic polished stone tools in Medog in 1973, there is still no record of when the first stone pot appeared (Shang et al. 1978). According to the local legend, the modern stone pot was moved to Medog in the late 18th century. The

Moinba tribe invented it. It is said that the ancestors of the locals moved from Menu and Tawang to Pemagang, which is now Medog, because they could not bear the oppression and exploitation of the nobles at that time and were also hit by natural disasters such as strong earthquakes (Wu 1987). After the Monba people moved to Medog, they used the local soapstone to make stone pots. In addition to stone pots, they also make stone bowls, stone basins, stone buckets and other living utensils. Cooking utensils made of this soapstone can withstand high temperatures of 2000°C and have natural characteristics such as fast heat transfer, non-stick pan, and color change, and are very popular among Medog.

The transition from "Medog stone pot" to "Klu-Nang stone pot chicken" is due to the integration of Chongqing hot pot culture. The local people depicted He Baiyun, a person from Chongqing, who combined the Chongqing hot pot cooking method with the Medog stone pot to form the Stone Pot Chicken. We have talked with He Daiyun many times and knew that he followed his relatives to Klu-Nang for business in 1986. At first, he opened a casserole tofu shop in Klu-Nang, and the business was good. In 1997, when he traveled to Medog and was a guest at a villager's home, he tasted delicious cakes and soup cooked in a stone pot. He immediately bought a pot from the villager. It was transported back to Klu-Nang and used as a cooking utensil to cook the ingredients in Chongqing hot pot to form a dish. This is the first trial. Because He Daiyun opened a tofu shop, he originally used "Medog Stone Pot" to stew tofu to form "Stone Pot Tofu" instead of the previous "casserole tofu." The casserole tofu was also very popular with customers because of its good taste. Its popularity is related to the local natural environment. On the section of 318 State Road (Klu-Nang and Nyingchi through the Sejila Pass), which is 4,728 meters above sea level, traffic jams are common around the year. So to avoid traffic jams at Sejila Pass, most travelers choose to rest and eat in Klu-Nang. Passing business travelers have high-calorie requirements for food, so the casserole tofu became very popular. But it could not satisfy customers with the growing demands, and then the "Stone Pot Tofu" appeared. Since He Daiyun replaced the casserole with the stone pot, the restaurant he runs has put other ingredients into the stone pot, such as trotters, fish, Tibetan chicken, etc. It was found that the local Tibetan chicken in Klu-Nang was stewed as an ingredient and tasted better, and it was more popular with diners.

Based on the availability of ingredients, the requirements of "food" and "flavor" in the diet, Klu-Nang Stone Pot Chicken was finally formed. Since the Klu-Nang area is densely forested, there are various edible fungi such as palm ginseng and mats growing in the forest, which are more delicious after being added to the Stone Pot Chicken. So, the Klu-Nang Stone Pot Chicken uses Tibetan chicken as the main ingredient and wild mushrooms, palm ginseng, corymbs, and red dates as supplements. Moreover, Tibetan chicken is a special local product of Klu-Nang and is easy to buy. Later, it has become the geographical indicator of Nyingchi in Tibet.

The Stage of Commercialization of Klu-Nang Stone Pot Chicken

The commercialization of Klu-Nang Stone Pot Chicken, formed by the integration and development of multiple cultures, has gone through the following three stages:

The first stage is the initial stage of commercialization. Klu-Nang Stone Pot Chicken as a commodity sold to customers is the starting point of its commercialization. The national highway "318" is the basis for the commercialization of Stone Pot Chicken, and the communication and interactions between Tibet and the interior of China are the "engines." Because the "318" national highway built-in 1954 connects Tibet with the mainland, most of the passing vehicles from Chengdu choose Klu-Nang to stay overnight or rest. As a result, the catering industry and hotel service industry in Klu-Nang Town has become the pillar industries there. However, at this stage, the economic value of Stone Pot Chicken has not been revealed, but like other foods, it was just used to fill the stomach. The number of local Stone Pot Chicken businesses is small, and the scale is not large, but Stone Pot Chicken "Guoji" has gained a little reputation. For non-local people, including truck drivers, migrant workers, and soldiers, eating Stone Pot Chicken is just a natural choice after a day's hard work or driving. Therefore, Stone Pot Chicken only meets the needs of diners passing Klu-Nang, and this state has continued until around 2006.

The second stage is the initial development stage of Stone Pot Chicken. In 2006, Nyingchi Airport was completed and opened. The reconstruction and expansion of National Highway "318" led to the rapid development of tourism in Tibet. Tourism to Tibet has shown explosive growth, and tourists to Klu-Nang regard Stone Pot Chicken as an object that satisfies their curiosity. In this context, the commercialization of Stone Pot Chicken has got initial development. On the one hand, it is reflected in the continuous expansion of the business scale of Klu-Nang Stone Pot Chicken.

Moreover, it is reflected in the gradual transformation of Klu-Nang Stone Pot Chicken from popularization food to a tourist cultural symbol. It is not only a piece of food but also has additional cultural value. Klu-Nang Stone Pot Chicken has become the necessary item in various cultural tourism festivals and the 318 National Road exploring trip. From the field investigation in Klu-Nang, it is confirmed that there are more customers and higher rents operating stone pot chicken restaurants along 318 National Road in Klu-Nang Town.[1] Through the 318 national highway and the tourists' exploration tour, locals are scrambling to show this "original" lifestyle to tourists and obtain transaction value from it. As a result, many changes have taken place in residents' livelihoods. They have shifted from primitive and traditional livelihoods to commercial livelihoods, and the local economic development model has shifted from collection in a forest to eco-cultural tourism. Occupation choices have changed from self-sufficient traditional agriculture and animal husbandry to a modern market economy, and the modernity of economic growth has been rapidly

[1] Xinguang Stone Pot Restaurant and Luklang Stone Pot Chicken Headquarters in Luklang Town Large-scale stone pot chicken restaurants such as Luklang Shiguo wang Main Store, some small and medium-sized restaurants with better business in the town, and Luklang ethnic characteristic restaurants at the entrance of Tashigang Village are all opened on both sides of the 318 National Highway.

improved. This situation continued until the eve of the construction of the "Klu-Nang International Tourist Town," which was based on the emergence of the Stone Pot Chicken as a cultural symbol of tourism, coupled with the excellent natural scenery of Klu-Nang.

The third stage is that the Stone Pot Chicken has been regarded as a geographically iconic food in Nyingchi. This is the finalized stage of commercialization of Stone Pot Chicken. As the largest single-investment and aid project in Tibet,[1] "Klu-Nang International Tourist Town" played a "catalyst" role in the commercialization of Stone Pot Chicken. The symbol of its finalization is that Klu-Nang Stone Pot Chicken has been rearranged in cooking methods to combine Medog's stoneware culture, Klu-Nang foraging culture and inland culinary cultures, making it have both the taste and consumption level preferred by high-end consumers and ordinary people, thus forming the geographical landmark in food and beverage of Klu-Nang Town. Through Guangdong's support of Nyingchi's, the local business environment has been improved and developed. The "Klu-Nang International Tourism Town" was completed and put into operation. The Klu-Nang Tourism Management Committee, exclusively responsible for Klu-Nang business management, was established and operated. This has created excellent conditions for the commercialization of Stone Pot Chicken, which has entered the finalized stage of development. At this stage, the large-scale, standardized production and operation of Klu-Nang Stone Pot Chicken and its integration with the festival economy reflect modern production and management characteristics. With the commercialization of Klu-Nang Stone Pot Chicken, the stone cooking pot and ingredients have been commercialized simultaneously. The establishment of the Stone Pot Cultural Industry Company marked the completion of the commercialization of Stone Pot Chicken (and Stone Pot), which indicates that an industrial chain has been formed.

---

[1] The project has invested more than 3 billion yuan. See Yang Minghong: "The Large-scale Development of Tourism Resources and the Conversion of Farmers' Livelihoods: A Case Study Based on Tibet's "International Tourist Town"," Journal of Ethnology, Issue 3, 2017.

In short, the starting point of Stone Pot Chicken is the "Medog Stone Pot," which is an ordinary cooking utensil for the locals in Medog. It was passed to Klu-Nang and combined with Chongqing hot pot cooking technology to form the Stone Pot Chicken. After decades of commercialization, it has become a geographical indicator of food culture in Nyingchi. This process shows the details of the generation of catering culture, especially the combination of traditional culture and modernization. It also shows Tibet's economic modernization process from one perspective.

Characterization of Commercialization

The commercialization of Klu-Nang Stone Pot Chicken has combined Medog's stone pot and Chongqing's hot pot cooking methods with the ingredients represented by Tibetan chicken to form a geographically iconic catering. Through this historical process, it can be observed that the commercialization of Klu-Nang Stone Pot Chicken is manifested in the trend of standardization in operation and production. At the same time, the complete industry chain has been formed based on the commercialization of Stone Pot and food materials. The commercialization of Klu-Nang Stone Pot Chicken has the following characteristics.

The Localization of the Stone Pot Chicken Development

Commercialization based on localization is the "code." Although the "initiators" who promoted the commercialization of Stone Pot Chicken were outsiders, the initiation and promotion of its commercialization reflected the local characteristics. The Stone Pot Chicken, created by Chongqing native He Baiyun, became popular in Klu-Nang, attracting diners. As the number of diners increased, He Daiyun's stores continued to expand, and his relatives and friends from Chongqing were also hired to participate in the business. Initially, these relatives and friends only participated in the operation of Stone Pot Chicken as assistants. Later, driven by considerable profits and market prospects, these people were separated and gradually developed into independent Stone Pot Chicken restaurant operators. According to Liu Yang, manager of Klu-Nang Stone Pot Chicken head office,[1] many people who open stone pot chicken restaurants in the town are their relatives and friends, accounting for about 1/3 of the total number of stone pot chicken restaurants in Klu-Nang Town. This kind of business proliferation based on geographical and kinship relationships has enabled the first wave of developing Klu-Nang Town's Stone Pot Chicken catering market.

The economic prosperity and increase in employment brought about by the Stone Pot Chicken restaurants have attracted the attention of the local government, and the local government has adopted the strategy to promote the Stone Pot Chicken business among local people. The Stone Pot Chicken cooking training was provided to farmers and herders as a result. Since 2013, He Baiyun, the founder of Stone Pot Chicken, has been entrusted by the local government to hold two training courses on cooking stone pot chicken for farmers and herders in Nyingchi. Farmers and herders from Tashigang, Zhongmai, and Narmai villages, who run family hotels, have received training. At the same time, farmers and herders in the villages of Klu-Nang Town in Bayi District of Bayi Town received a one-month training in tourism services,[2] including training in Stone Pot Chicken cooking techniques. So, Stone Pot Chicken began its second market expansion based on family hotels. In addition to organizing training for local farmers and herders, the local government also invites national media for interviews and reports. After being interviewed and reported by CCTV's food-related programs, Klu-Nang Stone Pot Chicken has become more and more influential in the market. It has become a special delicacy that tourists must eat in Tibet. Driving factors such as the potential market demand and considerable commercial profits have prompted more local people to open Stone Pot Chicken restaurants. Correspondingly, the Klu-Nang Stone Pot Chicken market scale expanded for the third time. This scale expansion results

---

[1] Liu Yang is the nephew and partner of He Daiyun, the founder of Luklang's Stone Pot Chicken.

[2] In 2015, the State Council agreed to rename Nyingchi County to Bayi District.

from the localization of Stone Pot Chicken operations. In 2017, the "Klu-Nang International Tourist Town" was completed. The operators of Stone Pot Chicken were uniformly moved to the "Food Street" of the new town. Localized Stone Pot Chicken operators opened stores here one after another. They have more advantages in terms of employment, ingredients and corresponding dining culture, which greatly promote the localization of the Stone Pot Chicken management. Local operators and out-of-town operators live in harmony and compete with each other simultaneously, thus improving the cooking level of Stone Pot Chicken.

The localization of the commercial development of Stone Pot Chicken is also reflected in the localization of food supply. The main ingredient of stone pot chicken has always been the local special Tibetan chicken, and other auxiliary ingredients include mushrooms, vegetables, tofu, etc., which have long been local sources. Since the local area does not produce vegetables, many vegetables must be purchased from the urban area of Nyingchi, which is dozens of kilometers away. The Tibetan chicken, vegetables, and other ingredients used in these Stone Pot Chicken restaurants come from local people. In recent years, Klu-Nang Town has begun to develop greenhouse vegetable cultivation, and local people have gradually supplied potatoes, cabbage, radish and other vegetables. Due to the small number of food ingredients, the procurement method was mainly farmers' door-to-door sales. Larger Tibetan chicken restaurants would go directly to the village to purchase the ingredients. Later, with the rapid increase in the number of Stone Pot Chicken restaurants in Klu-Nang Town, Tibetan chicken and mushrooms sales have increased rapidly, and batch purchases of Tibetan chicken and mushrooms from farmers have become the norm. In June 2019, according to Liu Yang, the manager of Klu-Nang Stone Pot Chicken's main store, when the local Tibetan chicken and mushrooms are in short supply during the tourist season, they need to go to Lhasa and Shannan to buy them.

Standardization of Stone Pot Chicken Production

There is standardization behind commercialization because standardized production is convenient for forming a brand and the implementation of specialized division of labor, which saves costs and expands the scale of operations. In the commercialization process, Stone Pot Chicken, under the sustainable promotion of customer needs and localization of ingredients, has gradually matured in production, and a certain standard cooking process has been formed. The cooking process and the selection of ingredients and stone pots are the accumulation of the long-term experience of the chef. The "Klu-Nang Training Course for Farmers and Herdsmen in Nyingchi Prefecture" is the catalyst for the standardization of "stone pot chicken production." It provides trainees with a series of material standards, cooking process standards, stone pot standards, tableware standards, etc. According to the requirements of the local government, the instructor should compile his lectures into handouts or teaching materials. The instructor improves and summarizes the experience and further regulates the production of Stone Pot Chicken.

In addition to the standardization of cooking technology, the first step to standardizing Stone Pot Chicken production is the standardization of stone pot production. The original "Medog stone pot" was produced by local farmers and herdsmen. Therefore, there is no uniform standard for stone pots produced. The standardization of Stone Pot Chicken is bound to require a standardization of stone pot production, which appeared with the introduction of machine tools into the stone pot production process. In 2013, Medog County established the Shiguo Professional Cooperative in Bangxin Township, Medog County. In December 2017, Medog County Metuo Shiguo Cultural Industry Co. Ltd. was established. It enables large-scale production and makes standardization of pot production come true. The standardization of Stone Pot Chicken production has promoted the standardization of food ingredient production. The raising of Tibetan chickens is a good example. Since 2017, the Tibetan chicken raising in Klu-Nang Town has changed from free-range style by villagers to collective style by chicken farms. According to the standard, the chicken farms have been established at fixed-point places, and chickens are raised together at the base. Stongmjug and Lagdong were the two villages mainly engaged in Tibetan chicken production, and they set up two new standard sites for raising Tibetan chicken in 2019.

Integration of Stone Pot Chicken Industry Chain

The formation of an industrial chain is the result of industrial development. By integrating the industrial chain, economies of scale can be formed for greater profits. In the Stone Pot Chicken industrial chain, the production and operation of ingredients including "Medog Stone Pot" and Tibetan fragrant chicken have been integrated into an industrial chain. This is an important characterization of the commercialization of Stone Pot Chicken. The industrialization of the Medog stone pot is a process from individual labor to socialized production. The stone pot was only used as a local non-consumable daily necessity with little market demand. It was produced by Medog local craftsmen of the Monba ethnic group who used stone pot production as a sideline for their use.

On the one hand, the commercialization of Klu-Nang Stone Pot Chicken expanded the demand for stone pots. Shopkeepers of Stone Pot Chicken from Klu-Nang began to place bulk orders to stone pot producers in Medog County. On the other hand, it endows the stone pot as a key component with additional commercial value. Moreover, with the further excavation and dissemination of the functional value of Medog stone pots, such as heat preservation and health care, the potential consumer market of stone pots has been further expanded. The production of stone pots has begun to have the division of labor and cooperation in the form of production organizations. Individual labor is difficult to meet the expansion of unsocialized needs. For example, Gongjiu, a stone pot manufacturer, and his family opened a "Medog stone pot" company in Bayi Town. Nine brothers in his family are engaged in stone pot production and operation, each respectively responsible for soapstone mining, stone pot production and processing, transportation and sales, etc. The continuous expansion and market segmentation of the stone pot market have made machine processing widely used in stone pot production, and large-scale production of stone pots has come, which has brought innovations in the organization of production and management of stone pots. For example, the Shiguo Professional Cooperative of Bangxin Township, Medog County, and Medogite Culture Industry Co., Ltd. signed a soapstone agreement. This integrated business model of supply, production and marketing of stone pots with the "farmers + cooperatives + companies" model marks the maturity of the industrialization of stone pots.

The industrialization of Stone Pot Chicken ingredients results from the integration of the Stone Pot Chicken industrial chain. The development of the stone pot chicken catering industry has directly promoted the large-scale development of the breeding industry of Tibetan chicken, Tibetan pig, forest crops, and organic vegetables in Klu-Nang Town. The industrialization of Tibetan chicken also brought about agricultural equipment and technological development. Take vegetable cultivation as an example. Greenhouse facilities and technologies have been widely used in Klu-Nang Town. At the end of 2017, Lagdong Village, Klu-Nang Town, completed the construction of 12 collective greenhouses of 4,000 square meters. At the end of 2018, with Stongmjug Village and Lagdong Village taking the lead, Klu-Nang town had 45 greenhouses covering an area of 35.5 acres. In the process of industrialization of foodstuffs, various business models such as "company + cooperative + farmer" and "catering association + cooperative" have emerged, providing a foundation for the integrated development of agricultural and animal husbandry with local special products. According to our investigation, since 2017, Stongmjug Village and Lagdong Village of Klu-Nang Town have planted vegetables in greenhouses. They have contracted with the Klu-Nang Town Catering Association to set up "farming by orders."

Normalization of the Selling Price of Stone Pot Chicken

With the standardization of the cooking process, the sales price of Klu-Nang Stone Pot Chicken has gradually become standardized. According to our investigation, the Klu-Nang Stone Pot Chicken operators now use small, medium, and large pots as the general specifications for stone pot chickens, as quoted by some consumers. The small pot is suitable for 1-3 people; the middle pot for 4-6 people; the large pot for more than six people, and the price corresponds to the specifications. Currently, there are two main business models of Klu-Nang Stone Pot Chicken, namely, the exclusive operation model of Stone Pot Chicken Restaurant and the concurrent operation model with family hotels. For the first model, the basic price varies slightly according to the restaurant grade, but it is stable at the standard of small pot/280 yuan, medium pot/380 yuan, and large pot/480 yuan. The price is slightly lower in the family hotel mode than in the first mode. As shown in Table 1, among the 17 family hotels in Klu-Nang Town randomly surveyed, 14 sold stone pot chickens, 11 of which have the same price. The prices of the small pot, medium pot, and large pot are respectively 180, 280 and 380 yuan. Of course, this specification is relative because there will be certain differences in price under different business models. In general, the operation of Klu-Nang Stone Pot Chicken has formed a standard that is commonly used in the industry.

Table 10.1

Name of Family Hotel	Operating stone pot chicken (Yes/No)	The price of stone pot chicken(yuan/pot) (Small/Middle/Large)
Tianfu clause	No	-
Tired inn	Yes	180/280/380
Dabian Bus Family Hotel	Yes	300/500
Dean of the inn	Yes	180/280/380
Yang Jin Family Hotel	Yes	180/280/380
Degi Family Hotel	No	—
Dragon Valley Inn	Yes	200/300/400
Baima Joe Family Hotel	Yes	180/280/380

Punima Family Hotel	Yes	180/280/380
Zhuo Family Hotel	No	—
The Argachimei Family Hotel	Yes	180/280/380
SanjiZhuoma Family Hotel	Yes	180/280/380
CangJie Family Hotel	Yes	180/280/380
Pingcuo Smart Family Inn	Yes	180/280/380
Lamb Family Hotel	Yes	200/300/400
The Pinso Family Hotel	Yes	180/280/380
Zhong Mai Family Hotel	Yes	180/280/380

Source: Compiled based on the authors' field survey data from June 20, 2019, to June 24, 2019.

Branding of Stone Pot Chicken Management

Branding food ingredients is the primary form of Stone Pot Chicken management. Driven by the local catering industry represented by stone pot chicken, special agriculture and animal husbandry in Stongmjug, Lagdong, Balmo, Badkar, Klum, and other villages in Klu-Nang Town are gradually forming an integrated local market system for agricultural products and green supply of catering industry. Klu-Nang has formed a self-circulating economic cycle with Stone Pot Chicken as the core. Its agricultural and livestock production and sales are expanding, and external markets are being explored or exploited based on branding. According to the mayor of Klu-Nang Town, the local government regards geographical indicator certification as a breakthrough to promote the brand effect of Klu-Nang agricultural and animal husbandry products. To achieve this goal, locally produced organic vegetables are uniformly printed with the Klu-Nang IP logo, and some products with local characteristics such as forest resources, Tibetan medicine, agricultural and livestock products, natural drinking water, fruits, tea, and other products are also actively involved in the trademark strategy, striving to establish a brand with regional characteristics to comprehensively enhance the added value and influence of Klu-Nang agricultural and animal husbandry products. The external export of brands reflects the advanced stage of branding of Stone Pot Chicken management. After the stone pot chicken was launched in Klu-Nang Town, it quickly became popular in the Nyingchi area.

At present, there are three major ways of exporting Klu-Nang Stone Pot Chicken to other places: one is that outsiders learn Klu-Nang Stone Pot Chicken cooking skills by themselves and independently operate stone pot chicken restaurants in other places, such as the restaurant in the urban area of Nyingchi; second, the local operator in Klu-Nang opened another stone pot chicken restaurant outside of Klu-Nang, such as He Daiyun who opened a branch of stone pot chicken in Chongqing; third, outsiders join the operation of stone pot chicken, such as the franchise store of Klu-Nang Stone Pot Chicken head office in Shanghai. According to the data from Dianping.com visited, in July 2019, there were 124 Stone Pot Chicken stores just in the urban area of Nyingchi. The commercial coverage of Klu-Nang Stone Pot Chicken is not only in the Nyingchi area but has appeared in inland cities such as Chongqing, Chengdu, and Shanghai in recent years. According to Liu Yang, the current business focus of He Daiyun, the founder of Klu-Nang Stone Pot Chicken, has begun to shift. His son mainly operates the stone pot chicken shop in Klu-Nang Town, and He Daiyun brought Klu-Nang Stone Pot Chicken to Chongqing, starting a new commercial layout. They not only directly operate the Stone Pot Chicken branch in Chongqing but also participate in the franchise preparation of Stone Pot Chicken restaurants in Shandong, Shanghai, and Xinjiang. At present, three restaurants have successfully joined the operation. He Daiyun and Liu Yang provide authorization on the use of trademarks, guidance on cooking methods, and stone pot equipment and ingredients.

Inherent Adaptability of Commercialization

When studying the inheritance of dietary cultures in Asian societies and the localization of foreign diets, Appadurai et al. emphasized that the production, manufacturing, and marketing aspects of diet reflect the inclusive and complex relationship between global integration and localization (Appadurai & Arjun,1988; Allison & Anne, 1991; Wu &Tan, 2001; Bestor, 2004). The emergence and development process of

Klu-Nang "Stone Pot Chicken" also has a complex relationship of compatibility and tension between modernization and localization, associated with the adaptability in the commercial development process from "Stone Pot" to Stone Pot Chicken.

Cultural Adaptation of Stone Pot Chicken Commercialization Process

Catering is not only a part of people's material life but also a kind of culture. Take cooking utensils as an example. The emergence of cooking utensils gives food the two opposite concepts of "raw" and "cooked." Levi-Strauss pointed out that the former belongs to the category of "natural" and the latter belongs to the category of "cultural." For human beings, the container is not only a tool but also an object with cultural significance (Levi-Strauss 1978). Therefore, as a diet, the inherent adaptability arising from the emergence and development of Klu-Nang Stone Pot Chicken must be reflected in a certain social culture. Klu-Nang Stone Pot Chicken itself is a product of multicultural integration, and this process itself is a manifestation of cultural adaptability. As a multicultural diet, residents can accept it, which also requires corresponding cultural adaptation. This reveals the important reason why Klu-Nang Stone Pot Chicken is an "omnivorous food" that integrates multiple cultures, stands out from many local traditional foods and has become an important geographical landmark in the Nyingchi area.

Firstly, it interacts with other food cultures. Although Klu-Nang Stone Pot Chicken is named Klu-Nang, it is a meal formed by using a Medog stone pot as a cooking utensil, using the Chongqing hot pot cooking method and cooking ingredients grown in Klu-Nang Town. "Medog stone pot" represents Medog's cooking culture, and the cooking method is the embodiment of Sichuan and Chongqing food culture. Klu-Nang Stone Pot Chicken is the result of multi-cultural integration, and the smooth progress of cultural interaction and integration stems from the openness and tolerance of culture in the process of Tibet's modernization. After China's reform and opening up in the early 1980s, the number of merchants entering Tibet to engage in commerce and trade activities continued to increase, especially those from the Sichuan-Chongqing area adjacent to Tibet (Liu 1989). The process of the formation of Klu-Nang Stone Pot Chicken implies a process from the closed to the open presented by residents with the development of the economy. Cultural communication and blending are based on human beings, and the food culture is based on human material needs. Therefore, the population flow between inland China and Tibet is driven by economic development also promotes the flow and integration of the food culture of the two places. The increase in openness and inclusiveness makes the local culture willing to accept and absorb the foreign culture, reflecting residents' modernity.

Secondly, the religious adaptability in food culture has increased. Among the many folk cultural items, food culture has the dual characteristics of material culture and spiritual culture. At the same time, food folklore is also the most lively. When people talk about food culture tradition, it is not a dogma but the result of people adapting to a specific environment under a certain time and space background (Wu 2001). Like the commercial development trend of Stone Pot Chicken, Klu-Nang's local food culture has also experienced the integration of "tradition" and "modern" in time and space of modernity. Among them, the part that conforms to the value orientation of modernity will be retained or naturally developed. The part that contradicts it will gradually disappear or be consciously downplayed by people.

Of course, this process is not a simple replacement of tradition by modernity, but rather that people continue to improve their openness of thought and tolerance to different cultures in the time and space environment that has been developed. On this basis, we need to compare the "other" and examine the "self," reposition one's material and spiritual needs, re-evaluate the value of traditional culture, and then make new choices.

As we all know, the production of Stone Pot Chicken involves the slaughter of live chickens, which conflicts with the taboo of killing in Tibetan Buddhism tradition. After the Stone Pot Chicken Catering

Management Training Course was offered to farmers and herders, residents of Klu-Nang continuously entered the business of Stone Pot Chicken catering. It made residents choose between "making money" and conservative religious dogma. Especially the family hotel and Stone Pot Chicken operators are mainly local Tibetan farmers. The religious adaptability they embodied in operating Stone Pot Chicken is divided into two types: one is to adapt to the commercial development of Stone Pot Chicken by breaking religious precepts to a certain degree. Take the Da Pemba Family Hotel in Narmai Village, Klu-Nang Town, as an example. The hotel owner Pemba believes in the Yellow Sect of Buddhism, which has the strictest precept on killing. His approach is to avoid killing a chicken on religious holidays. According to the Yellow Sect, Pemba said that they neither kill nor eat meat during the whole month of April in the Tibetan calendar. Once April is over, it is allowed to kill, eat, and sell "Stone Pot Chicken." The other is to resolve the conflict between religious beliefs and commercial profits through modern business methods. Starting in 2017, Klu-Nang Town established a chicken farm to raise Tibetan chickens at designated locations. Under this model, the farm is responsible for slaughtering chickens and uniformly delivering them to family hotels. As far as the local Tibetans are concerned and as long as the Tibetan chickens were not killed by themselves, they did not violate the religious precepts, thus solving the contradiction between religious beliefs and commercial profits.

The above two situations are manifestations of religious adaptation shown in the modernization process. The former uses religious breakthroughs to dilute the influence of religious beliefs on modern production methods. At the same time, the latter separate religious beliefs from the production methods to avoid conflict between the two. Both of these situations are examples of adaptability and development when the regional community's religious culture and modernization collide in modernization. Of course, some residents choose to simplify the way of observing religious precepts. For example, they choose the method of no killing when the date is "1, 3, 5" and its multiples. In the commercialization of Stone Pot Chicken, sporadic breakthroughs have converged into a secularized transformation of the religious life of local Tibetan residents. This is one of the impacts of the commercialization of Stone Pot Chicken.

Thirdly, there are memories of food culture. Some dietary anthropology researchers regard food as a kind of memory. For example, "the memory of food is the so-called 'habit memory,' a special 'memory on the tip of the tongue" (Peng 2013). Food is the result of a nation's historical and cultural choices. No matter how the folklore subjects change in space, once the memory of food is formed, it will be run through one's whole life like a shadow (Wang 2016). Still, at the same time, for individuals, food lets them participate in body feelings and the construction of experience through sense organs. The local special-featured catering is the "physical image" of the local food culture. When tourists try to perceive and experience local culture through catering, specialty food products related to the place become the local catering culture. At the same time, food memory will further deepen the "food image" of food in the culture. Thus the local catering culture would be transited to commercialization, "forming a series of commercial, economic activities with catering as the core, culture as the expression, and ethnicity as the characteristic, to promote tourism." The eating memory contained in food makes it easier for the locals to accept and promote it as local culture. Therefore, the Stone Pot Chicken, which has evolved from the integration and development of multiple cultures, can be regarded as the representative of local food culture recognized by the locals with the stone pot, Tibetan fragrant chicken, and mushroom with the memory of Tibetan special diets.

In short, the emergence of Klu-Nang Stone Pot Chicken and its commercialization process both reflect the enhancement of cultural adaptability in Tibet's modernization. This shows not only the gradual increase in cultural tolerance and openness and the interaction, integration, and development of food culture but also the secularization of local people's religious life in the modern economy and the transition of local food and beverage culture to commercialization.

Ecological Adaptation of Stone Pot Chicken Commercialization Process

The food system is not only a choice system for material survival but also a special cognitive system or a cooperative system that complements the ecological environment (Peng and Xiao 2011). In other words, choices of related materials, including food, utensils, and cooking methods, must be compatible with the local natural environment and have ecological adaptability to achieve social reproduction with natural resources. Klu-Nang Town is located in the southeast corner of Tibet, with an average elevation of 3,700 meters, a cold climate, and thin air. The special geographical location and harsh climatic conditions to a certain extent, determine the unique eating habits of the local Tibetans. Therefore, the commercialization process of Stone Pot Chicken shows a certain ecological adaptation.

On the one hand, the emergence of Stone Pot Chicken is a manifestation of the ecological adaptability of the local people in the choice of life tools. The stone pot can cook ingredients that can only be cooked in a pressure cooker. Due to the restrictions in high-altitude areas, the boiling point of water is lower than 100°C, so ordinary cooking tools cannot cook food. In addition, saponite, the raw material of stone pot, is rich in a variety of microelements required by the human body and has certain health-preserving properties (Huang and Lv 2011), which can meet people's needs for a healthy diet. The soapstone pot, which has fast heat transfer, slow heat dissipation, and pressure cooker performance, is a manifestation of the ecological adaptation of residents.

On the other hand, the commercialization of Klu-Nang Stone Pot Chicken stems from the sustainable supply of food resources. As the main material, the stone pot chicken is unique to the local area and can be raised in large numbers in local forests, which ensures the availability and sustainability of the supply of this food material and the existence and sustainability of the Stone Pot Chicken as a cultural symbol. Therefore, stone pot, Tibetan fragrant chicken and mushrooms have become the three standard items of Klu-Nang "stone pot chicken," deriving from the ecological adaptability that matches the local natural environment. This is the basis for the commercialization of Klu-Nang Stone Pot Chicken.

Economic Adaptation of Stone Pot Chicken Commercialization

Anthony Giddens believes that the emergence of modernity is, first of all, a modern economic order (Luo 2007). From a relative perspective, economic modernity can be seen as the changes in the external economic environment of mankind. Economic adaptation is the adaptability and development of local communities under the impact of changes in the external economic environment during the modernization process. Klu-Nang Stone Pot Chicken is both a delicacy and a commodity. It appeared in the early 1990s and entered the market as a commodity, and began to be commercialized at pace with China's reform and opening up. Therefore, the commercialization of Klu-Nang Stone Pot Chicken is also a process for residents and local migrants to adapt to changes in the external economic environment and the construction of modern economic order.

The first economic adaptation is to comply with the general trend of Tibet's opening to the outside world. In the 1980s, many people from Sichuan, Chongqing and other places entered Tibet for work and business. Due to low capital investment, low technical thresholds, and low cultural requirements, wholesale and retail, transportation and other business services have become the preferred industries for many migrant workers in Tibet. The regional aggregation of the population has caused rapid growth in consumer demand, thus creating conditions for the commercialization of stone pot chicken. The business experience of He Daiyun in Tibet, from "casserole tofu" to Stone Pot Chicken, illustrates this point. When he entered Nyingchi in early 1986, there were few restaurants on the 230-kilometer highway from Bomi County to Bayi Town, and his customers were only truck drivers running along National Highway 318. Owing to Tibet's opening to the outside world, Klu-Nang Town, which is uniquely located, has become a good location for catering operations.

The second adaptation is the interaction of culture and tourism. In the new century, the main customers of Klu-Nang Stone Pot Chicken have shifted from truck drivers to tourists, which means that Klu-Nang Stone Pot Chicken has transformed from serving specific types of consumer groups to serving mass diners and thus entered the commercialization stage. Through local commercial packaging and promotion, it is regarded as a part of the local food culture and presented to the public as a local business place card embodied with local characteristics. After decades of market selection and competition, it developed from an original soup pot restaurant to a large-scale industry that now spreads throughout Klu-Nang town and the famous Nyingchi Street market. This is inseparable from the development of local tourism.

The prosperity of the tourism industry has provided a relatively stable source of tourists for the commercialization of Klu-Nang Stone Pot Chicken. The central government arranged guangdong and Fujian provinces to assist Nyingchi since 1994. They were optimistic about the prospects of Nyingchi's tourism development and focused their efforts on this area. Especially in 2011, as the largest province in China that assists Nyingchi, Guangdong Province implemented the “Klu-Nang International Tourist Town” construction project. After its completion in March 2017, it received 110,000 tourists and achieved a total tourism income of 6.45 million yuan in that year. In 2018, Klu-Nang Town received 240,000 tourists and realized a total tourism income of 6.97 million yuan.

The third adaptation is the implementation of industrialized production methods. As a commodity, Klu-Nang's “Stone Pot Chicken” displays the scale and standardization of commercialized production and management. Its economic adaptation can be found in forming its industrial chain, which demonstrates modern industrialized production thoughts. Klu-Nang Stone Pot Chicken has evolved from the initial hand-made and small-scale operation to a large-scale operation with standardized cooking procedures and brand management. Later, it became a leading local industry. This shows that its commercialization process is the infiltration of modern industrial ideas. The commercialization of Stone Pot Chicken has led to the industrial development of Medog Stone Pot and Stone Pot Chicken ingredients. It has formed the integrated industrialization of supply, production and marketing of Stone Pot with the model of "farmers + cooperatives + companies." The Tibetan chicken and other food materials have also been industrialized, promoting the advancement of planting and feeding technology in local farming and animal husbandry. These characteristics that embody the thought of industrialization indicate that the operators of Klu-Nang Stone Pot Chicken adapt to the development of the market economy.

In short, the commercialization process of Klu-Nang stone pot chicken is a microcosm of the development of Tibet's economic modernization. It is a result of its adaptation to the modern development of Tibet's economy. On the one hand, the transformation of production methods has turned diet activities from a family basis into a commercial one. On the other hand, the flow of people and logistics in the development of the market economy provides the necessary material conditions and markets for its commercialization, enabling it to interact with market and tourism consumers. Therefore, the commercial performance of Klu-Nang Stone Pot Chicken also carries the characteristics of Tibet's economic modernization.

Conclusion

A panoramic display of the commercialization process of Klu-Nang "stone pot chicken" is a clear demonstration of the social adaptability of the local community in the face of external impact. Therefore we can see that the transformation from "Medog stone pot" to "Klu-Nang stone pot chicken" is the process of economic modernization in Tibet. In the process of modernization, the interaction between "old" and "new," "tradition" and "modern" is constantly increasing, and the collision and adaption within the society continue to occur in daily life, which constitutes the history of social change. Food is closely related to human survival and social development. By tracking the trade and flow of food between regions, anthropologists can combine observations of communities with the penetration of external capitalism, looking for collisions of external forces, adaptive changes and the development of communities in such collisions (Peng and Xiao 2011). The emergence and commercialization of Klu-Nang Stone Pot Chicken is a projection of this process in reality.

Klu-Nang Stone Pot Chicken is a reproduction of food culture. From the "stone pot" embodied in the traditional stoneware culture of Nyingchi to the Klu-Nang Stone Pot Chicken, which is one of the current symbols of Nyingchi food culture, it reflects the fluidity nature of food culture, which is the result of cultural convergence. The flow and aggregation of culture is an unstoppable historical torrent. Still, the specific picture presented in this process is based on social development background and presents different manifestations. The emergence and commercialization of Klu-Nang Stone Pot Chicken are based on the historical background of Tibet's economic modernization, making its commercialization obvious characteristics of commercialization under the conditions of the Chinese socialist market economy.

Similarly, in the interactive process of modernization and localization, the commercialization process of Klu-Nang Stone Pot Chicken is more embodied in the inherent adaptability of society rather than exclusion. Based on diet, the social adaptation and development of culture, ecology, and economy constitute not only the commercialization of Klu-Nang stone pot chicken but also a corner of the process of modern social changes in Tibet. This shows that in the process of modernization, social development promotes multicultural interaction, aggregation and development, and the result of cultural aggregation and development further promotes economic and social development under the effect of its inherent adaptability. The aggregation of multiple cultures and social development promote each other. The commercialization process of Klu-Nang Stone Pot Chicken shows the interaction and aggregation of multiple dietary cultures and, at the same time, being a primary local specific cultural form. It reveals the logic of the formation of specific ethnic cultures.

Epilogue

Jenny Banh

When the editors Chen Gang and Tian Guang of the *International Business Anthropology Journal* asked me to write this Foreword, I was delighted, honored and humbled. This book, *Business Anthropology: New Progress in China*, is a much-needed intervention in Anthropology and China studies. Perhaps they asked me because—as a Chinese American Anthropologist who edited the book *American Chinese Restaurants: Society, Culture and Consumption* (Routledge 2019)—I am also betwixt and between Anthropology and China studies.

What inspired me to edit the book was my background as a Chinese restaurant kid in Belleview, Illinois. We owned an American Chinese restaurant and lived in a sea of typical African and Anglo-American Midwesterners. But little did I know that this would lead to my work in Business Anthropology. The task of Business Anthropology is to adapt anthropological methods for the betterment of businesses, and I see Chinese restaurant families doing this all over the world to survive. I have traveled to 35 countries, and one of the first things I do is to visit Chinese restaurants to see how those families adapt and solve problems in those new countries. Every little kid in these families is an applied anthropologist who is tasked with solving problems to help their families. Americans like fried things with gravy, and Chinese restaurants sell things like egg foo young and pupu platters. As Chef Martin Yan says, "You sell people what they want to eat."

Every day since age 8, I have taken food orders and helped my family by translating what my primarily African-American and Anglo-American customers wanted. That included St. Paul Sandwiches or Egg Foo Young. There were good times when I felt so much older than my age, and I helped my parents solve problems. But there were also bad times when we were subjected to racism. I would change my persona based on the customer and social situation. Years later, in my Ph.D. studies, I learned that what I did was called "*code-switching.*" Code-switching means changing or shifting my language and persona, depending on who I was with or the conversational setting. When I took the orders of African American customers, I would be friendly and gracious. And they were always kind and warm to me. When Anglo-American customers committed macro/microaggressions, I ignored it and never told my parents what they said to me. In the company of my parents, I had to be the dutiful Cantonese daughter in the Confucian sense of always honoring my parents even though they were often sullen. As ethnic Chinese refugees from Vietnam, my dad and mom were severely traumatized when they had lost their class privilege. At Catholic school, I had to become the premier student, follow the nuns and priests, and then go back to being the dutiful daughter at home. I code switched three times a day.

This background led me to declare that I wanted to be an anthropologist at age eight. Or was it the endless *Star Trek* and *National Geographic* shows that I watched as a child? One thing I learned that is central to Anthropology is that culture is important and culture directs how you do things. There is a culturally relevant reason that people do important things to understand.

In China and throughout Asia, a common greeting when you meet up with a friend is, "Have you eaten rice yet?" [sihk jófaahnmeih a? 食咗飯未呀?] Which is somewhat the equivalent of asking "How are you?" in English, but to the Chinese, the question means so much more. In Asian contexts of famine, warfare and strife, to be asked, "Have you eaten?" is a sign of caring and concern. Treating someone to a meal is an extremely common practice among the Chinese, especially done by elders for the younger generation. Quite simply, food is the Asian love language. Having been a Chinese restaurant kid, this resonated with me deeply.

There are some people who would consider me a food-business anthropologist, but I consider myself to be undefined. However, I do use food as an entryway into investigating many transnational corporate practices. I ask, "Is the business selling culturally acceptable food to the consumer?" If it is not acceptable, what are ways the business can adjust to meet the cultural expectations of taste, price point and service? I find these skills that I learned as a Chinese restaurant kid very applicable to Business Anthropology.

This is why this book is so important—because it sheds light on Business Anthropology in China. China is one of the oldest civilizations in the world, and we can learn a great deal when we study how business is practiced in China. Transnational corporations that hope to conduct their businesses successfully in China would do well to study the lessons this book offers.

Jenny Banh

Associate Professor of Asian American Studies and Anthropology

California State University, Fresno

Author of "*I Have an Accent in Every Language I Speak*!": Shadow History of One Chinese Family's Multigenerational Transnational Migrations" *Genealogy* 3, no. 3: 36.https://doi.org/10.3390/genealogy3030036

Co-editor Anthropology of Los Angeles (Lexington, 2017) and American Chinese Restaurants (Routledge, 2019)

References

Aaker, D. A. 1991. *Managing Brand Equity: Capitalizing on the Value of a Brand Name*. New York, NY: Free Press.

Aaker, D. A.1996. *Building Strong Brands*. New York, NY: The Free Press.

Aaker, D. A. 2004. *Brand Portfolio Strategy: Creating Relevance, Differentiation, Energy, Leverage, and Clarity*. New York, NY: Free Press.

Aall, Pamela R. 1996. *NGOs and Conflict Management*. Washington, D.C.: United States Institute of Peace.

Alden, Chris. 2007. *China in Africa*, London: Zed Books.

Aldrich, Howard & Roger Waldinger. 1990. Ethnicity and Entrepreneurship. *Annual Review of Sociology*, Vol. 16:111-135.

Alexander J., Alexander P. 1994. Gender Differences in Tobacco Use and the Commodification of Tobacco in Central Borneo. *Social Science and Medicine* 38: 603–8.

Allen, A. J. 1985. Economic Anthropology. Translated by Tian Guang. *World Nations* 20 (4): 30-38.

Allison, A. 1991. Japanese Mothers and Obentsos: The Lunch-Box as Ideological State Apparatus. *Anthropological Quarterly* 64: 195–208.

An, Hexin, and Li, Zhe. 2013. A Study on Management of Customers' Experience with Classic Brands. *Management World* 2: 182-183.

Appadurai, A. ed. 1988. How to Make a National Cuisine: Cookbooks in Contemporary India. *Comparative Study of Society and History* 30 (1): 3–24.

Baba, M. 2006. Anthropology and Business. In *Encyclopedia of Anthropology,* edited by H James HJ Birx, 83-117. Thousand Oaks, CA: Sage Publications.

Baba, M. L. 2014. De-Anthropologizing Ethnography: A Historical Perspective on the Commodification of Ethnography as a

Business Service. In *Handbook of Anthropology in Business*, edited by Rita Denny and Patricia Sunderland, 43-68. New York, NY: Left Coast Press.

Babalola A. 1989. The Economic Behavior of Commercial Flue-cured Tobacco Farmers in the Oyo-North Division Nigeria. *Odu* 36:198–210.

Baer G. 1995. The Role of Tobacco in the Shamanism of the Matsigenka, Eastern Peru. *Acta Amazonica* 3:101–16.

Baleseng, Batlotleng. 2011. Minister Explains Appointment of New Board. Daily News, Tuesday, November 22, No 220: p. 2.

Balise, Joseph. 2011. BDC Glass Project Raises More Questions Than Answers." Sundaystandard News, June 26- July 2.

Balise, Joseph. 2011. DCEC Pounces on BDC Amid Alleged Corruption Reports. Sundaystandard News, October2-8.

Bao W. M. 1998. *Jiangnan Town and Its Modern Destiny (1840-1949).* Beijing: The Knowledge Publishing House.

Bao, L. 2020. Dulong Township of Gongshan County: the Mountains Unchanged but the World Changed. *Lujiang Grand Valley Website*. https://www.nujiang.cn/ 2020/1001/ 81745.html, accessed January 2, 2022.

Berry, Norman C. 1998 Revitalizing Brands. *Journal of Consumer Marketing* 5: 15-19.

Bestor, T.C. 2004. Tshuiji: *The Fish Market at Center of the World.* Berkeley, CA: The University of California Press.

Bian, Yianjie. 1998. Making Sense of China's Transformations. *Contemporary Sociology* 29: 613-624.

Bourdieu P. 2003. *Le Senspratique.* Translated by Jiang Z.H. Nanjing: Yilin Press.

Braudel F. 1993. *Civilisation Materielleeconomieet Capitalism XVe-XVIIIe siècle, tome 2*, Translated by Shi K. Q. Beijing: Joint Publishing.

Brown, Stephen, Kozinets, Robert V, and Sherry, John F. 2003. Teaching Old Brands New Tricks: Retro Branding and the Revival of Brand Meaning. *Journal of Marketing* 67: 19-33.

Cai, J. 2000. *Collection of Primitive Religion Information of all Nationalities in China: Dulong Volume*. Beijing: China Social Sciences Press.

Cameron D, Jones I.G. 1985. An Epidemiological and Sociological Analysis of the Use of Alcohol, Tobacco and Other Drugs of Solace. *Journal of Public Health* 7:18–29.

Cao H. L. 2005.Public Space in Rural Changes: a Study on the Reconstruction of the Village Order- Taking Yao village in North Jiangsu. *China Rural Survey* 6:61-73.

Casta-neda H, Nichter M, Muramoto M. 2008. Enabling and Sustaining the Activities of Lay Health Influencers: Lessons from a Community-Based Tobacco Cessation Intervention Study. *Health Promotion Practice* 11:483–92.

Caulkins, D. Douglas, and Ann T. Jordan, ed. 2013. *A Companion to Organizational Anthropology*. Malden, Massachusetts: Wiley-Blackwell.

Chan, Kwok Bun & Claire Chiang See Ngoh. 1994. *Stepping Out: The Making of Chinese Entrepreneurs*. Simon & Schuster (Asia) Ltd.

Chan, Kwok Bun.1991. *Smoke and Fire: Montreal Chinese*. Chinese University of Hong Kong Press.

Chen, G., & Guo, R. 2015. Business Anthropology Study on Transnational Operation: Based on the Case of a Chinese Enterprise in Southeast Asia. *The Journal of Beifang University of Nationalities* 3: 104-109

Chen, J. 2017. The Dulong People in Southern Himalayan Cultural Belt: An Anthropological Research into the Survival Strategies of Human Groups in Zomia. Ph.D. dissertation Yunnan University.

Chen, X.W. 2019. Protect and Play the Function of the Village, Build a Community of Shared Future in Cities and Village. Entrepreneur Daily 2019-09-20 (008).

Chen, Zhongping. 2001. The Origins of Chinese Chambers of Commerce in the Lower Yanzi Region. *Modern China* 27 (2): 155-201.

Chen, G., and Zhou, D. 2013. Editorial Commentary: The Rise of Business Anthropology in China. *International Journal of Business Anthropology* 4(1):11–14.

Chinese Ministry of Foreign Affairs. 2018. Bilateral Relations Between China and Botswana. *Ministry of Foreign Affairs of the People's Republic of China Website*, http://www.fmprc.gov.cn/chn/gxh/cgb/zcgmzysx/fz/1206_4/1206x1/t6498.htm, accessed June 24, 2018.

Chow, Nelson W.S. 2000. Socialist Welfare with Chinese Characteristics: The Reform of the Social Security System in China. Hong Kong: Centre of Asian Studies. The University of Hong Kong.

Chuanchuang, Bangfu. 2011. *China Tobacco's World*. Translated by Zhang Jing. Bejing: The Commercial Press.

Da Silva, T. and Duguid, P., ed. 2010. *Trademarks, Brands and Competitiveness*. London, UK: Routledge.

Daley CM. 2006. Tobacco Has a Purpose, Not just a Past: Feasibility of Developing a Culturally Appropriate Smoking Cessation Program for a Pan-tribal Native Population. *Medical Anthropology Quarter* 20:421–40.

Damon A. 1961. Constitution and Smoking. *Science* 134 (3475):339–41.

De Waal Malefyt, Timothy, and Robert J. Morais, ed. 2017. *Ethics in the Anthropology of Business: Explorations in Theory, Practice, and Pedagogy*. New York, NY: Routledge.

De Waal Malefyt. Timothy and Morais, R. 2012. *Advertising and Anthropology Ethnographic Practice and Cultural Perspectives*. New York, NY: Berg.

Denny, Rita and Patricia L. Sunderland. 2014. *Handbook of Anthropology in Business 1st Edition*. New York, NY: Routledge.

Dev, Chekitan S and Keller, Kevin Lane. 2014. Brand Revitalization. *Cornell Hospitality Quarterly* 55(4): 333-341.

Dikarabo Ramadubu. 2011. How the Chinese Trickled BDC. Botswana Guardian, November 11.

Dong, H.L. 2014. On the Political Governance of Northwest Ethnic Regions Led by the CPC after the Western Development. Ph.D. dissertation, Lanzhou University.

Drabek, A. Gordon ed. 1987. Development Alternatives: The Challenge for NGOs. *World Development* 15, special issue.

Durkheim, E., and S.Lukes. 2014. *The Division of Labor in Society.* New York: Free Press.

Economic and Commercial Counsellor's Office of the Embassy of China in the Republic of Botswana. 2012. The First Quarter of 2012 Witnessed Over 100 Million US Dollars of Sino-Botswana Bilateral Trade Volume. http://bw.mofcom.gov.cn/article/jmxw/201206/ 20120608197847. Shtml, accessed June 26, 2018.

Economist Intelligence Unit. 2011. The Democracy Index 2011: Democracy Under Stress. http://www.eiu.com//public/topical_report.aspx?campaignid=DemocracyIndex2011, accessed January 2, 2022.

Editorial Board of Ethnic Dictionary. 1987. *National Dictionary.* Shanghai: Shanghai Dictionary Publishing House, 08:229.

Estes, Richard J. 1998. Emerging Chinese Foundations: the Role of Private Philanthropy in the New China. *RDS: Regional Development Studies* 4: 165-180.

Fairbank K. J. 2008. *The United States and China.* Translated by Zhang L. J. Beijing: World Knowledge Press.

Fan S. Z. 2005. *Jiangnan Town: Traditional Transformation*. Shanghai: Fudan University Press.

Fan, X. Q. 2009 Economic Anthropology Research in China. *Journal of Huaihua University*, 28 (12): 21-24.

Fei X. T. 1992. *From the Soil: The Foundations of Chinese Society.* Berkeley: University of California Press.

Fei X. T. 2001. *Peasant Life in China*. Shanghai: The Commercial Press.

Fei X. T. 2003. Some Confessions about "Cultural Consciousness." *Academic Research* 7:31-33

Fei X. T. 2004. *Anthropology and Cultural Awareness*. Nanjing: Huaxia Publishing House.

Fei X. T. 2019. *Rural Recovery*. Beijing: China International Trust and Investment Corporation Press.

Fox, A.T. 1987. NGOs from the United States. *World Development* 15(1): 11-19.

Francois, P., & MacLachlan, D. L. 1995. Ecological Validation of Alternative Customer-Based Brand Strength Measures. *International Journal of Research in Marketing* 12(4): 321–332.

Franklin, Adrian 2002 Consuming Design: Consuming Retro. In *The Changing Consumer: Markets and Meanings*, 90-103. Edited by S. Miles, A. Anderson, and K Meehan. London: Routledge.

Franz, T. R.1987. The Role of NGOs in the Strengthening of Civil Society. *World Development* 15 (1): 121-128.

Freedman, Maurice. 1958. *Lineage Organization in Southeast China*. London: Athlone Press.

Freedman, Maurice. 1966. *Chinese Lineage and Society: Fukien and Kwangtung*. London: Athlone Press.

Freeman, Carla. 2000. *High Tech and High Heels in the Global Economy: Women, Work, and Pink-Collar Identities in the Caribbean.* Durham, North Carolina: Duke University Press.

Fu, Y. 2015. Entering Mysterious Dulong River in Yunnan. *Chinanews Website*. http://www.chinanews.com/tp/hd2011/2015/11-13/581050.shtml, accessed January 2, 2022.

Galletto, V. 2008. Distritos Industriales Innovacion. *Mediterraneo Economico* 13: 117–137.

Gao, Q. 2015. Study on Public Opinion Express Ways in Social Management among Dulong People. MA Thesis, Minzu University of China.

Gao, Z. 2003. The Brief Study of the Origins of Dulong and Nu Peoples. In *Collection of Historiography Essays, Volume 9*, edited by the Department of History of Yunnan University, Kunming: Yunnan University Press.

Golas, Peter J. 1977. Early Ch'ing Guilds. In *The City in Late Imperial China*, edited by G. William Skinner. Stanford, CA: Stanford University Press.

Gong G. 2001. The Development of Markets in North China in Modern Chinese History. *Modern Chinese History Studies* 1:141-167.

Gong, Guiying 2004. Situation and Development Strategy of Classic Brands in Beijing's Catering Industry. *China's Food* 4: 18-21.

Goody, Jack. 1991. Time: Social Organization. *International Encyclopedia of Social Sciences* Vol. 16: 31.

Guo, Y. 2006. Cultural Anthropology Reflections on "Eating"- Comments on Eugene Anderson's Chinese Food. *Folk Culture Forum 5*: 99–104.

Ha, Z, L. 2009. *Social Changes and Disciplinary Development: A Brief History of Taiwan's Ethnology Anthropology*. Beijing: The Ethnic Publishing House.

Habermas, Jurgen.1989. The Public Sphere. In *Jurgen Habermas on Society and Politics: A Reader*, edited by Steven Seidman. Boston: Beacon Press.

Hall, Edward T. 1959. *The Silent Language*. New York, NY: Anchor Books.

Hann, Chris and Keith Hart. 2011. *Economic Anthropology*. Cambridge: Polity Press.

Hann, Chris, and E. Dunn.1996. *Civil Society: Challenging Western Models*. Routledge.

Hao, Shiyuan. 2007. Ethnic Issues in the Construction of an Ethnic Country. China Ethnic News, 2007.01.16.

Harding, Harry. 1987. *China's Second Revolution*. Washington, D.C.: The Brookings Institute.

Hart, K. 1996. End of the World: Anthropologists Speechless. *Anthropology Today* 5:1-2.

He S. Y. 2011. *Probing Socio-Cultural Anthropology*. Beijing: China Social Sciences Press.

He, Jiaxun, and Li Yao. 2006. A Probe into the Principles of Brand Activation and Means of Decision-Making. *Journal of Beijing Technology and Business University* 21(6): 50-55.

Herskovits, M. J. 1936. Applied Anthropology and the American Anthropologists. *Science* 83:215-222.

Hirst, Paul and Grahame Thompson.1999. *Globalization in Question (second edition)*. Cambridge, U.K.: Polity Press.

Ho, Ping-ti. 1960. .*A Historical Survey of Landsmannschaften in China.* Taipei: Student Book Publication.

Hofstede, Geert. 1984. *Culture's Consequences: International Differences in Work-Related Values*. London: Sage Publications Inc.

Hofstedt, Todd A. 2009. China in Africa: An African Response. *Naval War College Review* 62(3): 79-100.

Hong, J. 1994. The Preliminary Study on the Origin of the Dulong People. In *Selected Works of Historical Accounts of Nujiang Prefecture*, edited by the Editorial Committee of Works of Historical Accounts of Nujiang Prefecture. Manshi: The Nationalities Publishing House of Dehong.

Hosking W., Borland R., Yong H.H., Fong G., Zanna M., et al. 2009. The Effects of Smoking Norms and Attitudes on Quitting Intentions in Malaysia, Thailand and Four Western Nations: a Cross-Cultural Comparison. *Psychol. Health* 24:95–107.

Howell, Jude. 1998. An Unholy Trinity? Civil Society, Economic Liberalization and Democratization in Post-Mao China. *Government and Opposition* 33: 56-80.

Howell, Jude. 1995a. Prospects for NGOs in China. *Development in Practice* 5(1): 5-15.

Howell, Jude. 1995b. Striking a New Balance: New Social Organizations in Post-Mao China. *Capital and Class* 54: 89-111.

Hsiao, Kung-chuan. 1960. *Rural China: Imperial Control in the Nineteenth Century*. Seattle: University of Washington Press.

Hsiao, Michael H.H. and Alvin So.1999. Economic Integration and the Transformation of Civil Society in Taiwan, Hong Kong, and South China. In *Imagining China: Regional Division and National Unity*, 221-252, edited by Huang and Hsu. Taipei: Institute of Ethnology, Academia Sinica.

Hu, P., and Long, X.Y. 2009. Community Participation from the Perspective of Public Crisis Management. *Journal of Sichuan Economic Management Institute* 1: 35-36.

Huan P. Q. 2005. The Changing of Rural Periodic Market and Transformation of Rural Social Structure in North China: a Case Study in Ting Hsien (Dingzhou). Ph.D. dissertation, Renmin University of China.

Huan P. Q. 2016. Rural Market Change, Social Transformation and Rural Construction in North China: a Case Study in Ting Hsien (Dingzhou). *Social Construction* 5:1-13.

Huang, A., & Lv, T. 2011. Study on the Dietary Application Value of Xizang Meituo Stone Pot. *Journal of Fuzhou University* (Natural Science Edition) *39*(4): 613–616.

Huang, G. 2006. Region and Boundary: Study on Salt Monopoly in Neighboring Areas of *Hunan, Guangdong and Jiangxi in Qing Dynasty*. Beijing: Lifes-Reading XinzhiSanlian Bookstore.

Huang Z. Z. 1986. *The Peasant Economy and Social Change in North China*. Beijing: Zhonghua Book Company.

Huang, Chien-yu Julia and Robert P. Weller. 1998. Merit and Mothering: Women and Social Welfare in Taiwanese Buddhism. *Journal of Asian Studies* 57: 379-396.

Huang, L., and Xia, W.T. 2020. Value Reshaping and Planning Response Under The Concept of 'One Health.' *Guangdong Urban & Rural Planning and Design Institute Co.Ltd. Website.* http://www.gdupi.com/Common/news_detail/article_id/7469.html, accessed May 3, 2021.

Huang, S, P. 2007. Mr. Fei Xiaotong's Contribution to the Theory of Anthropology in China. *Journal of the Central University for Nationalities* (Philosophy and Social Sciences Edition) 34 (4): 22-31.

Huang, Shu-min. 1994. Rural China in Transition. In *China Briefing, 1994*, edited by William A. Joseph. Boulder, San Francisco, and Oxford: Westview Press.

Huang, Shu-min. 1998. *The Spiral Road: Change in a Chinese Village through a Communist Party Leader* (second edition). Boulder: Westview Press.

Huang, Shu-min. 1993. The State-Society Relationship as Seen in Changing Marital Practices in Fengjia, Shangdong. *The Bulletin of the Department of Archaeology and Anthropology*, National Taiwan University 49: 12-169.

Huang, Y.H. 2007. Literature and Country. *Journal of Literary Review* 1: 54-56.

Jain S. 2003. "Come up to the Kool Taste": African American Upward Mobility and the Semiotics of Smoking Menthols. *Public Cult* 15:295–322.

Jian, W.X. 2009. Transcultural Management Research Based on the Analysis of Culture Difference. Ph.D. dissertation, North China Electric Power University.

Jiang Y. L. 2009. *The Economic and Cultural Life of the Pai-I.* Kunming: Yunnan People's Publishing House.

Jin B. H. 2007. *Policies of Nationalities*. Beijing: Minzu University of China Press.

Johansson, Johny K., Dimofte, Claudiu V., and Mazvancheryl, Sanal K. 2012. The Performance of Global Brands in the 2008 Financial Crisis: A Test of Two Brand Value Measures. *International Journal of Marketing Research* 29: 235-245.

Jordan A. 2017. The Significance of Enterprise Anthropology in Asia. *Global Economic Review* 11:1-8.

Jordan, A. 2013. *Business Anthropology (2nd Edition)*. Prospect Heights, Il: Waveland Press.

Joyce, Patrick D., 2003. *No Fire Next Time: Black Korean Conflicts and the Future of America's Cities*. Ithaca, NY: Cornell Univ. Press.

Kato F. 1973. Regular Markets in the Villages and Towns of the Qing Dynasty.In *A Research on Chinese Economic History* (volume 3). Translated by Wu J. Shanghai: The Commercial Press.

Kavahematui, Justice. 2011. Danger Lurks for Motlhale's BDC Motion. The Midweek Sun, Wednesday, December 7.

Keane, Michael.2001a. Broadcasting Policy, Creative Compliance and the Myth of Civil Society in China. *Media, Culture and Society* 23: 783-798.

Keane, Michael. 2001b. Redefining Chinese Citizenship. *Economy and Society* 30: 1-17.

Kelleher, David and Kate McLaren.1996. *Grabbing the Tiger by the Tail: NGOs Learning for Organizational Change.* Ottawa: Canadian Council for International Co-operation.

Keller, K. L. 1999. Managing Brands for the Long Run: Brand Reinforcement and Revitalization Strategies. *California Management Review* 41(9): 102-124.

Keller, K.L., and Lehmann, D.R. 2006. Brands and Branding: Research Findings and Future Priorities. *Marketing Science* 25(6): 740–759.

Keller, K.L., Aperia, T., and Georgeson, M. 2008. *Strategic Brand Management: A European Perspective*. Harlow, England: Pearson.

Kohrman M. 2004. Should I Quit? Tobacco, Fraught Identity, and the Risks of Governmentality in Urban China. *Urban Anthropology and Studies of Cultural Systems and World Economic Development* 33: 211–45.

Kohrman M. 2007. Depoliticizing Tobacco's Exceptionality: Male Sociality, Death, and Memory-Making among Chinese Cigarette Smokers. *The China Journal* 58:85–109.

Kohrman M. 2008.Smoking among Doctors: Governmentality, Embodiment, and the Diversion of Blame in Contemporary China. *Medical Anthropology* 27:9–42.

Kolrman, Matthew and Peter Benson. 2011. Tobacco. *The Annual Review of Anthropology* 40:329–44.

Kong, Lingren, and Li, Dezheng. 1998. *China's Classic Brands(Volume I)*. Beijing: Higher Education Press.

Kotler, P. & Keller K. 2005. *Marketing Management, 12th edition.* Upper Saddle River, New Jersey: Pearson Prentice Hall.

Kottak, Conrad Phillip. 2005. *Cultural Anthropology: The Exploration of Cultural Diversity*. Translated by Xu Yucun. Taiwan: McGraw-Hill International Co., LTD.

Kulp, D. H. 2011. *Country life in South China: The Sociology of Familism*. Beijing: Intellectual Property Publishing House. Translated by Zhou Daming.

Kwong, Peter, 1979. *Chinatown New York: Labor and Politics (1930-1950)*. New York: Monthly Review Press.

Kwong, Peter, 1987. *New Chinatown: Modern Chinese Communities in U.S.* WAP Press.

LaForet, S., and Saunders, J. 1994. Managing Brand Portfolios: How the Leaders Do It. *Journal of Advertising Research* 34(5): 64–76.

Lam Wai-Fung and James L. Perry. 2000. The Role of the Nonprofit Sector in Hong Kong's Development. *Voluntas: International Journal of Voluntary and Nonprofit Organizations* 11 (4): 355-373.

Lee J., 2002. *Civility in the City: Blacks, Jews, and Koreans in Urban America*. Cambridge, MA: Harvard Univ. Press.

Levi·Strauss, C. 1978. *The Origin of Table Manners*. London: Jonathan Cape.

Li J. F. 2011. Ethnic Interaction and National Identity in the Cross-border Trade between China and Vietnam-Taking the Market of the People on Northwest Border in Yunnan Province as an Example. *Study of Ethnicities in Guangxi* 4:47-50.

Li Qianwen. 2014. Research on the Cognitive Differences of Traditional Brand Value Based on Pearce's Symbol Theory: a Case Study of Wang Laoji. *Southeast Mass Communication* 1: 113-116.

Li Y. Y. 2014. *The Economy in the Area Blended by Han-Yi*. Kunming: Yunnan People's Publishing House.

Li Z. H. 1998. *Rural Market and Modern Society: a Study on the Markets of Villages in North China in the First Half of the 20th Century*. Beijing: Contemporary China Publishing House.

Li, B., & Ziliang, L. 2015. To Build a Moderately Prosperous Society in All Aspects, Not a Single Nationality Will be Left Behind: Reporting Notes on General Secretary Xi Jinping's Interview with

Representatives from Gongshan Dulong and Nu Autonomous County. Xinhua Daily Telegraph January 23, 2015.

Li, Fei 2015. A Study of the Lifecycle of China Time-Honored Brands. *Journal of Beijing Technology and Business University* (Social Sciences) 30(4): 28-34.

Li, G.P. and Zhao, Y.C. 2008. A Summary of the Grads Theory. *Human Geography* 1: 61-65.

Li, H.Y., and Lv C.Z. 2019. From Divide to Conquer: the Change and Trend of Urban-Rural Relationship in the Process of Modernization. *Journal of Henan Normal University* (Philosophy and Social Sciences) 46 (05): 8-15.

Li, Peter S. 1976. Ethnic Businesses among Chinese in the U.S. *Journal of Ethnic Studies* 4: 35-41.

Li, S. 2017. The Dulong Scenery Area in Yunnan is Closed to the Public from October 1 Temporarily. *EastdayWebsite*, http://news.eastday.com/eastday/13news/auto/news/society/20170922/u7ai7111114.html, accessed October 8, 2020.

Li, W.R. and Chen, G. 2014 Competition among Profit and Challenge and Pressure-Industry and Commerce Anthropology Case Study Based on Taxi Drivers from Kunming. *Qinghai Journal of Ethnology* 2014(01): 12-21.

Li, Y. 2019. Dulong River Scenery Site Opened Again after Two Years of Closing for Reconstruction. Xinjing Newspaper October 6. https://baijiahao.baidu.com/s?id=16466 22652542651178&wfr=spider&for=pc. accessed January 4, 2022.

Li, Y. H. 2013. Business Anthropology: From Tradition to Modern. China Social Science Daily November 20, Theory page.

Light, Ivan and Steven Gold. 2000. *Ethnic Economies*. San Diego: Academic Press.

Light, Ivan. 1972. *Ethnic Enterprises in America: Business Welfare among Chinese, Japanese, and Blacks*. University of California Press.

Lin, J. and Tian, G. 2016. Anthropological Studies of the Business Export Credit Insurance Business of Insurance - Based on the Case of Shantou. *China Market* 52： 30-43.

Ling, Z. 2016. The Livelihood Pattern of Dulong People and Its Changes. *Culture Journal* 7: 42-44.

Lipset D. 2006. Tobacco, Good and Bad: Prosaic of Marijuana in a Sepik Society. *Oceania* 76: 245–57.

Liu, R. ed. 1989. *China's Population: Tibet Volume*. Beijing: China Financial and Economic Press. Beijing: China Finance and Economics Press.

Liu S. H. 2010. Market and Modernity in Nuosu (Yi) Area, Southwest China. *Thinking* 1:22-17.

Liu X.X. and Li X.Y. 2009. An Overview of Studies on Anthropology of Development. *Journal of Guangxi University for Nationalities* (Philosophy and Social Science Edition), 31(5): 38-47.

Liu, Q. and Zhang, Y. F. 2016. Commodity Producing and Consuming: an Anthropology Perspective–Starting from the Development of the Western Business Anthropology. *Journal of the Renmin University of China* 2016(01)： 138-146.

Liu Y. H. 1993. Traditional Marketing and Social Structure in China: Reflect Skinner's Marketing Theory and Macro-Regional Theory. *Researches in Chinese Economic History* 4:133-139.

Liu, Z. 2012. Cultural Inheritance and Evolution of Tibetan Diet - An anthropological Field Study of a Tibetan Rural Community. *China Tibetology 1*: 92–109.

Llonch-Casanovas, Montserrat. 2012. Trademarks, Product Differentiation and Competitiveness in the Catalan Knitwear Districts during the Twentieth Century. *Business History* 2: 583–599.

Lu Y. L. 2012. Examing the Development of Rural Markets from the Changes of Village Markets: Taking Dingzhou Temple Fair in Hebei Province as an Example. *Jianghai Academic Journal* 3:113-121.

Lu, Y. 2014. Basic Information of Dulongjiang Township. *Yunnan Website*, http://special. yunnan.cn/feature11/html/2014-10/28/content_3425097.htm, accessed March 12, 2018.

Luo K. L. and Walle A. 2014. Traditional Economies and Mainstream Alternatives: Business Anthropology Looks at Dong Tree Farming. *Anthropologist* 18 (1): 25-31.

Luo, H. G. 2000. *Exchange of Unequal Values: Working and the Consumption of Wealth*. Hangzhou: Zhejiang People's Publishing House.

Luo, K. L. and Tian, G. 2014. The Path of Localizing Economic Anthropology in China and Its Theoretical Contributions. *Journal of Minzu University of China* 47 (3): 57-66.

Luo, Q. 2007. *On Marx's Criticism of Modernity and Its Contemporary Significance*. Shanghai: Shanghai People's Publishing House.

Luo, Ying. 2010. Analysis of Classic Brands in Drinking Industry and Investigation of Strategy Choice--with the Example of Classic Brands in Zhengzhou. *Economic Survey* 4: 40-45.

Ma X. D. 1987. Ancient Urban and Rural Markets in Yunnan. *Inquiry into Economic Issues* 6:50-53.

Mao, Zedong. 1956. On the Ten Major Relationships. *Marxists Internet Archives Website*, https://www.marxists.org/reference/archive/mao/selected-works/volume-/mswv5_51.htm, accessed January 3, 2022.

Mead, Margaret. 1975. Discussion. In *Anthropology and Society*, edited by Bela Maday. Washington, D. C. Anthropological Society of Washington.

Mendonc, A, S., Santos Pereira, T., and Mira Godinho, M. 2004. Trademarks as an Indicator of Innovation and Industrial Change. *Research Policy* 33(9): 1385–1404.

Mercer, John. 2010. A Mark of Distinction: Branding and Trademark Law in the UK from the 1860s. *Business History* 1: 17–42.

Merton. R. 2006. *Social Theory and Social Structure*. Translated by Tang S.J., Qi X.. Nanjing: Yilin Press.

Miller,M.C., and L. Mumford. 2016. *The Culture of Cities*. New York: Open Road Media.

Mock J. 2000.Thai Views of Wellness: Sabaay, Smoking, and Buddhist Health Promotion. Ph.D. dissertation. Program in Medical. Anthropology, University Califonia San Francisco.

Modise, Oliver. 2011. Parliament Investigates BDC. Sundaystandard December 4-10.

Moeran, Brian. 2005. *The Business of Ethnography: Strategic Exchanges, People, and Organizations*. Oxford, UK: Berg.

Mogapi, Spencer. 2011. Corruption Mars BDC Multi-million Pula Project. Sundaystandard May 22-28.

Morula, Morula. 2011. Embattled Shanghai Fengyue Glass Company Auctioned. Sundaystandard November 27-3 December.

Mumford, L. 1961. *The City in History: Its Origins, Its Transformations and Its Prospects*. New York: Harcourt, Brace and Company.

Mu, S. 2009. *China: Sugar and Society-Farmers, Technology and World Market*. Guangzhou: Guangdong People's Publishing House.

Munoz, Lina Galvez. 2005. Regulating an Addictive Product: the Spanish Government, Brand Advertising and Tobacco Business (from the 1880s to 1930s). *Business History* 3: 401-420.

National Bureau of Statistics. 2020a. Statistical Communique of the People's Republic of China on the 2019 National Economic and Social Development. *National Bureau of Statistics Website*, http://www.stats.gov.cn/tjsj/zxfb/202002/t20200228_1728913.html. Accessed January 3, 2022.

National Bureau of Statistics. 2020b. 2019 Migrant Workers Monitoring. *National Bureau of Statistics Website*, http://www.stats.gov.cn/tjsj/zxfb/202004/t20200430l742724.html, accessed January 3, 2022.

National Bureau of Statistics. 2020c. *China Statistical Yearbook 2019*. Beijing: China Statistics Press.

National Bureau of Statistics. 2020d. The Overall Plan For Epidemic Prevention Has Achieved Remarkable Results. The National

Economy Gradually Recovered in The First Half of the Year. *National Bureau of Statistics Website*, http://www.stats.gov.cn/, http://www.stats.gov.cn/tjsj/zxfb/202007/t20200716_1776194.html, accessed January 3, 2022.

National Bureau of Statistics. 2020e. Residents' Income and Consumption Expenditure in the First Quarter of 2020. *National Bureau of Statistics Website*, accessed May 3, 2021. http://www.stats.gov.cn/

Naughton, B. 1995. *Growing out of the Plan: Chinese Economic Reform, 1978-1993*. Cambridge: Cambridge University Press.

Naughton, B. 2007 *The Chinese Economy: Transitions and Growth*. Cambridge: The MIT Press.

Nee, V. and B. Nee. 1973. *Longtime California: A Study of an American Chinatown*. Standford University Press.

Niu H. B., Wang W. C. 2000. *Marketing in Yunnan*. Kunming: The Nationalities Publishing House of Yunnan.

Oarabile, Mosikare. 2011. Parliament to Probe BDC. The Botswana Gazette, Wednesday 07-13 December.

Ong, Aihwa.1999. *Flexible Citizens: the Cultural Logics of Transnationality*. Durham: Duke University Press.

O'Sullivan, D., Hutchinson, M. C., & O'Connell, V. 2009. Empirical Evidence of the Stock Market's (mis) Pricing of Customer Satisfaction. *International Journal of Research in Marketing* 26(2): 154-161.

Oxfam International-Hong Kong. 2007. *Committed Practice for Poverty Assistance: 20 Years of Oxfam International in China's Interior Regions*. Hong Kong: Oxfam International.

Pan, T.S. 2016. Disneyland Under the Ethnographic Gaze: a Laboratory of Business Anthropology. *Journal of Guangxi University for Nationalities* (Philosophy and Social Science Edition) 38(5): 58-59.

Peng, Z. 2013. *Anthropology of Diet*. Beijing: Peking University Press.

Peng, Z., & Xiao, K. 2011. A Review of Dietary Anthropology. *World Nationalities 3*: 48–56.

Piet, Bame. 2016. Fengyue Glass Project to Be Auctioned This Week. *Mmegi*, Feb 16.

Plattner, S. M. 1974. Formal Models and Formalist Economic Anthropology: the Problem of Maximization. *Reviews in Anthropology* 4:572-582.

Portes, Alejandro and Robert L. Bach. 1985. *Latin Journey: Cuban and Mexican Immigrants in the United States*. Berkeley: University of California Press.

Qi, X. G. 2016. *Study of Organizational Culture in the Chinese Operations of Multinational Companies: a Business Anthropology Perspective*. Beijing, PRC: People's Publishing House.

Qi, X. G., Wang, X. N. and Liu, Z. Y. 2012. The Dialogue between Management and Anthropology: the Rise of Industrial and Commercial Anthropology. *Journal of Dalian Maritime University* (social science edition) 11(03):48-51.

Qiang, K. 2015. How did Wheat Come to the Table of the Tibetan?--Modernization of Tibet and Changes of Tibetan Diet Culture. *Open Times 3*: 175–192.

Qu, X.X. 2014. Quality of Life Research in the Context Harmonious Society Construction. Ph.D. dissertation, Shandong University.

Quan, J.X. and Cui, H, Y. 2013. On FEI Xiao-tong's Anthropological Research Methods: a Detailed Interpretation of Peasant Life in China—a Field Study of Country Life in the Yangtze valley. *Journal of Guangxi University for Nationalities* 35(4):58-64.

Quintero G., and Nichter M. 1996. The Semantics of Addiction: Moving beyond Expert Models to Lay Understandings. *Journal of Psychoactive Drugs* 28:219–28.

Raine, Sarah. 2009. *China's African Challenges,* London: IISS/Routledge.

Ramadubu, Dikarabo. 2011. BDC Rots From the Head / Inside BDC's Shambles. Botswana Guardian November 4.

Rankin, Mary Backus.1993. Some Observations on a Chinese Public Sphere. *Modern China* 19: 158-182.

Redding, Gordon S. 1998. The Function of Business-Related Reciprocity in Chinese Non-Civil Societies. In *Democratic Civility: The History and Cross-Cultural Possibility of a Modern Political Ideal*, edited by Robert Hefner. Transaction Publisher.

Reid A. 1985. From Betel-Chewing to Tobacco-Smoking in Indonesia. *Journal of Asian Studies* 44:529–47.

Rowe, William T. 1989**.** *Hankow: Conflict and Community in a Chinese City, 1796-1895.* Stanford, CA: Stanford University Press.

Rowe, William T.1993. The Problem of "Civil Society" in Late Imperial China. *Modern China* 19:139-157.

Saich, Tony. 2000. Community-Based Poverty Alleviation: The Ford Foundation's Program in Southwest China. Paper presented for the 40th Anniversary of the Shanghai Academy of Social Sciences.

Salamon, Lester M., Helmut K. Anheier and Associates.1998. *Global Civil Society: Dimensions of the Nonprofit Sector*. Baltimore, MD: Johns Hopkins Center for Civil Society Studies.

Sassen, Saskia.1996. *Losing Control? Sovereignty in an Age of Globalization.* New York: Columbia University Press.

Schroeder, Jonathan E. 2009. The Cultural Codes of Branding. *Marketing Theory* 9(1): 123-126.

Scott, James C. 2009. *The Art of Not Being Governed: An Anarchist History of Upland Southeast Asia.* Yale Agrarian Studies. New Haven & London: Yale University Press. pp. 14–16.

Sefhako, Sefhako. 2012. Glass Project to Continue. Daily News, Friday, February 03.

Shang, J., Jiang, H., & Zhao, L. 1978. Another Batch of Neolithic Relics Found in Motuo County, Xizang Province. *Archaeology 2*: 136–137.

Shelley, Becky. 2000. Political Globalization and the Politics of International Non- Governmental Organizations: the Case of Village Democracy in China." *Australian Journal of Political Science* 35(2): 225-238.

Sherry, John and Bradford, Tonya. 2015. Domesticating Public Space through Ritual: Tailgating as Vestaval. *Journal of Consumer Research* 42(1): 130-151.

Shi, L. 2002. *Economic Anthropology*. Beijing: Minzu University of China Press.

Shi, L. 2002. Economic Anthropology: Its Beginning and Early Development in the USA. *Ethno-National Studies* 12 (2): 97-103.

Shi, L. 2011. Border Ethnography: Perspective and Methods of Economic Anthropology. *Journal of Guangxi University for Nationalities* (Philosophy and Social Science Edition) 3:35-38.

Shi, L. 2016. The "African Ideas" to Deal with Ethnic Diversity---The "Multidimensional" View of the Ethiopian National Governance Model. *Heilongjiang National Series* 3:59-67.

Shi, X.T. 2013. A Research on Fei Hsiao-tung's Family Sociology Thought. Ph.D. dissertation, College of Sociology, Shanghai University.

Shi, Z. Y. 1986. The "Accelerating Strategy" of Economic Development in the Western Minority Areas. *China's Ethnic Groups* 11： 8-10.

Shi, Z.Y. 1989. Gap Acceleration and Equilibrium-An Exploration of the Economic Development Strategy in the Minority Areas. *Heilongjiang National Series* 3:29-45.

Shi, Z.Y. 1993. *Introduction of National Economics*. Beijing: Nationalities Publishing House.

Shi, Z.Y. 2000. Some Relationships that Should Be Handled Correctly While Implementing the Development Strategy of the Western Regions: —Again on the "New Thoughts on the Development of Western Regions." *Journal of The Central University For Nationalities* 5:58-61.

Shi, Z.Y. 2002. Come up with Innovative Ideas for National Economy Research. *Ethnic Unity* 4:56-57.

Shu, Y. 2009. *The Meaning of "Salt": A Historical Anthropological Survey of Nuodeng Salt Industry in Yunnan Province*. Beijing: Great World Books Publishing Company.

Skinner, G. William. 1998. *Marketing and Social Structure in Rural China*. Translated by Shi J. Y., Xu X. L. Beijing: China Social Sciences Press.

Smart, Alan.1998. Guanxi, Gifts, and Learning from China: A Review Essay. *Anthropos* 93: 559-565.

Song, W. 2016. The Convergence of Regional Economic Growth and the Test of Knowledge Spillovers effect in China. Ph.D. dissertation, Jilin University.

Song, Xiyan, and Deng Ting. 2003. Wangmazi Scissors Company Applies for Bankruptcy. Jinghua Times January 23.

Statistical Bureau of Yunnan Province 2015. *Yunnan Statistical Yearbook 2015*. Beijing: China Statistics Press.

Stellman S., Resnicow K. 1997. Tobacco Smoking, Cancer and Social Class. *IARC Sci. Publ.*: 138:229–50.

Stewart, A. 2011 Foreword: Why Become a Business Anthropologist? In *Advanced Readings in Business Anthropology: 1-2*, edited by Tian, R., D. Zhou, and A. van Marrewijk. Miami, FL: North America Business Press.

Strickland S. 2002. Anthropological Perspectives on Use of the Areca Nut. *Addict, Biol.*: 7:85–97.

Sunderland, P., McCabe, M. and Malefyt, T. 2012. Business Anthropology in China, Anthropology News July 23, 2012.

Swan G.E., Hudmon KS, Jack L.M., Hemberger K, Carmelli D. 2003. Environmental and Genetic Determinants of Tobacco Use: Methodology for a Multidisciplinary, Longitudinal Family-Based Investigation. *Cancer Epidemiol. Biomark, et al., Prev.*: 12:994–1005.

Tang, Y. X. and Chen, W. J. 2017. The Originality and Development of Business Anthropology in China. *Journal of Xinan Minzu University* 4:1-7.

Tao, Jun and Li, Shanwen. 2012. Revival of China's Classic Brands: Brand Extension and Feedback. *Economic Management* 34(2): 97-106.

Tett, Gillian. 2009. *Fool's Gold: The Inside Story of J. P. Morgan and How Wall St. Greed Corrupted Its Bold Dream and Created a Financial Catastrophe*. New York, NY: The Free Press.

Tian, G. 2010. The Unique Contribution and the Unique Methodologies: A Concise Overviews of the Applications of Business Anthropology. *International Journal of Business Anthropology* 1(2): 70-88.

Tian, G. 2012. The Rising and Application of Business Anthropology. *An Academic Edition of Management* 12:39-48.

Tian, G. 2013. Business Anthropology and Cultural Different Management. *Nationalities Research in Qinghai* 24 (3): 1-9.

Tian, G. 2016. Anthropological Perspective on Market and Marketing. *Qinghai Journal of Ethnology* 3： 38-42.

Tian, G. and Chi, X.D. 2012. The Design Thinking and Teaching Practice of Business Anthropology Course. *Economic Research Guide* 12: 254-258.

Tian, G. and Liu, L.Y. and Liu, Y. 2015. The Development Track and Problems of Time-Honored Catering Brands in Shantou-Based on Ethnographic Research for Industry and Commerce. *Minzu Tribune* 9: 36-45.

Tian, G. and Liu, Y. and Wang, Y. F. 2015. Exploring New Pathway of Management: Qualitative Research Methods in Business Anthropology. *Chinese Journal of Management* 1: 1-10.

Tian, G. and Luo, K. L. 2013. *Economic Anthropology*. Yinchuan: Ningxia People's Publishing House.

Tian, G. and Wang, Y. F. 2014. Organizational Culture Change and Intervention Strategy: an Anthropological Perspective. *Chinese Journal of Management* 4： 525-532.

Tian, G. and Zhou D.M. 2013 China Needs Business Anthropology. *Minzu Tribune* 6： 5-8.

Tian, G. and Zhou, D, M. 2012. *Business Anthropology*. Yinchuan: Ningxia people's Publishing House.

Tian, G. and Zhu, T. T. 2014. Industry and Commerce Anthropology Approach of Product Design. *Qinghai Journal of Ethnology* 1: 7-11.

Tian, G., & Zhou, D. M. 2013. *General Business Anthropology*. Beijing: China Financial and Economic Publishing House.

Tian, G., Feng, J. and Wang, Y. 2017. *Marketing Anthropology*. Yinchuan: Ningxia People's Publishing House.

Tian, G., Zhou, T. and Ma, J. F. 2018. *Management and Business Anthropology*. Yinchuan: Ningxia people's Publishing House.

Tian, Guang 2016. Anthropological Perspective on Market and Marketing. *Qinghai Journal of Ethnology* 27(3): 38-42.

Tian, Guang, Trotter, Dan, and Liu, Yu. 2015. Anthropological Methods are Meaningful in Business Research: a Case Study of Foodservice at a Chinese University. *The Anthropologist* 19 (1): 11-24.

Tian, H. 2011. Empirical Study on the Relationship between Corporate Cultural Conflicts and Performance in Sino-Chinese Joint Ventures. *Systems Engineering* 9(1): 90-97.

Tian, R, Van Marrewijk, A.H. and Lillis, M. 2013. *General Business Anthropology*. Miami (2nd Edition), FL: North American Business Press.

Tian, R. & Walle, A. 2009. Anthropology and Business Education: Practitioner Applications for a Qualitative Method. *International Journal of Management Education* 7(2): 59-67.

Tian, Youqing, Ding, Ping, Zhang, Yunqing. 2015. Overview of Tobacco Medicinal Research. *Chinese Medicine* 5:25-27.

Ting, Jen-chieh. 1997. Helping Behavior in Social Context: A Case Study of the Tzu-Chi Association in Taiwan. Ph.D. dissertation, University of Wisconsin-Madison.

Tipps, Dean C. 1973. Modernization Theory and the Comparative Study of Societies: A Critical Perspective. *Comparative Studies in Society and History* 15 (2): 199-226.

Tylor, Edward Burnett. 1871. *Primitive Culture*. New York: G.P. Putnam's Son.

Van Marrewijk, Alfons. 2015. Introduction: a Megaproject as Culture Perspective. In *Inside Mega-projects: Understanding Cultural Practices in Project Management*, 13-33, edited by A. H. Van Marrewijk. Frederikberg: CBS Press.

Wakeman, Frederic Jr. 1993. *The Civil Society and Public Sphere Debate: Western Reflection on Chinese Political Culture. Modern China* 19: 108-138.

Walder, Andrew G. 1986. *Communist Neo-Traditionalism: Work and Authority in Chinese Industry*. Berkeley: University of California Press.

Waldron I., Bratelli G., Carriker L., Sung W.C., Vogeli C., Waldman E. 1988. Gender Differences in Tobacco Use in Africa, Asia, the Pacific, and Latin America. *Social Science & Medicine* 27: 1269–75.

Walle, Alf H. 2015. *Qualitative Research in Business: A Practical Overview*. Cambridge, UK: Cambridge Scholars.

Walle, Alf H. 2001. *Qualitative Research in Intelligence and Marketing*. Westport, CT: Quorum Books.

Walle, Alf H. 2009. Pro-Choice. *Cultural Survival Quarterly* 33(1) (Spring 2009).

Walle, Alf H. 2013. *Rethinking Business Anthropology: Cultural Strategies in Marketing and Management*. Sheffield: Greenleaf

Waller, Robert P. 1998. Horizontal Ties and Civil Institutions in Chinese Societies. In *Democratic Civility: The History and Cross-Cultural Possibility of a Modern Political Ideal*, edited by Robert Hafner. Frederikberg: CBS Press.

Wan H. 2004. On the Historical Formation of the Market in Southwest Minority Areas. *Guizhou Ethnic Studies* 3:100-106.

Wan H. 2006. *Studies of the Ethnic Markets in Southwest China*. Beijing: China Economic Publishing House.

Wang D. 1993. *Stepping Out of a Closed World--a Study of Regional Society in the Upper Yangtze River (1644-1911)*. Beijing: Zhonghua Book Company.

Wang Q. C. 2004. Markets and Market circles in North China in the Late Qing Dynasty. *Modern Chinese History Studies* 4:2-69.

Wang Q. C. 2005. An Analysis of the Growth of the Regular Markets in North China in the Late Qing Dynasty. *Modern Chinese History Studies* 6:1-38.

Wang, S. 1987. Investigation on the Origins of Minority Nationalities in Yunnan. *Journal of Yunnan Nationalities University (Social Sciences)* 1:30-41.

Wang, S.J. 2015. Field Research on Enterprise Culture Evolution Path and Influence on its Performance--The Analysis from the Perspective of Business Anthropology. *Journal of Shanxi University of Finance and Economics* 7: 71-84.

Wang X. Y. 2012. The Construction of Border Market and Village Community-Based on the Investigation of Zhenjiang Town on the Sino-Myanmar Border. *Minzu Tribune* 4:69-73.

Wang, Y. 2016. Changes of Mongolian Diet Culture in the Context of Urbanization. Ph.D. Dissertation, Minzu University of China.

Wang, Z. 1998. Food and Culture in Jingpo Ethnography. *Ethnic Art 3:* 103–111.

Wang, Zhuo 2015. THBV Evaluation and Promotion Strategy of Shenyang Old Brand's Value. *Journal of Beifang University of Nationalities* 6: 27-31.

Wansink, Brian, and Gilmore, Jennifer Marie. 1999. New Uses Revitalize Old Brands. *Journal of Advertising Research* 39(2): 90-98.

Wei, W., & Chen, Z. 2018. Rhythm and Identity of Food: An anthropological Study Based on the Diet of the Bouyei Nationality in Libo, Guizhou. *Journal of Southwest University for Nationalities* (Humanities and Social Sciences Edition) 39 (3): 30–36.

Weilin Sun. 2010. Promoting Social Organizations' healthy development. *Outlook Weekly*, September 13: 21.

Weiss, Thomas G., and Leon Gordenker, ed. 1996.*NGOs, the UN, and Global Governance*. Boulder and London: Lynne Rienner Publishers.

Weitzer, Ronald. 1997. Racial Prejudice among Korean Merchants in African American Neighborhoods. *Sociological Quarterly* 38:587–606.

Whiting, Susan H. 1991. The Politics of NGO Development in China. *Voluntas* 2: 16-48.

Wilkins, M. 1992. The Neglected Intangible Asset: the Influence of the Trademark on the Rise of the Modern Corporation. *Business History* 34(1): 66–95.

Win, Aye-Aye. 1998. The Growing Society in Asia. *Development* 41: 101-106.

Wong, B. P. 1988. Patronage, Brokerage, Entrepreneurship, and the Chinese Community of New York. New York: AMS Press.

Wong, Linda and Norman Flynn, ed.2001. *The Market in Chinese Social Policy*. New York: Palgrave Macmillan.

Wu X. Y. 2008. *Market Politics: the Power and Integration during an Exchange*. Beijing: China Social Sciences Press.

Wu, C. 1987. Historical Evolution of Monba in Medog County, Xizang Province. *Journal of Minzu University of China* (Philosophy and Social Sciences Edition) 1: 37-41.

Wu, D. 2017. From Burning Meats to Cheat Ghost to Banqueting Barbecue: An Interpretation of the Process of Cultural Homogenization and Heterogenization in Yi Diet from an Anthropological Perspective. *Northwest Ethnic Studies* 1: 148–155.

Wu, D.Y.H., & Tan Chee-beng. eds. 2001. *Changing Chinese Foodways in Asia*. Hong Kong: The Chinese University Press.

Xi, Y. 2015. Study on Supporting Policies for Ethnic Peoples in China: Taking Dulong People in Gongshan County of Nujiang Prefecture as an Example. Ph.D. dissertation, School of Public and Finance Management, Yunnan University of Economics and Finance.

Xiao, K. 2009. Empire, Jin Mercantile and Tea-The Dissemination Process of Wuyi Tea in Russia before the Middle 19th Century. *Journal of Fujian Normal University* 2: 113–118.

Xie, Y. J. 2005. Fei and His Peasant Way. The Beijing News, 2005-4-26.

Xu T. 1998. *The Development of Commodity Economy in Shandong Province during Ming and Qing Dynasties*. Beijing: China Social Sciences Press.

Xu, W. 2016. China and Africa: Can They Cross the Borders of System and Culture—A Business Anthropology Research of a Glass Factory Project Owned by a Sino-Botswana Joint Venture. *Qinghai Journal of Ethnology* 3: 43-48.

Xu, Yanfeng, Du Hengbo and Zhao Xiaokang. 2015. Research on Impact of Mechanism of China's Time-honored Catering Brand Extension upon Brand Image Base on Perspective of Perceived Fit. *Journal of Beijing Technology and Business University* (Social Science), 30(5): 99-107.

Xu, Z. G. and Huang, Y, G. 1999. *The Development of Anthropology in Taiwan - Review and Prospect*. Taipei: Institute of Ethnology, Academia Sinica.

Yan, Y. X. 1996. *The Flow of Gifts: Reciprocity and Social Networks in a Chinese Village*. Stanford, CA: Stanford University Press.

Yang C. K. 1934. A Study of Periodic Markets in Chowping Hsien. M.A. thesis, Department of Sociology, Peking University.

Yang M. C. 2001. *A Chinese Village, Toutai, Shandong Province*. Nanjing: Jiangsu People Publishing LTD.

Yang Tingshuo. 1995. *Economic Anthropology in China: Xiangji Operation Principles*. Guiyang: Guizhou Renmin Publishing House.

Yang, Baojun and Ma Yulong. 2015. Empirical Research on Hui-Honored Consumers Intergenerational Transmission and Brand Loyalty. *Journal of Capital University of Economics and Business* 17(2): 102-107.

Yang, J., & Jinming, L. 2010. Dulong People Living across the China-Myanmar Border: Interpretation of Self-Identification and Other-Naming. *World Ethno-National Studies* 4: 78-83.

Yoon Jung Park. 2009. Recent Chinese Migrations to South Africa: New Intersections of Race, Class & Ethnicity. In *Representation, Expression and Identity. Interdisciplinary Perspectives*, 153-168, edited by Tina Rahimy. Oxford: Inter-Disciplinary Press.

Yoon Jung, Park and Chen Anna Ying. 2009. Recent Chinese Migrations in Small Towns of Post-apartheid South Africa. *Revue Europeene des Migrations Internationals*(REMI), 25(1): 25-44.

Yoon, I.J. 1997. *On My Own: Korean Businesses and Race Relations in America*. Chicago: University Chicago Press.

Yuan Chaoyang. 2008. Frontier Sociological Analysis on Smoking and Health for Women of Ethnic Minorities in Yunnan. *Journal of Kunming University* 4: 54-56.

Yuan Y. X. 2017. *Private Life under Socialism: Love, Intimacy and Family Change in a Chinese Village,1949-1999*. Translated by Gong X. X. Shanghai: Shanghai People's Publishing House.

Zaloom, Caitlin. 2006. *Out of the Pits: Traders and Technology from Chicago to London*. Chicago, IL: University of Chicago Press.

Zeng, Manlu 2008. Brand Resource Development Shantou Activates Election of 'Classic Brands' in Chaoshan. Dawa News November 26.

Zhang H., Gu J. R. 2012. A Study of Social Interactions and the National Identity of the People on Yunnan and Myanmar Border.' *Journal of Yunnan University of Nationalities* (Social Sciences) 1:17-22.

Zhang Jijiao. 2016. Time-Honored and Old Commercial Streets in the Urban Transformation: Comparison between Seoul and Beijing. *Journal of Beifang University of Nationalities* (4): 17-20.

Zhang Y., Wang X. Y. 2010. An Analysis of Cultural Connotation of Markets in Minority Areas-Taking Yi People's Marketing in Tanhua. *Thinking* 6:122-126.

Zhang, C. 2018.The Experience Reference of "Leave Blank" in Urban Planning at Home and Abroad and Its Enlightenment to Chongqing. In *Sharing and Quality-Proceedings of the 2018 China Urban Planning Annual Conference* (14 Planning Implementation and Management). China Association of City Planning, China Urban Planning Society, 633-640.

Zhang, Chunwei, and Lin Pandeng. 2007. Brand Ally: Market Expanding Approach for China's Classic Brands—with the Example of Beef Industry in Pingyao, Shanxi. *Journal of the Postgraduate of China's University of Economics and Law* 5: 100-104.

Zhang, D.Z. 2014. A Study on the Culture of Integrative Model of Chinese Corporates Cross-border M&As. Ph.D. dissertation, Nan Kai University.

Zhang, H. 2015. The New Transition of Local Research Paradigm of Economic Anthropology. *Journal of Minzu University of China* (Philosophy and Social Sciences Edition) 42(6): 100-107.

Zhang, J. F. 2015. Solidification and Reconstruction: the Research of Dulong's Identity and Border in Northwest Yunnan Province. *Qinghai Journal of Ethnology 26*(3): 60-65.

Zhang, J. J. 2018. Beehive Society: A New Concept for Observation of China's Social-economic Transformation. *International Journal of Anthropology and Ethnology* Vol.2.

Zhang, J. J. 2015. A Study on "Cellular" Development Model of the Time-honored Brands: From Enterprise Anthropology Perspective. *Journal of Guangxi Economic Management Cadre College* 4： 50-54.

Zhang, J. J. 2014. "Umbrella Society"--a New Concept to Observe China's Economic and Social Structure Transformation. *Thinking* 4： 54-61.

Zhang, J. J. 2013. Insight into the Development of Enterprises with Classic Brands from the Perspective of Relationship between Enterprises and Government--A Comparison between Heniantang and Tongrentang. *Ideological Front* 39(3): 34-40.

Zhang, J. J. 2011. Industrial Transfer between Eastern China and Midwest: An Analysis of Influencing Factors. *Guizhou Social Sciences* 2011(01): 69-73.

Zhang, J. J. 2009. The "Success Cases" from the Perspective of Enterprise Anthropology—Interviews of the 28 Overseas Chinese Businessmen and Managers in Malaysia and the Analysis of Their Cases. *Academic Exploration* 4: 68-73.

Zhang, J. J. 1998. The Changes of Private Lending, Private Credit and Financial System. *Social Science in Yunnan* 5: 46-52.

Zhang, Jijiao, Ding Huimin, and Huang Zhongcai. 2011. *A Blue Book for Classic Brands—A Report of Enterprise Development of China's Classic Brands.* Beijing: China's Academy of Social Sciences.

Zhang, J. J. and Huang, Y.Y. 2015. How Do Anthropologists Conduct Business Research? *Minzu Tribune* 2015(11): 31-35.

Zhang, Jijiao, and Li Yujun. 2012. Will Chinese Enterprises Flourish For Long?--a Sociology-Based Analysis on the Secret of Longevity and Development of Classic Brands. *Ideological Front* 38(4): 48-53.

Zhang, Jijiao and Yin Peng, 2013. Ethnic Migrants' Employment and Industry Distribution in the Cities of China, *The Review of Black Political Economy* April Volume: 81-106.

Zhang, J.M. 2014. Research on the Residentialization of the Hui Migrant Labor Immigrants in Ningxia. Ph. D. dissertation, Lanzhou University.

Zhang, Ke. 2001. Alliance of 100 China's Classic Brands. *Management and Wealth* 4: 46-47.

Zhang, Q. 2000. *The History of the Dulong Culture*. Kunming: The Nationalities Publishing House of Yunnan.

Zhang, X.Y. 2015. A Research on National Identity of Minority Nationalities in Ethnic Regional Autonomy. Ph.D. dissertation, Shanxi Normal University.

Zhang, Y. 2020. The Employment Situation Is Gradually Improving, The Employment of Key Groups Still Needs Attention. *China*

Economic Net. http://www.ce.cn/xwzx/gnsz/gdxw/202007/17/t20200717_35346643.shtml, accessed January 3, 2022.

Zhang, Y., Qian, Y., Ming, C., Xizhi, W., & Nan, M. 2014. The Past and Today of Dulong River Highway: from State-Owned Horse Caravan to the Real Highway. *China Highway Website*. http://www.chinahighway.com/news/2014/822952.php, accessed January 3, 2022.

Zhang, Y.J., Zhou, J.X. and Lin, H. 2003. A Study on the Localization of Anthropology Theory and Method in China. *Journal of Guangxi University for Nationalities* (Philosophy and Social Science Edition) 2: 1-27.

Zhang, Z. 2001. Hakka Restaurant and Social Change. *Journal of Guangxi University for Nationalities* (Philosophy and Social Sciences Edition) 4: 39–41.

Zhao, Jianhua. 2013. *The Chinese Fashion Industry: An Ethnographic Approach*. London: Bloomsbury Academic.

Zhao, T.L. 2020. The Economy Was Affected by the Impact of the Epidemic in the First Quarter; the Long-term Development Trend Has Not Changed. *China Economic Net*. http://www.ce.cn/xwzx/gnsz/gdxw/202004/19/t20200419_34722139.shtml,accessed January 3, 2022.

Zhao, Y. 2011. Tsamba, Rice and Vegetable -- A Dietetic Anthropological Study in Naga, The village, Duilong Deqing County, Tibet. Ph.D. dissertation. The Minzu University of China.

Zhao, Z.X. 2016. Research on Urbanization Social Cost and Regulation-Using a Case of Chongqing City. Ph.D. dissertation, Chongqing University.

Zhou, D. M. 2012. Thinking on the Discipline Position of Anthropology. *Journal of Guangxi University for Nationalities* (Philosophy and Social Science Edition) 1: 79-83.

Zhou, D. 2004 The Follow-up Investigation of Fenghuang Village. *Journal of Guangxi University For Nationalities* (Philosophy and Social Science Edition) 1: 33-38.

Zhou, D. 2002 Farmer Entrepreneurs from Perspective of Cultural Sociology. *Journal of South-Central University for Nationalities*(Humanities and Social Sciences) 2: 32-37.

Zhou, D. 1996. Chinese Anthropology and the Localization of Anthropology. *Journal of Guangxi University for Nationalities* (Philosophy and Social Science Edition) 3: 30-35.

Zhou, D. 1992. Study on Migrant Labor in the Pearl River Delta. *Sociological Research* 5: 71-79.

Zhou, D. M. and Tian, X. Y. 2015. Modern Family Business and Family Culture in China. *Journal of Northern Minzu University of Nationalities* (Philosophy and Social Science) 3: 98-103.

Zhou, D. M. and Zang, M.N. 2006. The Anthropological Investigation of the Vocational Skills Training-Taking Nanning and Liuzhou as Examples. *Journal of Southwest University for Nationalities* (Humanities and Social Science) 12: 38-43.

Zhou, Min. 1992. *Chinatown: The Socioeconomic Potential of an Urban Enclave*, Philadelphia: Temple University Press.

Zhou, Y. 2009. A Brief Study of the Dulong People's Christian Faith. *Journal of Religion Studies* 4: 200-205.

Zhou, Y. 2010. Study of Roads and Roadology. *Twenty-First Century Bimonthly*, Chinese University of Hong Kong 120(August): 71-79.

Zhu, G.J. 2001. Concepts and Methods of Taiwan Anthropology Fieldwork. *Guangxi Minzu Yanjiu* 1:32-37.

Zhu, Liye. 2008. Origin and Structure of Classic Unique Brand Property. *Economic Survey* 1: 117-120.

Index

A

academic research, 22, 87
adaptive, 126, 130, 260
administrative system, 89
Africa, 12, 23, 24, 33, 36, 210, 215, 216, 219, 221, 224, 227, 230, 232, 233, 234, 265, 272, 288, 291, 292
agricultural modernization, 78, 79
agricultural product, 64
agricultural production, 65, 68, 79, 94, 121
agricultural products, 64, 69, 70, 91, 106, 250
alcohol, 29, 100, 122, 123, 148
ancestor, 155
ancestors, 30, 116, 155, 239
applied anthropology, 5, 41
Awakening Age, 22

B

basic research, 54
beehive society, 132, 145
Belt and Road Initiative, 21
Border Market, 289
border markets, 8, 23, 27, 87, 92, 93, 96, 98, 100, 107, 110, 111, 113
Border Markets, 87
Botswana, 11, 24, 32, 33, 54, 215, 216, 217, 218, 219, 220, 221, 222, 223, 224, 225, 226, 227, 228, 229, 230, 231, 232, 233, 268, 269, 281, 282, 291
bourgeois society, 125
Brand Management, 163, 173, 275
business anthropology, 5, 6, 7, 11, 24, 35, 41, 43, 44, 45, 46, 48, 49, 50, 51, 52, 53, 54, 55, 56, 57, 58, 59, 60, 309
Business Anthropology, 1, iii, iv, vii, 6, 12, 13, 15, 23, 41, 42, 43, 48, 52, 53, 56, 59, 217, 261, 263, 267, 268, 274, 277, 278, 279, 281, 282, 285, 286, 287, 288, 289, 291, 309
business organization, 6
Butterfly, 143

C

cash crop, 126
cash crops, 121
catering industry, 140, 240, 248, 250
central government, 143, 258
Central Place Theory, 89
Chen Gang, iii, vii, 12, 23, 50, 52, 54, 56, 261, 309
Chinatown, 128, 130, 276, 281, 296
Chinese Anthropological Society, 2

Chinese anthropologists, 1, 3, 4, 5, 53, 309
Chinese anthropology, 3, 4, 17, 44, 59
Chinese economic reforms, 46
Chinese immigrant, 130
Chinese immigrants, 128, 130, 143
Chinese intellectual, 1
Chinese peasants, 45
Chinese society, 1, 3, 4, 63, 67, 68, 89, 189, 197, 211
Chinese traditional culture, 68
Chongqing hot pot, 239, 243, 252
Christianity, 30, 123, 126, 137, 210
city-state, 74
Civil Society, 192, 203, 270, 271, 272, 275, 283, 288
Classic Brand, 163
collaborative theory, 48
collective consciousness, 74, 85
collective decision-making, 19
collective enterprise, 183
commercial culture, 93
commercial trade, 30, 134
commercialization, 11, 33, 95, 235, 237, 240, 241, 242, 243, 246, 247, 255, 256, 257, 258, 259, 260
Commercialization, 235, 238, 240, 243, 251, 252, 256, 257
commodity circulation, 63, 88, 90
commodity economy, 48, 91
common people, 131
commune system, 65
community development, 10, 191, 195
community with a shared future for mankind, 17, 22
comparative study, 127, 131
conflict, 57, 130, 196, 202, 254
conflicts, 11, 19, 20, 21, 130, 131, 142, 196, 201, 216, 217, 232, 234, 253
consumer behavior, 5, 23, 52
consumer market, 72, 79, 247
consumers' rights, 32, 205, 211
consumption group, 8, 61
Contemporary China, 13, 275, 276
corporate culture, 54, 137
COVID-19, 7, 8, 21, 61, 62, 70, 72, 74, 75, 84, 85
critical theory, 125
cross-border exchanges, 8, 87
cross-border peoples, 97
cross-border trading, 98
cultural adaptation, 54, 252
cultural analysis, 42, 150
cultural and social resources, 47
cultural characteristics, 53, 96, 142, 236
cultural disrupt, 123
cultural heritage, 139, 144, 165, 204, 212
cultural identity, 9, 80, 96, 137, 143, 145
Cultural Impacts, 147, 150
cultural preservation, 10, 191, 195
Cultural Revolution, 24, 26, 29, 46, 94, 170, 171, 172, 174, 175, 176

D

daily necessities, 95, 97, 98
Daniel Harrison Kulp, 43
decision-making, 45, 60, 231
democratization process, 203
development, 3, 4, 5, 6, 7, 8, 10, 12, 17, 19, 21, 23, 26, 27, 35, 41, 42, 43, 44, 46, 47, 48, 50, 51, 52, 53, 54, 55, 56, 57, 59, 60, 61, 63, 64, 65, 66, 67, 68, 69, 73, 74, 77, 78, 79, 80, 81, 82, 83, 84, 85, 86, 87, 90, 91, 92, 93, 95, 96, 99, 101, 102, 103, 105, 107, 108, 111, 112, 115, 126, 128, 129, 130, 131, 132, 136, 140, 145, 153, 164, 192, 193, 194, 195, 200, 202, 204, 205, 207, 208, 209, 211, 213, 215, 217, 218, 219, 220, 225, 227, 228, 229, 232, 236, 237, 240, 241, 242, 245, 247, 248, 251, 252, 253, 254, 255, 257, 258, 259, 260, 289, 309
Development, 3, 12, 13, 38, 41, 50, 67, 82, 149, 165, 195, 222, 225, 226, 228, 242, 243, 269, 270, 271, 272, 275, 276, 278, 280, 284, 285, 286, 290, 291, 292, 293, 294, 295
digital China, 20
digitalization, 17
dimensions model of cultures, 58
division of labor, 82, 143, 246, 247
domestic violence, 200
driving force, 80, 131, 141, 204
Dulong people, 9, 115, 116, 117, 120, 121, 122, 123, 124, 125, 126
Dulong People, 115, 267, 270, 272, 278, 290, 292, 296
Dumplings, 166, 167, 169, 171, 172, 176, 178, 182

E

Earthly Branches, 93
Ebola, 84
ecological environment, 93, 121, 142, 256
ecological environments, 8, 74, 87
economic and social change, 5
economic and social transformations, 51
economic anthropology, 41, 42, 44, 45, 46, 48, 49, 50, 55, 56, 57, 60, 162, 309
economic development, 8, 48, 60, 61, 131, 253
economic exchange, 64, 99
Economic Hub, 104
economic life, 44, 68
economic reform, 5, 164
ecosystem, 9, 83, 115
elite classes, 125
empirical data, 90
empirical research, 90, 91, 128, 203, 204
empty nest villages, 66
enclave, 9, 127, 128, 129, 130, 132, 133, 145
enclaves, 30, 43
Enlightenment, 18, 22, 293

entrepreneurship, 127, 142, 143
environmental conservation, 10, 191, 195, 200, 211
epidemic prevention and control, 72, 74, 76
epidemic's impact, 71, 72, 75
Ethnic character, 145
ethnic characteristics, 144
ethnic consciousness, 99
ethnic enclave, 129
ethnic enterprises, 9, 51, 127, 131, 132, 142, 143, 144, 145
Ethnic Enterprises, 127, 277
ethnic entrepreneurs, 9, 30, 127, 129, 145
ethnic group, 9, 43, 93, 99, 115, 120, 125, 144, 247
ethnic groups, 1, 3, 10, 30, 41, 55, 59, 93, 95, 97, 98, 99, 100, 115, 127, 131, 133, 134, 142, 149, 150, 151, 152, 156, 191, 217
ethnic identity, 124, 129
ethnic minorities, 1, 9, 23, 24, 25, 26, 31, 42, 43, 46, 47, 48, 49, 50, 57, 59, 92, 94, 97, 100, 105, 125, 127, 133, 135
ethnic villages, 154, 155, 156, 159
ethno-economics, 41, 42, 56, 57, 60
ethnographic method, 42, 49
ethnography, 28, 31, 32, 33, 34, 56, 217, 237

F

face tattoo, 115
Familism, 43, 276
family businesses, 51
Fei Xiaotong, 1, 17, 45, 59, 61, 62, 63, 88, 97, 98, 101, 273
female smokers, 23
Female Smokers, 147
festival, 112, 117, 236, 242
fictitious commodities, 24
field survey, 88, 237, 250
financial turmoil, 137
fishing, 121
flowing population, 134
food culture, 52, 166, 237, 243, 252, 253, 255, 258, 260
foodservice industry, 10, 135, 161, 162, 163, 173, 174, 185, 188, 189
Foodservice Industry, 161, 168
formalist, 44, 48
formalists, 41
fragmentation, 127
frontier regions, 88
fruits of business anthropology, 35
Fudan University, 6, 269
future challenges, 18

G

gathering, 75, 87, 102, 113, 121, 128, 143
gatherings, 75
gender equality, 213

gift-giving, 24, 49
global economy, vi, 57, 164
global future, 213
global village, 17
globalization, 5, 9, 17, 21, 57, 66, 83, 116, 122, 125, 236, 309
gradient theory, 48
grassroots organizations, 195, 196, 212
Gregorian calendar, 95, 103
grid management, 63
guanxi, 24
Guanxi, 2, 285

H

Habermas, 192, 194, 196, 203, 204, 212, 271
Han people, 93, 94, 97, 136, 140, 150, 155, 159
Handbook of Anthropology in Business, 42, 43, 266, 268
handicraft production, 96, 208
harmonious society, 80
health education, 75, 77, 149, 160
heavy industry, 64
hegemony, 125
highland, 97
historical changes, 90, 92
Hong Kong, 2, 38, 43, 181, 182, 183, 204, 205, 209, 236, 267, 268, 272, 276, 281, 290, 296
household appliances, 98
Household Contract Responsibility System, 65
Household Registration, 65
Hui, 13, 30, 133, 134, 151, 291, 294
human civilization, 21, 82
Human Destiny, 17, 18, 19, 21
human governance, 19, 20, 21, 22
human progress, 22
humanity, 17, 18, 19, 20, 22
Humanity, 3, 17, 21, 81
Hunting, 121

I

indigenous culture, 33, 148
industrial anthropology, 51
industrial development, 64, 82
Industrial Revolution, 82
industrialization, 45, 53, 59, 231, 247, 248, 259
information network, 77, 107
information networks, 10, 30, 107, 191, 195
infrastructure, 21, 73, 75, 79, 116, 120, 140, 153
interaction, 8, 35, 61, 64, 76, 77, 78, 79, 80, 87, 91, 96, 107, 108, 109, 110, 129, 130, 154, 235, 237, 252, 255, 258, 259, 260
interdisciplinary field, 56
internal mechanism, 81
international conference on business anthropology, 6
International Journal of Business Anthropology, 12, 268, 286

International Union of Anthropological and Ethnological Sciences, 3
interpersonal communication, 63, 82
interview, 136, 141, 149, 181, 218, 237
interviews, 117, 125, 132, 154, 168, 174, 180, 184, 206, 215, 216, 244
iron-bowl, 193

J

James C. Scott, 125
Japanese, 1, 31, 49, 87, 131, 136, 171, 265, 277
Jiangnan Town, 90, 266, 269
Jingpo people, 101, 236
Jishou University, 7, 15, 309
joint venture, 11, 215, 217, 222, 229
Joint Venture, 215, 291

K

kinship, 3, 100, 101, 110, 142, 143, 197, 244
Klu-Nang Town, 235, 237, 240, 241, 242, 244, 245, 246, 248, 249, 250, 251, 252, 254, 256, 257, 258
Korean, 30, 130, 131, 133, 134, 135, 136, 137, 138, 139, 144, 274, 290, 292
Koreans, 130, 131, 135, 136, 137, 138, 139, 276
Kunming, 29, 30, 54, 126, 132, 133, 205, 270, 274, 276, 277, 281, 292, 294

L

labor market, 128, 129, 130
Laos, 23, 26, 98, 100
life history, 174, 180, 188
livelihood, 9, 92, 120, 121, 126, 132, 143, 152, 172, 185
living condition, 220
living conditions, 71, 120, 128, 152, 216, 218
localizing (*bentuhua*) anthropology, 4
Longyuan Village, 117, 121, 122
Low-carbon, 74
lunar calendar, 94, 103, 183
lunar system, 93

M

macroscopic and microscopic approaches, 90
manufacturing sector, 133, 136, 225
Margaret Mead, 59
market economy, 6, 8, 66, 87, 92, 103, 105, 112, 126, 132, 193, 205, 229, 241, 259, 260
market hierarchy system, 106
market research, 90, 92
market society, 100
market trade, 88, 96, 103
marketing cultural circle, 93
marketing theory, 89
Mexican, 282
Mexicans, 131
migrant worker, 135

migrant workers, 26, 51, 65, 71, 80, 128, 129, 135, 241, 257
Minzu University of China, 6, 270, 274, 279, 284, 289, 290, 293, 295
modern changes, 9, 87, 110
modern transformation, 8, 87, 107, 110, 111, 112, 113
Modernization, vii, 64, 78, 277, 282, 287
Mongolian, 30, 133, 134, 140, 141, 142, 144, 151, 289
Multi-disciplinary, 149
multinational enterprises, 54
multi-point ethnological approaches, 149
mutual dependence, 63
mutual exchanges, 98
Myanmar, 23, 26, 98, 100, 115, 125, 289, 292

N

natural environment, 68, 93, 148, 239, 256, 257
natural resources, 142, 256
New Culture Movement, 18
New Era, 18
NGOs, 10, 23, 32, 191, 192, 193, 194, 195, 196, 197, 198, 199, 200, 201, 202, 203, 204, 205, 206, 207, 208, 209, 210, 211, 212, 213, 265, 269, 270, 272, 275, 290
Ningxia University, 7
non-market economies, 44
North China, 49, 87, 90, 91, 106, 271, 273, 274, 276, 289
Nu people, 116
Nyingchi, 235, 237, 239, 240, 241, 242, 243, 244, 245, 246, 251, 252, 257, 258, 260

O

open-door policy, 2
opening up, 66, 67, 252, 257
operation, 11, 65, 68, 80, 87, 89, 110, 129, 188, 191, 193, 195, 197, 206, 209, 215, 220, 224, 225, 242, 243, 247, 249, 251, 258, 275
operations, vi, 10, 53, 191, 208, 245, 246, 257
organic cycle, 8, 62, 63, 70
Organizational Culture, 53, 282, 286
overseas, 2, 99, 171, 234

P

pan-human, 209
participant observation, 42, 117, 168, 215
participatory management, 213
Party-State, 32, 191, 192, 193, 197, 198, 199, 200, 202, 203, 211, 212, 213
patrilineal lineages, 197
Pearl River Delta, 90, 296
peasant society, 96

Peking University, 6, 48, 49, 55, 281, 291
people-centered, 17, 20
periodic markets, 87
physical facilities, 85
planned economy, 64, 103, 132, 162, 163, 164, 186, 188
policymakers, 161, 164, 187
political control, 125
post-epidemic, 8, 62, 74, 77, 78, 79, 80, 81, 83
Post-Epidemic, 77
postindustrial and commercial society, 53, 59
post-socialist society, 191, 193
poverty, 10, 35, 67, 86, 90, 116, 120, 128, 191, 194, 195, 202, 208, 209, 229, 230
poverty alleviation, 86
power vacuum, 193
prejudice, 131
primary market, 96, 100, 103
primary markets, 88
private businesses, 164
Private Enterprises, vi
product design, 5, 54
production materials, 64, 65, 83
Public health, 75
public sphere, 72, 196

Q

qigong, 32, 199
Qing Dynasty, 90, 96, 273, 274, 289
Qingdao, 30, 132, 133, 135, 136, 137, 138, 139, 144
Qinghai, 12, 52, 116, 134, 277, 286, 287, 291, 293
qualitative research, 42, 55
quantitative, 42
queen, 30, 135, 143

R

raw materials, 8, 26, 45, 61, 69, 71, 140, 221, 222, 223
reciprocal relations, 24
reform, 3, 19, 21, 44, 65, 66, 67, 103, 164, 171, 192, 194, 199, 203, 204, 205, 211, 212, 229, 252, 257
refugee, 130
refugees, 2, 125, 262
religious affiliations, 201
religious culture, 138, 254
Renaissance, 17, 18, 22, 85
resilient social structure, 70
rise and fall, 90, 92, 166
risky society, 83
road construction, 115, 118
Road Construction, 118
Rural China, vii, 89, 272, 273, 285
rural community, 73, 88
rural industry, 45
rural market, 44, 89, 91, 96, 112
rural markets, 8, 44, 87, 88, 90, 91, 93, 98, 99
rural population, 27, 65
Rural Rebuilding, 77

rural revitalization, 63, 67, 68, 77, 78, 79, 80, 86
rural surplus laborers, 66
Russell Belk, 15, 23, 36, 37, 42

S

SARS, 76, 84, 85
scissors-like trend, 64
Shantou University, 6, 10, 52, 55
shelters, 128
Shi Zhengyi, 46, 57, 59
sideline products, 70, 71, 97, 98
Sino-African relations, 215, 216
Skinner Model, 89
slash-and-burn, 97, 121
smoking control policy, 160
social and political functions, 88
social capital, 85, 194
social cohesion, 80, 85
Social Gender Analysis, 156
social interaction, 108
social organism, 70
social resilience, 115
social responsibility, 54, 220
social security, 68, 72, 109
Social Status, 36
social structure, 61, 65, 73, 74, 75, 85, 89, 90, 111, 131
social transformation, 5, 91, 102, 194
social welfare, 10, 191, 197, 209
Social Welfare, 192, 273
Socialism with Chinese Characteristics, 18, 20, 47
socialist modernization, 61, 64, 66, 72, 78, 85, 86
socio-cultural changes, 9, 115, 116, 117, 126
Southwest China, 35, 91, 115, 191, 194, 206, 278, 283, 288
Spanish flu, 85
spatial arrangement, 95
Spring Festival, 62, 70, 75
state-owned enterprises, 32, 164
stone pot chicken, 23, 24, 33, 34, 235, 239, 241, 244, 245, 246, 248, 249, 250, 251, 256, 257, 259, 260
Stone Pot Chicken, 11, 33, 235, 237, 238, 239, 240, 241, 242, 243, 244, 245, 246, 247, 248, 249, 250, 251, 252, 253, 255, 256, 257, 258, 259, 260
structure and function, 92, 105
subsidiary business, 45
subsidiary businesses, 45
subsistence farming, 126
substantive, 44, 49
substantives, 42
suicide, 122, 126
suicides, 30
Sun Yat-sen University, 2, 55, 56
surpass theory, 48
surplus products, 71, 89, 97
surviving ability, 129
sustainable development, 85
SWOT, 165

T

Taiwan, 1, 10, 44, 89, 201, 204, 205, 212, 271, 272, 274, 275, 287, 291, 296
technical personnel, 134, 219, 237
temporal system, 95
the Middle Ages, 17, 85
theoretical analysis, 55, 90
Tian Guang, iii, vii, 6, 7, 10, 12, 23, 46, 50, 51, 52, 55, 56, 217, 261, 265, 309
Tibet, 3, 11, 24, 28, 33, 34, 115, 119, 134, 150, 235, 237, 240, 241, 242, 243, 244, 252, 255, 256, 257, 259, 260, 278, 282, 295
time-honored brands, 163
Time-Honored Brands, 277
Tobacco, 31, 147, 148, 152, 265, 266, 267, 268, 275, 278, 280, 283, 285, 287, 288
tourism development, 126
Township enterprises, 66
trade partners, 26, 135
trading centers, 103
trading circles, 96, 97
traditional cultures, 3, 110
transformation, 5, 61, 76, 78, 91, 92, 102, 110, 111, 113, 131, 135, 141, 144, 191, 192, 204, 207, 220, 241, 255, 259
Transformation, 38, 102, 269, 272, 273, 292, 293
transitional stage, 203
transnational business transactions, 57
transparent governance, 213
travel bans, 71
two-step theory, 48

U

umbrella society, 51, 131, 135
urban economy, 144
urban landscape, 209
urban migrants, 9
urban society, 82
urban-rural integration, 8, 61, 63, 77, 78, 80, 83, 86
urban-rural relationships, 8, 61, 86
Urban-Rural Relationships, 61

V

vegetable gardens, 120
Vietnam, 23, 26, 98, 100, 262, 276
Village cadres, 74
village enterprises, 66
voluntary citizen groups, 196

W

Wang Jing, 15, 17
WeChat, 28, 107
Western business anthropologists, 43
Western China, 23, 24, 25, 50, 59
women smoking, 149, 156
world anthropology, 3, 4, 5
World War II, 195, 236

WTO, 66

Y

Yan Yunxiang, 49
Yang Tingshuo, 50, 291
Yangtze River, 90, 288
Yi people, 112, 155, 156, 236
Yunnan, 1, 3, 7, 8, 9, 10, 11, 15, 24, 26, 27, 28, 29, 31, 34, 45, 49, 52, 55, 87, 88, 92, 93, 94, 95, 96, 97, 98, 99, 100, 101, 102, 103, 104, 105, 106, 107, 108, 110, 111, 112, 113, 115, 116, 117, 147, 148, 149, 150, 151, 152, 156, 158, 160, 191, 194, 205, 206, 267, 270, 274, 276, 277, 279, 281, 284, 285, 289, 290, 292, 293, 294, 309
Yunnan University, 56, 270, 292

Z

Zhang Jijiao, 9, 50, 51, 165, 292
Zhou Daming, 6, 50, 52, 217, 276
Zhou Yongming, 126
Zhuang People, 150
Zodiac system, 103
Zomia, 125, 267

Afterword

It has been over a decade since business anthropology was introduced and promoted in universities in China in the early 2000s. With a grant from Sen Yat-sen University located in Guangzhou, China, the first issue of the International Journal of Business Anthropology was published in 2010. The goal of this journal is to generate an exchange of ideas among scholars, practitioners and industry specialists in the field of applied and business anthropology, to provide a vehicle of communication for anthropologists working within the practitioner world in different parts of the world, and to provide a forum for work concerned with qualitative business analysis inspired by anthropological theory and methods. Since its first issue, this journal has published numerous articles by Chinese anthropologists. This book, edited by Chen Gang and Tian Guang, current and former chief editors of this journal, aims to introduce how business anthropology rose in China and explain how business anthropology has been practiced in China by providing case studies from articles selected from this journal.

Chen Gang is a professor at the Economic Research Institute of Yunnan University of Finance and Economics in China. He received a MA in anthropology from Iowa State University in the USA in 1993 and a Ph.D. in anthropology from Ohio State in the USA in 2000. His main research interests are business anthropology, food safety and culture, development anthropology and cultural tourism, and globalization and culture change.

Tian Guang currently serves as a specially appointed professor at the School of Business, Huaihua University in China. He also serves as the Dean of the Advanced Research Institute for Applied Anthropology at Jishou University and the Doctoral Supervisor at Hebei Unversity. His research interests are regional development, cross-cultural marketing management, and economic anthropology. He received his Ph.D. in social anthropology from York University in 1995 and an MBA from Wilfried Laurier University in 1999.

Made in United States
Orlando, FL
04 November 2026

90200102R00177